Russia and the Outbreak
of the Seven Years' War

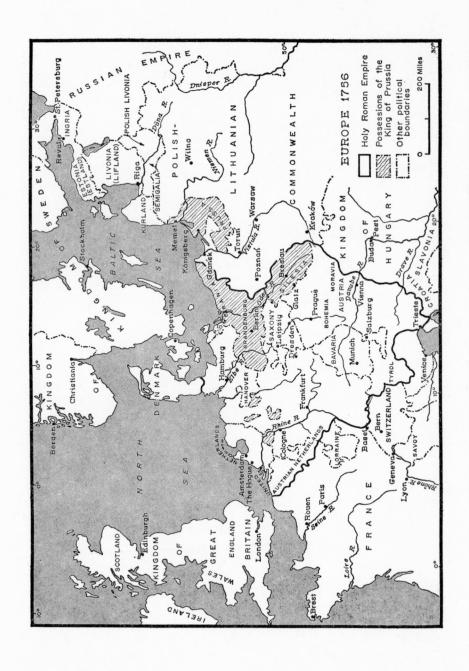

EUROPE 1756

Holy Roman Empire
Possessions of the King of Prussia
Other political boundaries

0   200 Miles

RUSSIAN EMPIRE

Dnieper R.

SWEDEN

St. Petersburg
Reval
INGRIA
ESTONIA (ESTLAND)
LIVONIA (LIFLAND)
POLISH LIVONIA
Dvina R.
Riga
KURLAND
SEMIGALIA

KINGDOM OF SWEDEN

Stockholm

BALTIC SEA

Memel
Königsberg

POMERANIA
Gdansk

POLISH-
Wilno
Niemen R.
LITHUANIAN
Warsaw
Torun
Poznań
Vistula R.
Kraków
COMMONWEALTH

KINGDOM OF HUNGARY

Brandenburg
Berlin
Oder R.
Breslau
SILESIA
Glatz
Prague
BOHEMIA
MORAVIA
AUSTRIA
Vienna
Danube R.
Budapest
Drave R.
CROATIA-SLAVONIA
Trieste
Venice

KINGDOM OF DENMARK

Christiania
KINGDOM OF NORWAY

Bergen

Copenhagen

Hamburg
Elbe R.
HANOVER
SAXONY
Leipzig
Dresden
Munich
BAVARIA
Salzburg
TYROL

NETHERLANDS
Amsterdam
The Hague
AUSTRIAN NETHERLANDS
Cologne
Rhine R.
Frankfurt
LORRAINE
Bern
Basel
SWITZERLAND
Geneva
SAVOY
Lyon
Rhône R.

NORTH SEA

SCOTLAND
Edinburgh
KINGDOM OF GREAT BRITAIN
ENGLAND
WALES
London

IRELAND

Brest
Rouen
Paris
Seine R.
FRANCE
Loire R.

Russia and the Outbreak of the Seven Years' War

Herbert H. Kaplan

BERKELEY AND LOS ANGELES / 1968
UNIVERSITY OF CALIFORNIA PRESS

UNIVERSITY OF CALIFORNIA PRESS
BERKELEY AND LOS ANGELES, CALIFORNIA

CAMBRIDGE UNIVERSITY PRESS
LONDON, ENGLAND

COPYRIGHT © 1968, BY
THE REGENTS OF THE UNIVERSITY OF CALIFORNIA

LIBRARY OF CONGRESS CATALOG CARD NUMBER: 68–12249
PRINTED IN THE UNITED STATES OF AMERICA

FOR BARBARA

Preface

> We might wonder whether the world in an absentminded way had not known all the time that Russia was the real culprit, though failing to focus attention on this side of the problem—failing to see that the story needed to be told around Russia. The key to the riddle lies in something which Russia did, not merely as the associate or auxiliary of Maria Theresa, but of her own motion and on her own account. It is just the evidence of the Russian documents which is necessary, therefore, to enable us to see what the narrative is like when it is viewed so to speak from its own centre, and is reconstructed in its proper bearings.[1]

Historical treatments of the Seven Years' War have focused primarily on the mutually dependent relationships among Austria, France, Great Britain, and Prussia. Little attention has been devoted to Russia's influence in shaping the incipient stages of this major European conflict. Consequently, Russia's role has been greatly understated and seriously misunderstood.

Whereas no attempt has been made to retell the whole story of the coming of the Seven Years' War, certain events must be recapitulated to bring into focus the real position of Russia and the manner in which other countries chose to weigh and contemplate her power. The addition of new source materials necessitated, after an intensive examination of all the evidence, a new appraisal of Russia's relations with Austria, France, Great Britain, and Prussia. Not since the time of Peter the Great had Russia so fully and deliberately participated in European affairs as during this period.

[1] Herbert Butterfield, "The Reconstruction of an Historical Episode: The History of the Enquiry into the Origins of the Seven Years War," *Man on His Past* (Cambridge, 1955), pp. 163–164.

A close examination of Russia's involvement in the Seven Years' War illuminates several crucial aspects in the formulation of her foreign policy and in the conduct of court politics. Empress Elizabeth considered Russia's participation in the war so important that she drastically reformed the administrative and decision-making apparatus because she feared it could not meet the challenges of war. Her chief advisers disagreed with each other on how and who should implement her diplomacy. Their divisive views on diplomacy merely sharpened the conflict in the power struggle which had already begun at the court. The outcome of this controversy led to a distinctive reorientation in Russian foreign policy and to a change in those responsible for directing it. Empress Elizabeth, who had been sickly for some time, suddenly fell critically ill and her death was expected at any moment. Grand Duke Peter and Grand Duchess Catherine, who had until then remained off stage, quickly stepped into leading roles. At that juncture the question of succession to the imperial throne produced sharply conflicting political configurations which could have changed again the foreign policy of Russia.

No attempt has been made to examine Russian military history beyond its relationship to court politics and foreign policy. An intensive study of the state of the military at that time would require a knowledge and understanding of fields that lie outside the present study.

All dates used are adjusted to the New Style calendar. All proper names in the text are spelled in their native language (the Russian being transliterated), except a few for which there are other firmly established forms in English, for example, Michael for Mikhail.

Acknowledgments

Several people have aided me in the writing of this study. I am particularly indebted to my wife Barbara, who read all the drafts from beginning to end. She was a constant source of encouragement and a stern critic, and it is superfluous to say that wifely criticism is the most difficult to accept. I have also benefited greatly from the wise counsel of E. J. Hollingsworth and Stuart Loory, who read the final draft of the manuscript. Sister Alphonsus Ciborski and Lawrence D. Orton assisted me in verifying factual data and in proofreading galleys. I owe Diane F. Beck of the University of California Press my special thanks for her meticulous editorial advice and her cooperation in preparing this study for the Press.

I would also like to thank the librarians and archivists of the various institutions that permitted me to carry on my research. Their cooperation and assistance allowed for this work to be accomplished quickly and efficiently. In particular I should like to extend my appreciation to the members and associates of Moscow State University who offered me their assistance for two years.

During the past few years I have been awarded several grants and fellowships which enabled me to do the research for this book. I gratefully acknowledge the American Philosophical Society, the Graduate Research Board of the University of Illinois, and the Inter-University Committee on Travel Grants.

Finally, I would like to mention specifically my debt to Professor Herbert Butterfield of Peterhouse, Cambridge University. It was his stimulating article on the historiography of the Seven Years' War which led me to inquire further into the prob-

lem. During the past few years I benefited from the conversa-
tions we had on this subject and from the kindness he has
shown me.

While I have gained greatly from my association with those
people and institutions herein mentioned, I am solely responsible for the views expressed and data presented.

Contents

Russia and the Outbreak of the Seven Years' War

I British and French Missions to Russia

Peter the Great was primarily responsible for Russia's becoming one of the most powerful states of Europe during the eighteenth century. The legacy he bequeathed to his successors was a Russia radically transformed from that which Muscovite society had previously known. Economic and political institutions were altered and attempts were made at efficient administration. Although absolutism still remained one of Russia's essential features, it was now thoroughly secularized. "Western" ideas were introduced into Russia which undermined traditional cultural patterns in the hope that they would lead to greatness and to equality with the other states of Europe.

The legacy was a burden as well; for not all of Peter's successors had equal courage, determination, and foresight. Those who followed him on the Russian throne were faced with the heavy responsibility of ruling a country that had enormous potential for continued and accelerated growth. Just to maintain the prominence Russia had achieved by the end of Peter the Great's reign in 1725 required considerable endeavor on the part of successive sovereigns, not all of whom were capable of such endeavor and not all were desirous of even trying.

Peter the Great successfully undermined the power of Sweden, which for decades had dominated the Baltic and had been influential in European affairs. Sweden's decline allowed the influence of Russia to increase in both these areas, but it also permitted the state of Brandenburg-Prussia to take her share of the spoils. In Frederick II, Brandenburg-Prussia found a leader as determined, courageous, and ruthless as Russia had found in Peter. Frederick became a formidable opponent to Russian power and expansion in western Europe, the Polish-Lithuanian

Commonwealth, and the Baltic. This alone can explain Empress Elizabeth's desire to see Brandenburg-Prussia weakened and even dismembered. But the daughter of Peter the Great also personally detested Frederick and looked on him as an insulting *parvenu*. His treatment of the Habsburg ruler Maria Theresa was sufficient evidence that the Hohenzollern could not be trusted and should therefore be feared. During the early years of Elizabeth's reign, these emotional and national objectives culminated in a series of foreign policy commitments: By the middle of the eighteenth century Elizabeth had united Russia with Frederick's enemies, Austria and Great Britain, and had broken diplomatic relations with him and his ally, Louis XV of France.

If Elizabeth could deliver a blow to Brandenburg-Prussia as her father had done earlier to Sweden, she could then stand proudly as his daughter. To achieve this end she was willing to go to war. Her aggressive foreign policy had been calculated as early as 1753.[1] Thus, no one at the Russian court was surprised when, in 1755, Elizabeth reaffirmed her opposition to the further aggrandizement of Frederick's power. Each time she solemnly declared it her aim to reduce his possessions to their former size and never again allow him to threaten Russia.

Through military victory, Elizabeth hoped to wrest East Prussia from Frederick and give it to Poland. Poland, in turn, was to cede Kurland and Semigalia to Russia and to adjust the Polish-Russian frontier to Elizabeth's satisfaction. In carrying out her aggressive aims, Russia first needed allies; secondly, through subtle manipulation she needed to make Frederick appear to be the aggressor.

In the early months of 1755 the peace of Europe was threatened by Anglo-French colonial rivalries in North America. This conflict indirectly provided Russia with a patiently awaited opportunity to carry out her designs. Perceiving that the war erupting between Britain and France in the colonies might easily spread to Europe, several statesmen and diplomats made frantic efforts to avert such a catastrophe. In doing so, however,

---

[1] See advice and opinion of the Senate given to Empress Elizabeth's court conference held on May 14 and 15, 1753, in SIRIO, CXLVIII/ 293/ 458–462.

they unwittingly assisted Elizabeth in the realization of her goal.

The unfortunate problem facing British statesmen was in having a king who was also the elector of Hanover. Hanover was contiguous with the Brandenburg possessions of King Frederick II of Prussia. He had threatened Hanoverian independence before and, as an ally of King Louis XV of France, might do so again in the near future. Given the meager armed forces at her disposal, Hanover alone was no match for the military might which could be mobilized against her by Frederick and Louis. Thus, the British were constantly aware that, if they went to war, Hanover would be in danger. The primary task of the British and Hanoverians in 1755 was the protection of their respective countries from the dangers implicit in dynastic union. Great Britain was capable of protecting herself and her colonies, but the defense of Hanover would require British troops or foreign armies subsidized by Great Britain.

Archduchess Maria Theresa of Austria—ruler of Bohemia and Hungary as well as the Austrian Netherlands—was a traditionally important ally of George II of England. Like Empress Elizabeth, Maria Theresa felt only contempt for Frederick. She longed for the moment when she could humble the aggressive Hohenzollern and recover Silesia and Glatz. Chancellor Wenzel Kaunitz, director of Maria Theresa's foreign policy, had for a long time argued that the old system of power relations was dead and should not be revived merely for the sake of tradition. He suspected that Great Britain's friendship for Austria was not entirely genuine. Great Britain had always been reluctant to see an increase in Habsburg power, and had at times flirted with Prussia. Kaunitz considered France less dangerous to Austria than Prussia, and he believed France had more to fear from Great Britain than from Austria. Moreover, both Bourbon and Habsburg houses had suffered from the increase of Hohenzollern power. Thus, if the Franco-Prussian alliance could be broken, Austria would benefit greatly from a rapprochement with France.

Kaunitz knew, however, that before his ideas could be realized a long, arduous, and uncharted road would have to be traveled. He looked to Russia, with her enormous military potential, as the key to the containment of Prussia. He felt that it

was necessary for Russia to remain perpetually convinced that
Frederick was the greatest threat to peace and that his power
should be reduced. If France chose not to act openly against
Frederick when the time came, she might be inclined to lend
her support indirectly by persuading some of the German states
and princes not to give Frederick aid. Russia could be counted
on to invade and occupy East Prussia, while Austria was con-
centrating her efforts in the south and west against Frederick's
forces.[2]

Against the backdrop of Kaunitz' reasoning, Maria Theresa
did not respond favorably to Great Britain's request for assistance in April 1755. She declared that neither a groschen nor
a grenadier would be expended for the defense of either the
Netherlands or Hanover without first obtaining from Great
Britain certain guarantees in the form of actions, not paper
promises. First, for the defense of Hanover and the Netherlands,
Austria wanted Great Britain to obtain the services of several
thousand mercenaries from friendly German principalities. Secondly, Great Britain would also have to employ 60,000 Russian
troops who would be ready at a moment's notice to attack Prussia in the event of a European war. The rationale for this *démarche* was Austria's fear that she would weaken the defenses of
her own hereditary realms and leave them open to Prussian attack if she were to deliver arms and funds for the defense of the
Netherlands and Hanover. However, if Russia could be enticed
into an agreement to attack Frederick as soon as he moved one
soldier across his frontier, Austria would feel secure enough to
assist England.[3]

This forceful presentation upset Britain, despite the sound
logic of Austria's argument. The Austrians did have something
to fear from Frederick, too; and perhaps the Russians might
serve to keep him in check. The expense of subsidizing mercen-

[2] For a good description and analysis of the development of Kaunitz'
views on foreign policy, see William James McGill, Jr., "The Political Education of Wenzel Anton von Kaunitz-Rittberg" (unpublished Ph.D. dissertation, Harvard University, 1960).

[3] BMAddMSS 6870/ 305, 90–93; 32854/ 150–151; 33020/ 200–201;
and 43435/ 125–129. Holdernesse to Keith, May 31, 1755, and Keith to
Holdernesse, June 4, 1755, PROSP 80/ 196. VA, Vorträge, 1755, *faszikel*
120/IV: 21–40, 42–44, 47, 64, 72–73.

aries would be a considerable drain on the British treasury, but the loss of Hanover and the Netherlands would be far more serious. Moreover, the demand to employ Russian troops against Frederick was for Great Britain neither a startling nor a new idea. During the previous few years Great Britain had been trying to effect that very thing. The first step in this direction had been taken as early as 1753, when the British feared that Frederick would attack Hanover.

In March of that year the British had begun negotiations for the employment of Russian troops against Prussia in the event Frederick attacked Hanover. However, by August, before any concrete Anglo-Russian measures could be agreed on, Frederick gave strong assurances that he would not move against Hanover. The British, with an eye to the future, decided to keep the subsidy negotiations alive without specifically designating the king of Prussia as the enemy. The ostensible reasons for the subsidy arrangement were declared to be the preservation of peace and maintenance of a solid and useful alliance between Great Britain and Russia.[4]

Subsequent negotiations bogged down due to disagreements not only over the amount of the subsidy but also over what constituted the *casus foederis* for the deployment of Russian troops outside Russia or Russian-controlled territory. By the beginning of 1755 nothing had been effected, other than the mental and physical exhaustion of the British envoy in Russia Colonel Guy Dickens. In February he officially requested his own recall. The British ministry replaced him with Sir Charles Hanbury Williams, the British envoy to Poland.[5] Williams was instructed to bring the subsidy treaty to a "speedy conclusion." To facilitate this, he was empowered not only to raise the amount of the subsidy, but also to offer Russia's grand chan-

[4] BMAddMSS 33021/ 30–37. See also Newcastle to Dickens, Oct. 2, 1753, *ibid.*, 32859/ 305–311; and CHW 20–10884/ 2–4, 9–16; and SIRIO, CXLVIII, *passim.*

[5] PROSP 91/ 57, 58, 59, 60, *passim*; SIRIO, CXLVIII, *passim*; and AVPR, f. Snosheniia . . . Angliei, 1755, *op.* 35/ 1, d. 770/ 2–3 (Feb. 4, 1755). Dickens to Holdernesse, Feb. 18, 1755, PROSP 91/ 60; and CHW 20–10884/ 160–161. Dickens to Holdernesse, April 15, 1755, CHW 20–10884/ 190; AVPR, f. Snosheniia . . . Angliei, 1755, *op.* 35/ 2, d. 111/ 1 (April 10, 1755); and AVPR, f. Snosheniia . . . Angliei, 1755, *op.* 32/ 2, d. 112/ 1 (April 10, 1755).

cellor 10,000 pounds upon the ratification of the treaty. The Duke of Newcastle, the king's chief minister, wrote Williams on April 11: "Never were [there] greater offers, either publick, or private, than those which you are now authoris'd to make. And, if they are not accepted, the Court of Russia must have chang'd their System, or forgot their interests."[6] For Russia to remain inactive and to provide "the King of Prussia an opportunity of putting in execution His ambitious, dangerous, long-concerted schemes of aggrandizement" would make her no better than an Asiatic power.[7]

Thus, in April 1755 when the Austrians requested Great Britain to undertake the employment of Russian troops to act as a check on the king of Prussia, they were only asking the British to conclude their original negotiation. Both in 1753 and 1755 the British clearly recognized Prussia as the real threat to their interests, and on both occasions Russia was willing to cooperate with Great Britain to meet this challenge. In fact, Russia maintained 79,404 troops in the Lifland Command (Kurland, Lifland, Estland, Polish frontier) that were waiting to be called into action.[8] Only two weeks before Williams arrived in St. Petersburg, Guy Dickens was told by some of the most important

[6] BMAddMSS 32854/ 97.

[7] See several letters from Holdernesse to Williams, April 11, 1755, PROSP 91/ 60; and BMEg 3426/ 52–53.

[8] See War College report of August 2, 1755, in AVPR, *f. Snosheniia . . . Angliei*, 1755, *op.* 35/ 1, *d.* 770/ 157–164. See also Dickens to Newcastle, Dec. 6 and 8, 1753, PROSP 91/ 57; and Dickens to Holdernesse, Nov. 2 and 9, 1754, PROSP 91/ 59. Since early in the eighteenth century the Duchy of Kurland, a fief of the Polish crown, had been directly or indirectly under Russian influence. In 1710 Peter I's niece, Anna Ivanovna, married the Duke of Kurland, Frederick Wilhelm of the house of Kettler; but within one year she was widowed. Frederick Wilhelm's uncle, Ferdinand, succeeded as duke but resided most of the time in Gdańsk (Danzig). For all practical purposes Kurland was ruled by Peter Bestuzhev-Riumin, the Russian agent at the ducal court and Anna's lover. When Ferdinand died childless in 1737, Anna, Empress of Russia, procured from Augustus III, the King of Poland, the investiture of the duchy for her favorite, Ernest Biron. Biron's rule lasted only three years, for with Anna's demise in 1740 he was exiled to eastern Russia. Henceforth, for almost two decades, Kurland was without a duke; but Russia continued to treat the duchy as if it were her own, maintaining large numbers of troops there. See Ernst Seraphim, *Geschichte Liv-, Est-und Kurlands* (Reval, 1895–1896), II; Claude de Rulhière, *Histoire de l'anarchie de Pologne* (Paris, 1819), I, II; and B. Bilbassoff, *Geschichte Katharina II* (Berlin, 1891–1893), II, pt. 1.

members of the Russian court that, if the struggle between France and Great Britain were to develop into a war in Europe, "they hoped they should not be idle spectators; that their troops were in compleat order, provided with everything, and ready to march at the shortest warning."[9]

Newcastle informed the Austrian court that the king of England was pressing for the immediate conclusion of the Russian subsidy treaty. He hoped Austria would take measures for sending assistance to Hanover and the Netherlands.[10] But again the Austrian court disappointed Great Britain. Kaunitz declared that he could not commit Austrian forces until the subsidy treaty with Russia was in fact concluded and signed, and until Russian troops were in a position to protect Austria from any aggressive action on the part of Prussia.[11] This the British would not accept as the final word. Through their ambassador at Vienna, Robert Keith, they continually tried to convince Kaunitz that the lands belonging to Maria Theresa were safe. Keith argued that it was "next to certainty, that we should have the Russian troops immediately at our command, and ready to make such a diversion against His Prussian Majesty, as would make Him think twice, before He engaged Himself in an offensive war against Her Imperial Majesty."[12] Despite this urging, Kaunitz would not retreat from his former position. Besides, for him there were different ways to defend oneself from the king of Prussia. Kaunitz let slip to Keith that one was "En attaquant le Roi de Prusse, morbleu."[13]

Williams' mission did not go unnoticed in other parts of

[9] Dickens to Holdernesse, June 3, 1755, CHW 20–10884/ 208–209.

[10] BMAddMSS 32996/ 79–80 (April 17, 1755). VA, Vorträge, *faszikel* 121/ VI: 163–164 (June 17, 1755). Newcastle to Yorke, April 18, 1755; Newcastle to Keith, April 28, 1755, BMAddMSS 32854/ 169–170, 182, 311–312, respectively. Holdernesse to Keith, April 25, 1755, PROSP 80/195.

[11] Keith to Holdernesse, May 22, 1755, PROSP 80/ 196; and Holdernesse to Newcastle, May 28, 1755, BMAddMSS 32855/ 236; and VA, Vorträge, *faszikel* 121/ VI: 125–155, 159–161, 163–169, 171–189 (June 17, 1755).

[12] Keith to Holdernesse, June 19, 1755, BMAddMSS 32856/ 353; and PROSP 80/196.

[13] Keith to Holdernesse, June 27, 1755, BMAddMSS 32856/ 520; and Newcastle to Yorke, June 11, 1756, *ibid.*, 32865/ 258.

Europe. Before he reached the Russian capital, two significant
events took place—one originating at the Prussian court and
the other at the French court—which were to upset the time-
table of British diplomacy if not all Europe.

Frederick was well aware that in the event of war Great
Britain would not hesitate to conclude subsidy conventions with
Saxony, Austria, and Russia. For several months he had been
apprised of the flurry of negotiations which were meant to accelerate the Anglo-Russian subsidy arrangements.[14] He had also
received several disturbing reports that tens of thousands of
Russian troops were being mobilized and stationed along the
frontiers near East Prussia.[15] In early May, Frederick, through
his envoy, informed the French court that he wanted no part
in any future military expedition against Hanover. His reasons
were quite understandable. There were, he said, 60,000 Russian
troops in Kurland and Livonia (Lifland and Estland), and Austria herself had assembled about 80,000 troops on her frontiers.[16]

Frederick had also learned of George II's intended visit to
Hanover.[17] Here was a splendid opportunity for Frederick to
meet with him and he even went so far as to suggest that the

[14] PC XI/ 6579–6708/ 1–100, *passim*; Frederick to Klinggraeffen, April
5, 1755, *ibid.*, 6720/ 107; Frederick to Maltzahn, Knyphausen, and Klinggraeffen, April 19, 1755, *ibid.*, 6742, 6745, 6747/ 124, 126, 127, respectively; Frederick to Maltzahn and Haeseler, April 22, 1755, *ibid.*, 6751–
6752/ 130–131; Frederick to Klinggraeffen, April 25, 1755, *ibid.*, 6757/
133; Maltzahn to Frederick, April 18, 1755, *ibid.*, 6759/ 134–135; Frederick to Maltzahn and Klinggraeffen, April 29–May 2, 1755, *ibid.*, 6765–
6767/ 139–140, respectively; Frederick to Podewils, May 5, 1755, *ibid.*,
6772/ 142; Podewils and Finckenstein to Frederick, May 23, 1755, *ibid.*,
6806/ 163; and Frederick to Department of Foreign Affairs and Maltzahn,
May 24, 1755, *ibid.*, 6806–6807/ 163.

[15] Frederick to Klinggraeffen, Jan. 7 and 11, 1755, PC XI/ 6586, 6591/
5, 9–12, respectively; Frederick to Maltzahn, Feb. 14 and March 14,
1755, *ibid.*, 6650, 6687/ 56, 85, respectively; and Haeseler to Frederick,
March 29, 1755, *ibid.*, 6729/ 117.

[16] Frederick to Knyphausen, May 6 and 10, 1755, PC XI/ 6774, 6781/
143–145, 148–149, respectively; and Knyphausen to Frederick, April 25
and May 9, 1755, *ibid.*, 6774, 6796/ 143–144, 156–157, respectively.

[17] Frederick to Knyphausen, March 18, May 14 and 29, 1755, PC XI/
6692, 6787, 6814/ 89, 152, 169, respectively; Frederick to Michell, April
1, 22, and 29, 1755, *ibid.*, 6713, 6748, 6762/ 102, 128, and 136–137,
respectively; and Frederick to Klinggraeffen, April 22 and 25, May 6, 1755,
ibid., 6749, 6757, 6776/ 128, 133, 146, respectively.

French court send an envoy to Hanover to talk to the king of England.[18] On his own initiative Frederick made plans to visit Saltzthal, a palace belonging to his brother-in-law the Duke of Brunswick, on June 6. Through a secret correspondence handled by Prince Ferdinand of Brunswick and his brother the duke, it was learned in Hanover that Frederick wished to receive a "compliment" from George while he was at Saltzthal and even an invitation to visit Herrenhausen or Hanover. This request, of course, was meant to initiate discussions that would include the European crisis. George was considerably irritated by Frederick's bold proposal. It was a matter of protocol. Through the secret correspondents the king of England sent the following message to Frederick: "that if the King of Prussia chose to pass *incognito* thro any part of His Maty's dominions . . . all the honours due to his rank should be paid him . . . the King would not begin the compliment; but that if the King of Prussia would send notice of his intended journey to Saltzthal the King would then send a proper person with a compliment to him."[19]

It was ironic that the formality of a "compliment" played such an important role at a time when war was imminent. But George did not take Frederick's inquiry lightly. Save for his entourage at Hanover he wanted no one—not even the British ministry—to know of this incident. Despite this order the Earl of Holdernesse, Secretary of State, who had accompanied him to Hanover, chose to reveal the information to Newcastle and requested that his letter be shown to no one except Lord Chancellor Hardwicke and be returned to him by the next courier.[20] Pleased with the confidence that Holdernesse bestowed upon him and greatly satisfied with the important news from Hanover, Newcastle made the following observation to Holdernesse concerning Frederick's intrigues:

> I shall most freely own that I think, this overture from the King of Prussia must have the happiest Effect upon both sides of our Question. It is not that I promise myself any very solid advantage from the King of Prussia; tho' in the present disposition of the

---

[18] Frederick to Knyphausen, May 14, 1755, PC XI/ 6787/ 152.
[19] Holdernesse to Newcastle, June 1, 1755, BMEg 3428/ 208–209. See also Holdernesse to Newcastle, June 7, 1755, BMAddMSS 32855/ 375.
[20] Holdernesse to Newcastle, June 1, 1755, BMEg 3428/ 208.

Court of Vienna; if anything solid could be built upon it, It might be such to be wished. But this Advance, (for such It is,) will puzzle France; make them more cautious, how they act, or attempt any offensive Measures against the King in Germany; and It will certainly do good at Vienna; and be the likeliest means to force them into His Majesty's Measures; and that, I am sure, would be a good effect of it. I should have been the last, to have advised any advance from the King to the King of Prussia: But I am very glad to find, that His Majesty reasons so rightly; and will not discourage any overture, that may come from thence. I should even hope (tho' I know, It would be disagreeable to the King) that His Majesty would rather forward, than decline, an Interview, which could end in nothing, but mutual civilities; and those civilities would have their use.[21]

But the interview did not take place because neither king would make the first compliment. Frederick was merely saluted by cannon as he passed through a part of Hanover. Both Newcastle and Holdernesse still wished that something might materialize.[22] Their wish was in fact to be realized; for Frederick's initiative was the first move toward negotiations leading ultimately to the Convention of Westminster on January 16, 1756.

Williams' mission to Russia excited the French court also. Although France had been instrumental in placing Elizabeth on the Russian throne in 1741, subsequent relations between the two countries had not gone smoothly. Russian foreign policy was directed by the notorious Francophobe Grand Chancellor Alexis Petrovich Bestuzhev-Riumin. In 1748 Russian troops in the pay of Great Britain had moved westward and threatened France; and in the years that followed, contact between France and Russia of any kind was practically nonexistent. By 1755 it seemed to Louis XV that the events of 1748 were being repeated and that France once again might be endangered by British-paid Russian troops. In order to gain more information about the recent Anglo-Russian negotiations, France decided to send

[21] Newcastle to Holdernesse, June 6, 1755, BMAddMSS 32855/ 365. See also Newcastle to Holdernesse, June 13, 1755, *ibid.*, 32855/ 477; and BMEg 3428/ 283.

[22] Holdernesse to Newcastle, June 18 and 22, 1755, BMAddMSS 32856/ 38, 105, respectively; and Newcastle to Holdernesse, June 24, 1755, *ibid.*, 32856/ 155.

to Russia a secret agent whose identity would be known to only three people: the king himself; his Secretary of State for Foreign Affairs, Antoine Louis Rouillé; and the king's cousin and director of his Secret Correspondence, Prince de Conti (Louis François de Bourbon).

Conti did not hold an official post in the Ministry of Foreign Affairs; yet as much as anyone else he guided the destiny of French foreign policy in Eastern Europe. For some time Conti had aspired to the Polish throne, but he knew that Russia's blessing was necessary before anything could be accomplished. Thus, Russia became as much the object of his thoughts as Poland. Owing to Louis XV's public commitment to the Saxon house, which gave every indication of wishing to continue its decades-long hold on the Polish throne, Conti could not expect to gain official sanction for his goal. Nevertheless, in order for Conti to succeed in his intrigues, Louis allowed him to conduct secret and unofficial activities through an intricate web of agents in both France and Eastern Europe. Conti had vast personal wealth, and his secret *corps diplomatique* was supplied with more than enough funds to carry on its work. Because of his close relationship with the king of France, he was influential in the appointment of official diplomats who not infrequently became his agents as well as agents of the Ministry of Foreign Affairs. As a result what developed was a whole system of secret diplomacy that came to be known as "the King's Secret," "the Secret Correspondence," or merely "the Secret." A recent authority on the subject has succinctly described its significance in this manner:

> The whole structure of the Secret grew and functioned unknown to the Secretary of State for Foreign Affairs and the other ministers—and, indeed, unknown to all those outside its carefully chosen ranks. The completeness of this secrecy was astonishing.
>
> As a result, by 1755 the agency in France with most concern in Eastern Europe and the only agency in France with even a remote idea of affairs in Russia was that organization under Conti and the King known as the Secret. Any alteration in the relationship of Russia and Eastern Europe, and especially of Russia and Poland, was of immediate concern to this organization. Its ultimate aim seemed always to be the exclusion of Russian influence

in Poland if any success was to be expected for a French candidate for the Polish throne.[23]

Naturally, when Louis XV decided to send an agent into Russia, he consulted Conti. The man chosen for the role was Alexander Peter Mackenzie Douglas, a renegade Scotsman who, because he had involved himself in pro-Stuart activities, had sought refuge in Paris and had taken a position in the household of Conti. Douglas was to act as agent for both the Secret and the Ministry of Foreign Affairs.[24]

Posing as a surveyor of mines in Eastern Europe and Russia, Douglas' task was to determine the number of Russian troops stationed in Kurland and the number of Russian vessels harbored off the coast. In St. Petersburg he was to obtain the latest information on the Anglo-Russian negotiations and the total number of troops Russia had actually mobilized. He was to use a quaint allegorical code to relate his reports. Williams was to be known as the "black fox," and, if he was progressing in his negotiations, Douglas would report that "the black fox would be expensive because they give the English commissions to buy them." If Grand Chancellor Alexis Bestuzhev-Riumin dominated affairs then "the grey wolf also has his price," but if he did not "the price of Martens is going down." Three thousand Russian mercenary troops who would be hired by the British were one "little grey skin." All his reports would be sent first to agents in Amsterdam who would then forward them to Paris, either for Rouillé or Conti upon instructions from Douglas.[25]

Thus, by the time Sir Charles Hanbury Williams reached St. Petersburg on June 16, 1755, France and Prussia were well aware of the implications of his mission and were taking steps to guard themselves against its menacing results if he proved successful.

[23] L. Jay Oliva, *Misalliance. A Study of French Policy in Russia During the Seven Years' War* (New York, 1964), pp. 10–11 and also pp. 2–10.

[24] *Ibid.*, pp. 11–13.

[25] *Ibid.*, pp. 13–14, and L. Jay Oliva, "French Policy in Russia: 1755–1762" (unpublished Ph.D. dissertation, Syracuse University, 1960), pp. 23–24.

II Russian Intrigue; British Overtures to Frederick

Sir Charles Hanbury Williams, British ambassador-designate to the court of St. Petersburg, had never been to Russia. He arrived well prepared to avert domestic deprivations. He was accompanied by several servants in and out of livery for whom he wanted just "ordinary beds." His baggage wagon contained many damasks as well as a service of 5,893 ounces of white plate and 1,060 ounces of gilt. While his wine shipment was to follow along with his furniture and chimney pieces, Williams chose to take with him Lord Chesterfield's gift of goldfish, which Horace Walpole said could not live in Russia.[1]

The appointment of Williams was a mistake; his health was poor—as was his judgment—and he had failed in earlier missions. At Berlin he had infuriated King Frederick II and had been recalled. Subsequently, in Dresden he involved himself in Saxon and Polish domestic intrigues beyond the call of duty. That he owed his appointment to his connections in the British ministry and Parliament cannot be doubted. Sir Richard Lodge referred to Williams as one of the "very pretty young men" surrounding King George II's chief minister, the Duke of Newcastle.[2] Nevertheless, he was entrusted with a mission upon which depended at least the safety of Hanover and possibly the peace of all Europe.

[1] See PROSP 91/ 60, *passim*; CHW 22–10885, *passim*; and the Earl of Ilchester and Mrs. Langford-Brooke, *The Life of Sir Charles Hanbury-Williams: Poet, Wit and Diplomatist* (London, 1928), p. 310.

[2] Sir Richard Lodge, *Great Britain & Prussia in the Eighteenth Century* (Oxford, 1923), p. 78. For Williams' early life and background, see the Earl of Ilchester and Mrs. Langford-Brooke, *The Life of Sir Charles Hanbury-Williams: Poet, Wit and Diplomatist*; and David Bayne Horn, *Sir Charles Hanbury Williams & European Diplomacy (1747–58)* (London, 1930).

Williams' instructions were to conclude the pivotal subsidy treaty with Russia.[3] In July he had a series of talks with Grand Chancellor Alexis Petrovich Bestuzhev-Riumin and was able to reach an understanding with him and to exchange drafts of the treaty. A subsidy of 100,000 pounds per annum for a period of four years would be paid for the maintenance of 55,000 Russian troops and about 50 galleys. An additional 400,000 pounds per annum would be paid when those same Russian forces were requisitioned by the king of Great Britain to move out of Russia or Russian-controlled territory. In order to insure Bestuzhev-Riumin's continued support in this negotiation, Williams promised to give the grand chancellor 10,000 pounds upon the exchange of the ratifications. In essence, the ambassador had thus far followed the letter and spirit of his instructions.[4]

Despite this agreement with the grand chancellor, Williams knew that the final word rested with Empress Elizabeth and that she might also make some additional demands on Great Britain before acceding to the treaty. A certain amount of patience and further negotiation would perhaps be needed before it could actually be drafted and signed by both countries.[5]

While Williams continued his negotiations in St. Petersburg, the rest of Europe was in diplomatic ferment. Austria still refused to undertake the defense of the Netherlands and Hanover until Great Britain actually had the Russian troops in her employ.[6] Faced with this obstinancy, British and Hanoverian statesmen finally came to the conclusion that Austria could not be relied on as an ally. In fact, these statesmen charged that the Austrian court was ruining the plans of Great Britain[7] and was offensive, ungrateful, and impolitic.[8] Moreover, the British min-

[3] See several letters from Holdernesse to Williams and Dickens, April 11, 1755, PROSP 91/60.

[4] Williams to Holdernesse, July 4, 1755, and Holdernesse to Williams, June 17 and July 24, 1755, *ibid.*; Williams to Keith, July 8, 1755, BMAdd-MSS 35480/ 21–22; and CHW 22–10885/ 328–330, respectively; and LOII, *f.* 36, *op.* 1, *d.* 91/97–98 (July 17 and 18, 1755).

[5] Williams to Holdernesse, July 25, 1755, PROSP 91/61.

[6] See Newcastle to Holdernesse, July 18, 1755, BMAddMSS 32857/ 162–164.

[7] Holdernesse to Newcastle, June 29, 1755, *ibid.*, 32856/349–350. See also "Memorandum," July 13, 1755, 32996/ 170–172.

[8] Holdernesse to Keene, July 2, 1755, *ibid.*, 43435/ 1–3.

istry was being reminded by its own countrymen as well as the Hanoverians that the war that threatened to break out with France was Great Britain's affair and need not concern Hanover. Therefore, if European politics were to be so unjust as to involve Hanover, Great Britain should do everything in her power to provide for Hanover's safety and to defend her from attack.[9] At the same time, there were already indications of dissension in Parliament over the additional expense Great Britain was to shoulder in order to defend Hanover.[10] Nevertheless, on several occasions Newcastle outlined the policy that was to become Great Britain's: "We entirely agree with [the Hanoverian ministers] that the present Quarrel, is a Quarrel of this country . . . and that is an additional Reason, why we should now assist, and defend, the King's German Dominions, if attack'd";[11] and "if the King's German Dominions are attack'd for this cause; it is attacking the King, and His Majesty will and must be defended."[12]

In the opinion of British and Hanoverian statesmen the greatest and most immediate threat to Hanover was, of course, Prussia; thus, an agreement with Prussia could possibly resolve the whole issue. Although the interview between Frederick and George had not taken place in June 1755, the idea of such a meeting suggested the plausibility of future negotiation. Already in the latter part of June, Newcastle was contemplating just such an arrangement. He believed that the impending treaty with Russia could be used as an important, if not decisive, trump card in the diplomatic game to force Frederick to agree not to attack Hanover, since there would soon be at his back 55,000 Russian troops in the pay of George II.[13] Although mercenaries were to be obtained from other principalities in Europe to defend Hanover, Newcastle was convinced that the effect on

[9] See Holderness to Newcastle, July 30, 1755, *ibid.*, 32857/ 446–448.
[10] See Sir John Bernard's comments in Newcastle to Holdernesse, July 11, 1755, *ibid.*, 45–46, and 43, 53–55; Holdernesse to Newcastle, July 30, 1755, *ibid.*, 446–448; and Hardwicke to Newcastle, July 28, 1755, BMAddMSS 32857/398.
[11] Newcastle to Holdernesse, July 18, 1755, BMAddMSS 32857/ 160–162, and 162–164.
[12] Newcastle to Holdernesse, Aug. 1, 1755, *ibid.*, 502.
[13] See Newcastle to Hardwicke, Feb. 20, 1757, *ibid.*, 32870/ 202–203.

Prussia of an English subsidy treaty with Russia would "contribute to the preservation of the general peace."[14] Writing to Lord Chancellor Hardwicke more than a year later, he pointed out that "long before we had the least certainty of our Treaty with Russia being likely to succeed . . . my Idea *then* was to combine those two treaties [an Anglo-Russian subsidy treaty and the Convention of Westminster] together."[15]

It seemed that Newcastle's hopes and predictions were being realized when, in early July, it became known in London through an intercepted letter written by Frederick that Prussia desired that war "not be brought into Germany."[16] At this crucial moment, Newcastle decided to arrange an agreement with Prussia for the peace of Germany, utilizing the pending Anglo-Russian negotiations to help Frederick see where his real interests lay.[17] Despite the possibility of success, Lord Chancellor Hardwicke dissented and even warned Newcastle against acting hastily by using the Anglo-Russian negotiations as a club hanging over the head of Frederick. "The King of Prussia may ly by, and yet France may send such a force that way, as may strike so much fear that the King [George II] may insist our Requisition being made. On the other hand may not the Czarina be revolted and disgusted, when She hears such a private bargain is struck up with the King of Prussia; for She certainly flatters herself with the expectation that the great Subsidy of 500,000 pounds will come into her coffers."[18]

Hardwicke's pessimistic, although prophetic, views were in the minority. When Newcastle received the news from Williams that the conclusion of the subsidy treaty was imminent, he was further encouraged. He wrote Secretary of State Holdernesse, "The possibility of having Such a Force at the King's Disposi-

---

[14] Newcastle to Holdernesse, July 11, 1755, *ibid.*, 32857/ 5.

[15] *Ibid.*, 32870/ 202–203 (Feb. 20, 1757), and Hardwicke to Newcastle, Feb. 21, 1757, *ibid.*, 210. See also Newcastle to Mitchell, May 28, 1756, *ibid.*, 32865/ 128.

[16] Newcastle to Holdernesse, July 11, 1755, *ibid.*, 32857/ 43. See also Frederick to Mitchell, June 24, 1755, PC XI/ 6835/ 184.

[17] See Newcastle's letters of July 25 and 26, 1755, to Muenchausen, Holdernesse, and Hardwicke, BMAddMSS 32857/ 349–352, 354, 357, 359–360, 385.

[18] *Ibid.*, 397–398 (July 28, 1755).

tion, will, We humbly hope, prevent certain Powers from making any Hostile Attempts, either upon His Majesty, or His Allies."[19]

Newcastle's policy gained more support as the days passed. Most important was the acceptance of Newcastle's scheme by Holdernesse, who had considerable influence with the king. Holdernesse wrote to Newcastle:

> Fears of Prussia and pacifick councils authorize the King to take any measures to keep that powerful enemy quiet. . . . I quite agree with your grace that no better use could be made of the *Russian Treaty* in the *present circumstances*. I say in the present circumstances because . . . the moment *we* cannot make up our matters with Vienna, the only thing left is to keep terms with *Prussia*: . . . if His Pr. Majesty thinks us still well with our *old friends* he must see the possibility of his having the two Empress's and Saxony upon his back at a time and will the more readily hear reason, when he has much to fear and little to hope from a general *crash*.[20]

Finally, on August 9, Hardwicke withdrew his reservations.[21] Within the week King George ordered Holdernesse to explain Great Britain's position to the Duke of Brunswick, who immediately sent a messenger to Berlin to inform Frederick of the overture of Great Britain.[22] The duke disclosed that the English ministers recognized that the tranquility of Germany and especially that of Hanover depended on Prussia; Great Britain feared that the colonial war would be extended to Europe and sincerely hoped that Frederick would not support such an injustice committed in Germany. Frederick was asked, therefore, to subscribe to British views for the preservation of the peace of Germany. Specifically, he was asked not to threaten Hanover either by his own aggressive designs or through assistance to France.[23] The king of Prussia answered the Duke of Brunswick that he believed the issues involving Germany were unclear at this time;

[19] Newcastle to Holdernesse, July 29, 1755, *ibid.*, 403–404.
[20] *Ibid.*, 555–556 (Aug. 3, 1755).
[21] Hardwicke to Newcastle, *ibid.*, 32858/ 74.
[22] Holdernesse to Newcastle, Aug. 14, 1755, *ibid.*, 32858/ 141.
[23] Duke of Brunswick to Frederick, Aug. 11, 1755, PC XI/ 6923/ 251–252.

nevertheless, he would offer his services as a mediator in the Anglo-French crisis.[24]

Frederick's reserve with the British could have been expected; the British had not made any concrete proposals that would necessarily benefit Prussia. But it would be incorrect to accept Frederick's professed indifference to the British as a true barometer of his feelings or thoughts. The slightest movement of diplomats or military operations did not escape his attention. When he received a report early in July that General George Browne, who held a command in the Russian army in Livonia, was traveling incognito to Vienna, Frederick speculated that George II was ready to wage war against France in Europe. He suspected that Browne's mission was to assist in coordinating the military activities of Russia, Austria, and Great Britain. He further calculated that, if the Vienna court were to send troops to the Netherlands, Russia would send her own troops to the Habsburg dominions to replace them. Or as an alternative, the Russian army would encamp on the borders of Livonia or Kurland and would march in accordance with the demands of circumstance. Frederick made it clear that he was not treating these matters as simple conjectures. His oppressive fears were relieved only when he learned that General Browne had traveled to Prague to visit relatives and would later take the waters at Karlsbad.[25]

Frederick was acutely aware of his own vulnerability. He reacted to his fears concerning a possible invasion of his territories by Russians troops by putting his army officers in Königsberg on a 24-hour alert and prohibiting them from leaving that

[24] *Ibid.*, 6923, 6924/ 252–254, 254–255, respectively (Aug. 12, 1755). See also Frederick to Eichel (and enclosure from Prince Ferdinand of Brunswick, Aug. 7, 1755), Aug. 10 (?), 1755, *ibid.*, 6920/ 246–248; and Frederick to Prince Ferdinand of Brunswick, Aug. 10, 1755, *ibid.*, 6921/ 248; Frederick to Klinggraeffen and Knyphausen, Aug. 12, 1755, *ibid.*, 6926, 6927/ 256, 256–258, respectively; and Frederick to Klinggraeffen and Knyphausen, Aug. 16, 1755, *ibid.*, 6832, 6833/ 259–260, 260–261, respectively.

[25] Frederick to Maltzahn, July 5, 1755, *ibid.*, 6851/ 197; Frederick to Klinggraeffen, July 5, 8, 12, and 15, 1755, *ibid.*, 6850, 6855, 6864, 6872/ 196, 198–199, 199, 204, 209, respectively; and Frederick to Knyphausen, July 15, 1755, *ibid.*, 6871/ 209.

province on furlough.[26] He also instructed his envoy to France to refrain from making any commitment which might in any way involve Prussia in a war.[27] In fact, Frederick wished that France and Great Britain would allow Prussia and Austria to mediate their quarrel in the hope of avoiding a war in Europe.[28] In keeping abreast of British subsidy negotiations, especially those with Russia, he received information that Williams was making continued progress at St. Petersburg and that the conclusion of the convention was only a matter of time.[29] He was distressed when the false rumor reached him that an Anglo-Russian subsidy treaty had been concluded and a courier had already left St. Petersburg carrying official documents to the British.[30] Subsequent information arrived in Berlin that the Russian court had already ordered the augmentation and mobilization of Russian troops in Livonia and Kurland. The Russian army there, according to Frederick's reports, was to reach a total of 70,000 men with an additional 16,000 to man 50 Russian galleys.[31] Frederick envisaged Russian troops being transported by sea to Lübeck and hence into the Netherlands and Hanover.[32] Nor was that the only avenue of approach for Russian armies.

[26] Frederick to General von Lewaldt, Aug. 4, 1755, *ibid.*, 6909/ 235. See also Maltzahn to Frederick, Aug. 11, 1755, *ibid.*, 6934/ 261–262.

[27] Frederick to Knyphausen, Aug. 2, 1755, *ibid.*, 6904/ 232.

[28] Frederick to Knyphausen, Michell, and Klinggraeffen, Aug. 2, 1755, *ibid.*, 6904, 6905, 6906/ 232, 233, 233, respectively.

[29] Maltzahn to Frederick, June 30, 1755, *ibid.*, 6851/ 196; Frederick to Knyphausen, Michell, and Klinggraeffen, July 1, 1755, *ibid.*, 6843, 6844, 6845/ 192–193, 194, respectively; Frederick to Michell, July 8, 1755, *ibid.*, 6857/ 200; Frederick to Maltzahn, Aug. 16, 1755, *ibid.*, 6934/ 261–262; Michell to Frederick, Aug. 1 and 15, 1755, *ibid.*, 6925, 6953/ 255, 275, respectively; and Maltzahn to Frederick, Aug. 11, 1755, *ibid.*, 6934/ 261–262.

[30] Frederick to Michell, Aug. 18, 1755, *ibid.*, 6937/ 264–265; and Frederick to Hellen, Klinggraeffen, Maltzahn, and Knyphausen, Aug. 19, 1755, *ibid.*, 6938, 6939, 6940, 6941/ 265, 265, 265–266, 267, respectively.

[31] Frederick to Knyphausen, Aug. 23, 1755, *ibid.*, 6942/ 267–268; and Onzier to Frederick, Aug. 21, 1755, *ibid.*, 6955/ 277–278. See also Frederick to Podewils, Aug. 28 and 30, 1755, *ibid.*, 6955, 6956/ 277–278, respectively; and Podewils to Frederick, Aug. 29, 1755, *ibid.*, 6956/ 278–279.

[32] Frederick to Knyphausen, Aug. 19, 1755, *ibid.*, 6941/ 266–267; and Frederick to Haeseler, Aug. 23, 1755, *ibid.*, 6944/ 269.

Frederick was convinced that Polish forces could not prevent a Russian invasion if Russia chose to use Poland as a route to western Europe.[33]

Thus, by the end of August Frederick was deeply troubled. Everything suggested that his salvation from a Russian attack could be gained only through a rapprochement with Great Britain. Prussia now feared the British, who threatened to use Russian troops against her, more than the British feared Prussia. The courtship had already begun—the marriage had yet to take place.

Meanwhile in St. Petersburg, on August 9 Williams scored a short-lived victory—he thought he had concluded an Anglo-Russian subsidy treaty. Since his arrival in St. Petersburg, Williams had worked industriously for the speedy conclusion of the treaty in the hope that his reputation would be enhanced at home. Williams was more concerned with merely concluding the treaty than with the essential assumptions and purposes for which it was being negotiated. Had he sufficiently scrutinized the commitments he was making, he would never have made them even provisionally.

The treaty essentially provided for the maintenance of 55,000 Russian troops and 40 or 50 galleys at a cost of 100,000 pounds per annum for four years, with an additional 400,000 pounds when King George called them into his service outside Russian territories. As far as these provisions were concerned, Williams had carried out his instructions and served the king well. However, Williams allowed Empress Elizabeth to make further demands, the inclusion of two additional separate and secret articles plus a declaration. Although Williams had signed these two articles *sub spe rati*, they, together with the declaration, modified its substance and spirit when appended to the body of the treaty.

The first of these articles was based on the notion that, since Russia would take part militarily in the forthcoming war, she should also have a voice in the eventual peace negotiations. Elizabeth desired neither that negotiations be held nor peace be made with the enemy without the consent of both Great

[33] Frederick to Knyphausen, Aug. 30, 1755, *ibid.*, 6959/ 281–283.

Britain and Russia. The motivation for the second of these articles was Elizabeth's fear of depleting the military forces maintained near East Prussia once war broke out in Europe. Although the War College could not estimate how long it would take to replace from other parts of the Russian Empire some 50 or 60 thousand troops in the Lifland Command (Kurland, Lifland, Estland, Polish frontier), Elizabeth calculated that it would take no less than three months. Thus, the troops already encamped in the Lifland Command to be used by Great Britain would be allowed to move outside the frontiers only after a three-month waiting period from the day the requisition was made. Regarding the eventual war in Europe, Russia by her appended declaration sought to exclude as a *casus foederis* a war confined only to Italy and America.[34]

The least offensive Russian demand concerned the exclusion of Italy and America as a *casus foederis*, if the Russian court interpreted this to mean that their troops would not be sent into Italy or to America. But, as Holdernesse explained to Williams, "The use of the Treaty itself would be entirely lost, if the Russian succours were not forthcoming, in case an American or an Italian war should induce certain powers to make hostile attempts against any part of His Majesty's Dominions in Europe, or against the King's Allies."[35] Concerning the first additional separate and secret article, the British could not accept the rigid limitations that the Russians had proposed for future peace negotiations. The British view was included in a new draft proposal to which they hoped the Russians would agree. It merely bound each party to communicate to the other any negotiations that took place with the common enemy and to cooperate in arriving at an honorable and advantageous peace for both countries.[36]

The British would under no circumstances accept any part of the second additional separate and secret article, for it would

[34] Williams to Holdernesse, Aug. 9 and 11, 1755, PROSP 91/ 61, and LOII, *f*. 36, *op*. 1, *d*. 91/ 98–100. For the request to the War College and its reply see AVPR, *f. Snosheniia . . . Angliei*, 1755, *op*. 35/ 1, *d*. 770/ 156–157 (Aug. 1 and 2, 1755).
[35] PROSP 91/ 61 (Aug. 19, 1755).
[36] Holdernesse to Williams, Aug. 28, 1755, *ibid*.

destroy "at once the principal end for which the Treaty is made."
Williams was reminded that the king of England was paying
a subsidy to enable Empress Elizabeth "to keep a body of
troops near at hand to come immediately to His Majesty's assistance, and to act by diversion in case of an attack upon His
Majesty or his allies." Furthermore, it was pointed out that it
was expressly stated within the body of the treaty that "the
general who commands this corps shall have previous orders to
act immediately upon His Majesty's requisition, even without
waiting for fresh instructions from Her Imp. Majesty." Thus,
the three-month waiting period was strictly outside the original
purpose of the treaty; and as far as Empress Elizabeth's maintaining an active defensive force on her frontiers was concerned, "His Majesty does not well see what enemy the Czarina
can have to fear in Livonia."[37]

Williams could do nothing but apologize and promise that in
the future he would execute his instructions to the letter.[38] Subsequent discussions held at the Russian court led finally to an
agreement that satisfied the British in all matters. The treaty
was signed on September 30, 1755, and forwarded to London
for ratification.[39]

Four days later Mackenzie Douglas arrived in St. Petersburg
and precipitated a negotiation that eventually put an end to all
that Williams had thus far accomplished. More than that, Douglas was to find himself a party to an intrigue that led to a coup
of such major proportions that it changed the face of the Russian court and its foreign policy. He had traveled for three
months and had not hesitated to mix pleasure with business, an
indulgence that was to have political consequences. Although
Douglas had been committed to the strictest secrecy, he revealed the nature of his mission to a lady with whom he had an
affair in Dresden. He had promised to meet her in Berlin but
never appeared, and she, angered by this affront, not only wrote

[37] *Ibid.*
[38] Williams to Holdernesse, Sept. 13, 1755, *ibid.*
[39] Williams to Holdernesse, Sept. 16 and 30, Oct. 2, 1755, *ibid.*; LOII,
f. 36, *op.* 1, *d.* 91/ 100–101; and AVPR, *f. Snosheniia . . . Angliei,* 1755, *op.*
35/ 1, *d.* 770/ 198–215, 218, 225–226, 230–249.

privately to the French Ministry of Foreign Affairs, but also publicized the nature of the Douglas mission.[40]

Douglas was immediately thwarted and insulted by Williams. Since he was a British subject, Douglas could not obtain an audience at the Russian court without first obtaining the English ambassador's permission. But he could not produce any credentials from London, and his former association with the Stuart cause made Williams even more suspicious. Douglas even believed the Grand Chancellor Alexis Bestuzhev-Riumin and Williams had discovered the real purpose of his mission. Williams refused to give Douglas permission to have an audience at the Russian court and ordered him out of the country within a week.[41]

Before Douglas left St. Petersburg, however, he succeeded in a way he never thought possible. During his short-lived visit to Russia, he found out more about the clandestine activities at the Russian court than had Williams or even the grand chancellor himself. And everything that he learned was to be of extreme value and importance for Louis XV. He discovered that the 62-year-old grand chancellor was in a desperate struggle for his political life. Alexis Petrovich Bestuzhev-Riumin had served in the Russian bureaucracy from the time of Peter the Great. He became vice-chancellor after Elizabeth took the throne and was elevated to the office of grand chancellor three years later. Since that time, his influence had prevailed in the conduct of Russia's foreign affairs. He had early committed himself and Russia to a pro-Anglo-Austrian policy in opposition to France and Prussia, with whom Russia had severed diplomatic relations years before. However, he was now on the verge of losing all before the vicious intrigues and cabals of the younger Michael Vorontsov, the Vice Chancellor. Bestuzhev-Riumin was unaware of the enormous gravity and urgency of the situation.

Michael Ilarionovich Vorontsov hated Alexis Bestuzhev-

[40] L. Jay Oliva, *Misalliance: A Study of French Policy in Russia During the Seven Years' War*, pp. 14–15. See also Williams to Holdernesse, Oct. 7, 1755, PROSP 91/ 61.

[41] Douglas to Rouillé, Jan. 6 and 7, 1756, BN SM NAF 22009/ 3–14, 17–31, respectively; Williams to Holdernesse, Oct. 7, 1755, PROSP 91/ 61; and Oliva, p. 20.

Riumin. He wanted to remove the old man from his all-powerful position and fill the vacancy himself. Vorontsov, a leading member of a distinguished and wealthy family, owed his rise to political prominence to his involvement in placing Elizabeth on the throne. He was handsomely rewarded for that assistance with extensive estates, and in 1744 he was appointed vice chancellor at the age of thirty. Furthermore, he cemented his close association with Empress Elizabeth by his marriage to her first cousin. In domestic affairs he frequently caballed in economic and political ventures with the well-known Shuvalov family. In foreign affairs he was anti-Prussian and pro-Austrian but, significantly, also pro-French, which placed him in opposition to the grand chancellor. Moreover, Vorontsov led a group at the Russian court which favored a rapprochement between France and Russia and worked continuously but secretly toward its realization.

Douglas met these people soon after his arrival. The liaison was made through Michel de Rouen, Vorontsov's close associate and secretary. Michel de Rouen, then a private merchant in Russia, had built up a lucrative trade with members of the Russian court, in particular with Michael Vorontsov who later vigorously supported his commercial ventures. Michel de Rouen had made several trips to France, where he frequently stopped at the Ministry of Foreign Affairs to relate the news from Russia. Perhaps the most important communication he made to the ministry was that Russia was interested in renewing her former friendship with the Versailles court. Now, with Douglas in St. Petersburg, the pro-French interests at the Russian court were on the ascendancy.[42]

Vorontsov, practically taking charge of Douglas, held a dinner for him attended by several members of the Russian court and informed Empress Elizabeth of Douglas' arrival. Taking her cue she requested that the Scotsman appear at court to hear a program of Italian music, thus effecting an informal meeting not requiring an introduction from Williams. Douglas learned that the Shuvalovs, Narishkins, Razumovskiis, Dolgorukiis, and Michael Petrovich Bestuzhev-Riumin, the estranged brother of

[42] BN SM NAF 22009/ 4; LOII, f. 36, op. 1, d. 1071/ 192–200; and Oliva, pp. 6–8, 14–15, 20–22.

the grand chancellor, wanted French support for their intrigues against the grand chancellor and his policies. Vorontsov, it seems, was already aware of Douglas' connection with the Prince de Conti and wanted to know whether Douglas had a letter from the prince or some evidence of the prince's confidence in him. Douglas, of course, did not have such credentials but had to promise Vorontsov that he "would return one more time, but recommended by [his] family and friends."[43]

Vorontsov also told Douglas that he could tell the French Ministry of Foreign Affairs that the "Empress of Russia had the most sincere will and ardent desire to see a union established between the two states." In order to accomplish this, France was to send a representative incognito to Russia with authorization to open diplomatic negotiations between the two courts. To prevent mishaps, Vorontsov suggested that the representative write ahead of time that he was the person "charged to produce a librarian and send the burgundy wines." Vorontsov desired to keep Alexis Bestuzhev-Riumin from any knowledge of these plans lest he try to ruin them. "It is of the utmost consequence that he never be informed of this coup until it is accomplished and he learns of it from the lips of the Empress herself." The vice chancellor was of the opinion that the French, if they so desired, could demolish the Anglo-Russian Subsidy Treaty and the power of the grand chancellor who was its prime advocate.[44]

This was undoubtedly a crucial moment at the Russian court. The pro-French clique led by Vorontsov saw its opportunity to reestablish the French in Russia. The possible advantages to be derived from such a coup were enormous, for it could lead to the overthrow of the grand chancellor and enable Vorontsov and his associates to take complete control of Russian affairs. For years Bestuzhev-Riumin had been able to keep Russia and France apart and to ally his court with France's chief enemies— Great Britain and Austria. If suddenly a Franco-Russian rapprochement were established, the grand chancellor would certainly be humiliated. It would signify the end of his influence in

[43] Douglas to Rouillé, Jan. 6 and 7, 1756, BN SM NAF 22009/ 3–14, 17–31, respectively; and Oliva, pp. 20–22.
[44] *Ibid.*

Russian foreign policy. But France would be interested in re-asserting herself in Russia only if England could be removed from the scene. Vorontsov was aware of this fact and that it would present a major problem for him. For with England's departure Russia would lose the great sum of money for sub-sidizing her troops against Prussia. Moreover, as great an ob-stacle to his success was France's alliance with Prussia, against whom Russia wanted to go to war. It would be sheer fantasy to conclude that France would willingly take Great Britain's role and financially underwrite the use of Russian troops against Prussia. Thus, before Vorontsov and his associates could suc-ceed in their coup, a change in the European balance of power would have to take place. In this whole affair, Vorontsov demon-strated that he was one of the shrewdest politicians at the Rus-sian court.

III The Convention of Westminster Concluded

Early in September 1755, Frederick received confirmation of the rumors trickling into Berlin that an Anglo-Russian subsidy treaty had been concluded.[1] Weeks were to pass before Frederick would learn that the pact Williams had signed on August 9 in St. Petersburg was not acceptable to the British ministry. Frederick thought of himself as the object of a hostile world. Great Britain had 55,000 Russian mercenaries who were ready to strike a death blow at Prussia.

Frederick wrote to the Duke of Brunswick that he had reconsidered George II's inquiry. Since his alliance with France was scheduled to terminate the following spring—"allowing me," as he put it, "the liberty to act then in conformity to my interests and to my convenience"—Frederick hinted that the Duke of Brunswick could, on his own responsibility, suggest to the English ministry that it make "reasonable propositions" to him concerning the neutrality of Hanover.[2] At the same time, Frederick asked his envoy in London to find out whether the British would be interested in concluding a treaty for the security of Hanover.[3]

On receiving Frederick's message through the Duke of Brunswick, Holdernesse was perplexed by the vagueness of the communiqué and wrote Newcastle:

I am at a loss to guess what His Highness means by *Propositions équitables* which I have underlined in the copy; if it is no more

[1] See Maltzahn to Frederick, Aug. 29, 1755, PC XI/ 6970/ 290.
[2] *Ibid.*, 6966/ 286–287 (Sept. 1, 1755).
[3] Frederick to Michell, Sept. 2, 1755, *ibid.*, 6968/ 289.

than a security for *Silesia* and a promise that the King will not countenance any attack made upon any part of the *present* Prussian possessions it might possibly be worthwhile to give some opening of that kind; I think it not unlikely that the King may order me to write from Helvoet to the Duke of Brunswick to get him to explain these vague conjectures a little more fully.[4]

Holdernesse assumed correctly. George II ordered him to inform the Duke of Brunswick that he was pleased with Frederick's continued interest in preserving the general peace in Europe and above all in Germany, and that he further believed that no power would attempt to break the peace in Germany without first obtaining the support of Prussia. He wished, therefore, that the king of Prussia would explain his position more fully on the security of Germany, to clarify what he meant by "acceptable [sic] propositions."[5]

Newcastle was excited about these recent developments. He declared that "Negotiation must be push'd in earnest."[6] Even Chancellor Hardwicke was comforted. "I like your going on with your negotiation with Prussia extremely," he wrote to Newcastle on October 6; "If you can keep *Prussia* quiet on the one side, and Spain on the other, Surely that is all, that Great Britain wants and the other powers declaring a Neutrality may only put France more at her ease."[7]

About the same time Michell, the Prussian envoy to Great Britain, wrote Frederick that, if the king of Prussia would remain tranquil in the event of a war breaking out in Europe, he believed the king of England would make Prussia an acceptable proposition. Michell said that the British were somewhat apprehensive, however, concerning Prussia's alliance with France, since the British were not confident that it could be broken. Nevertheless, if there was the slightest possibility of success in

[4] BMAddMSS 32859/ 34 (Sept. 9, 1755). The Duke of Brunswick communicated Frederick's message on September 5 to Holdernesse. See *ibid.*, 30. See also Duke of Brunswick to Frederick, Sept. 5, 1755, PC XI/ 6984/ 303.

[5] Holdernesse to Duke of Brunswick, Sept. 30, 1755, BMAddMSS 32859/ 275–278. The Duke of Brunswick transmitted this letter to Frederick on October 8. See PC XI/ 7024/ 331–332.

[6] Newcastle to Hardwicke, Oct. 3, 1755, BMAddMSS 32859/ 360.

[7] *Ibid.*, 399.

this matter, the British would attempt to arrange the security of Hanover with Prussia.[8]

Frederick was ever cautious in his replies to the British, since he wanted them to make the first proposals. He made it known that he was well aware that the king of England wanted him to declare for the neutrality of Hanover; but, he wrote the Duke of Brunswick, "we never had any direct or indirect design on the German possessions of the King of England, on which we have neither rights nor pretentions; thus, I am able to say that Prussia desires certainly only to maintain the peace." Frederick dramatically continued, "I govern the State of which the happiness and the protection are confined to me, my first duty is to think of no action contrary to its interests, that I am obliged to sacrifice my desires, my hates, my person and in a word all my passions; that also, if the King of England or some Prince of Europe makes propositions to me, they must have all that is in accordance with the interests of Prussia."[9]

Frederick was candid in stating that France intended to renew her alliance with Prussia and that Louis was sending an envoy to negotiate the particulars with him. Therefore, if the king of England wished to arrange an agreement with Prussia, he must speak more openly on the matter—he had begun the negotiation and, therefore, should be the first to speak. Frederick apologized for his "pompous politic," but admitted his situation was critical: "it is not convenient for me to be ventrous and to make thoughtless [moves] which I would perhaps regret."[10] Frederick instructed his London envoy Michell to inform the British ministry that, if the Russians invaded Germany, he would have no alternative but to enter the war.[11]

Russia was preparing for that very thing. In the autumn of 1755, reports flowed out of St. Petersburg that the Russians were intensifying military preparations and were actually planning to attack the king of Prussia. On October 7 Empress Eliza-

[8] PC XI/ 7045/ 350–351 (Oct. 10, 1755). See also Frederick to Michell, Sept. 23, 1755, ibid., 6996/ 312; and Michell to Frederick, Sept. 30, 1755, ibid., 7027/ 338.

[9] Ibid., 7025/ 334–336 (Oct. 13, 1755); and ibid., 7024/ 332–334.

[10] Ibid., 7025/ 334–336 (Oct. 13, 1755); and ibid., 7026/ 337.

[11] Ibid., 7027/ 338 (Oct. 14, 1755); and BMAddMSS 32860/ 38.

beth convened a conference of the leading members of her court to discuss the methods that Russia should employ to fulfill her commitments to her allies in the event of a war in Europe. Grand Chancellor Bestuzhev-Riumin set the tone of the meeting by recalling the advice given to Empress Elizabeth by a similar conference held in Moscow on May 14 and 15, 1753, which declared itself opposed to further aggrandizement of Frederick's power. Once again the Russian court announced its desire to reduce his territories to their former modest size, and to return Silesia and Glatz to Maria Theresa. Magazines were to be established in Riga, Mittau, and Libau which would supply 100,000 men. Russia would immediately attack the king of Prussia if he were to attack an ally of Empress Elizabeth or if one of her allies attacked him.[12] Although several weeks passed before Frederick learned of these decisions,[13] he was distressed by the news that an Anglo-Russian subsidy treaty had been drawn up again and signed in St. Petersburg on September 30. He knew that the fate of Prussia would be sealed when the treaty was finally ratified.[14]

All that was taking place vindicated Newcastle's strategy regarding the utility of the Anglo-Russian negotiations against Prussia. As he aptly stated to Horace Walpole, "the King of Prussia sees, that by His Neutrality, He may be assured, beyond any doubt, of the most ample Security for His Present great acquisitions, and that by taking part with France, and introducing a War in the Empire, He may draw upon Himself, Seventy thousand Russians."[15]

On November 7 the English ministry agreed to submit the

[12] Williams to Holdernesse, Oct. 7 and 11, 1755, PROSP 91/ 61; Maltzahn to Frederick, Dec. 5, 1755, PC XI/ 7134/ 430–431; Frederick to Podewils, Dec. 20, 1755, PC XI/ 7147/ 439–441; and Evgenii Shchepkin, *Russko-Avstriiskii soiuz vo vremia Semiletnei Voiny, 1746–1758 gg.* [The Russo-Austrian union during the Seven Years' War] (St. Petersburg, 1902), pp. 244–245, 252–253.

[13] See Maltzahn to Frederick, Dec. 5, 1755, PC XI/ 7134/ 430–431; and Frederick to Podewils, Dec. 20, 1755, *ibid.*, 7147/ 439–441.

[14] Frederick to Knyphausen, Oct. 25, 1755, *ibid.*, 7044/ 350. See also Frederick to Knyphausen, Nov. 22, 1755, *ibid.*, 7090/ 388; Frederick to Klinggraeffen, Nov. 8 and 28, 1755, *ibid.*, 7071, 7106/ 370, 404–405, respectively; and Williams to Holdernesse, Oct. 25, 1755, PROSP 91/ 61.

[15] BMAddMSS 32860/ 151 (Oct. 25, 1755).

subsidy treaty to Parliament and the king for ratification.[16] Several days later Holdernesse informed Frederick through the Duke of Brunswick of King George's recent views on the European situation. Because the king was interested in preventing a war in Europe, circumstances prohibited him and parliament from being indifferent to the defense of Hanover. Logic demanded that Great Britain negotiate defensive alliances with other European powers for this purpose. The treaty with Russia had been concluded solely to defend Hanover; and Russian troops would be requisitioned only if some power attacked Hanover. Thus, Holdernesse wished that Frederick would be more explicit regarding those issues which could be arranged between Prussia and Great Britain for the peace of Europe.[17]

At the end of November Holdernesse told Michell that Frederick was in a "brilliant position" to determine whether Europe should have peace or war. Frederick, Holdernesse said, held the "olive branch in one hand and the sword in the other." A favorable reply from Frederick would reward him with not only the glory of having preserved the peace in Germany, but also the advantage of confirming the conquests in Silesia which he had made in the last war.[18]

Frederick could not afford to disregard the advantages of such a generous invitation, the acceptance of which gave him everything while he lost nothing. An alliance with Great Britain at this critical moment—when the Russian army seemed ready to pounce on Prussia—was calculated to save Prussia from destruction. Once Frederick guaranteed that he would not attack Hanover, would there be cause for Frederick to fear a Russian attack?

In one of the most important dispatches in the entire Anglo-Prussian negotiation, Frederick wrote to Michell on December 7 that he intended to contribute to the peace of Europe: "I do not find anything more reasonable than to begin by affirming the tranquility of Germany." Frederick was pleased with the British offer of a new guarantee of Silesia and that some minor

---

[16] BMEg 3426/ 80, 82. See also BMEg 3426/ 78, 84; and Frederick to Michell, Nov. 4, 1755, PC XI/ 7064/ 364.

[17] PC XI/ 7113/ 413 (Nov. 21, 1755).

[18] Mitchell to Frederick, Nov. 26, 1755, ibid., 7119/ 418–419.

differences between Great Britain and Prussia would be reconciled by this new alliance. So as not to offend them, Frederick suggested that no mention of the French or the Russians be made in the treaty. He believed it would be sensible and appropriate to exchange ambassadors in order to conclude the negotiation.[19]

The British ministry received with alacrity this declaration from Frederick[20] and immediately drafted the future Convention of Westminster.[21] Holdernesse told Michell that the proposed convention soon to be forwarded to him would include the important phrase "to preserve the peace of Germany in the present crisis." Moreover, Great Britain had every intention of sending an ambassador to the Prussian court.[22]

The principles of the Anglo-Prussian convention were agreed on and what remained was merely the exchange of draft and final projects and the signatures. During the next few weeks each side anxiously awaited the arrival of diplomatic couriers, hoping that no time would be lost.[23]

In the meantime Frederick was flooded with reports about Russian and Austrian military operations.[24] He had received the

[19] Ibid.
[20] BMEg 3459/ 14 (Dec. 15, 1755).
[21] Ibid., 3426/ 92, 97; and ibid., 3459/ 21.
[22] Mitchell to Frederick, Dec. 23, 1755, PC XII/ 7167/ 1–5.
[23] See BMEg 3459/ 1–55; King George II to Holdernesse and Holdernesse to King George II, Jan. 14, 1756, ibid., 57; "Minute," ibid., 3426/ 103–104; Newcastle to Devonshire, Jan. 2, 1756, BMAddMSS 32862/ 6–7; Frederick to Eichel and Eichel to Podewils, Jan. 1, 1756, PC XII/ 7167, 7168/ 1–5, 5–6, respectively; Frederick to Maltzahn and Podewils, Jan. 3, 1756, PC XII/ 7174/ 11–12; and Frederick to Michell and King of Great Britain, Jan. 4, 1756, PC XII/ 7175, 7176/ 12–16, 17, respectively.
[24] Frederick to Klinggraeffen, and Haeseler, Dec. 6, 1755, PC XI/ 7115, 7116/ 416, 416, respectively; Haeseler to Frederick, Dec. 13, 1755, ibid., 7156/ 446; Frederick to Knyphausen, Dec. 16, 1755, ibid., 7139/ 434; Frederick to Knyphausen, Klinggraeffen, Maltzahn, and Solms, Dec. 23, 1755, ibid., 7153, 7154, 7155, 7157/ 445, 445, 446, 447–448, respectively; Frederick to Haeseler, Dec. 24, 1755, ibid., 7158/ 448–449; Frederick to Knyphausen and Klinggraeffen, Dec. 27, 1755, ibid., 7161, 7162/ 452, 453, respectively; Frederick to Knyphausen and Klinggraeffen, Dec. 30, 1755, ibid., 7165, 7166/ 455, 456–457, respectively; Frederick to Knyphausen and Klinggraeffen, Jan. 3, 1756, ibid., XII/ 7171, 7172/ 8–9, 10, respectively; Frederick to Klinggraeffen, Jan. 6, 10, and 13, 1756, ibid., 7178, 7190, 7197/ 18, 29, 35, respectively; and Frederick to Knyphausen, Jan. 12, 1756, ibid., 7196/ 33–34.

crucial information that the Russian court conference held on October 7 in St. Petersburg had declared Russia's intention of attacking him.[25] This convinced him more than ever that Grand Chancellor Alexis Bestuzhev-Riumin was leading a conspiracy against him and that Russia was his worst enemy.[26] Russia and Austria had now contrived a project which was undoubtedly directed against him.[27] He envisaged large numbers of enemy troops advancing toward him from several directions: 50,000 Austrians entering Silesia, another 50,000 of them marching through Saxony directly toward the mark of Brandenburg, and 60,000 Russians overrunning East Prussia.[28]

Frederick had been desperately searching for ways to circumvent the Russians and, in doing so, the British, whom he knew were agreeing to pay them, and the Austrians, whom he suspected were clandestinely collaborating with them. Each day's post, the arrival of each courier, brought him the depressing news that the house of Hohenzollern was in imminent danger of destruction. Thus, when the Convention of Westminster was signed on January 16, 1756, Frederick must have been somewhat relieved; for Great Britain held the purse strings which supposedly held the Russians. But only time would tell whether Britain could be trusted and could restrain Empress Elizabeth's aggressive intentions.

[25] See Maltzahn to Frederick, Dec. 5, 1755, *ibid.*, XI/ 7147/ 430–431, and Frederick to Podewils, Dec. 20, 1755, *ibid.*, 439–441.

[26] Frederick to Maltzahn, Dec. 23, 1755, *ibid.*, XII/ 7155/ 446.

[27] Frederick to Klinggraeffen, Jan. 6, 1756, *ibid.*, 7178/ 18.

[28] Frederick to Knyphausen, Jan. 3, 1756, *ibid.*, 7171/ 8–9.

IV Britain vs. France at the Russian Court

"The Empress went into the country the beginning of this week, she has catched a violent rhumatism [sic], which is very unluckily fallen into her right arm which prevented her signing the ratifications last Thursday, as she intended to do," Sir Charles Hanbury Williams naïvely explained to Holdernesse in December 1755. And, as he was "thoroughly persuaded, that, that is the only reason why the ratifications are not yet signed," he was "less uneasy at this delay."[1] Empress Elizabeth's right arm seemed to be plagued with mishaps. Williams related that shortly before she was afflicted with rheumatism, she had a bad fall which left "a pain in her right arm." Then, a large pole in the Grand Duke Paul's nursery "fell down and would have hit the Empress on the head if she had not paryed the blow with her right arm." The pain was allegedly so great that Elizabeth thought her arm was broken, and on her birthday "her subjects had not the honour of kissing her hand as usual, since even that must have given Her Imperial Majesty some pain."[2]

The lame right arm was, indeed, but a lame excuse and so were the others that followed.[3] Williams had transmitted the British ratification on December 11,[4] and nearly two months had elapsed without a reciprocal gesture on the part of the Russian court. Had Williams been more alert, he might have suspected that these excuses were not genuine and would have attempted to discover the real reasons for the delay. He might have fur-

[1] Williams to Holdernesse, Dec. 27, 1755, PROSP 91/ 61.

[2] *Ibid.*, Dec. 30, 1755. See also Williams to Holdernesse, Dec. 12, 16, 20, and 23, 1755, *ibid.*

[3] Williams to Holdernesse, Jan. 3, 6, 10, 13, 20, 27, and 31, and Feb. 19, 1756, *ibid.*, 91/ 62.

[4] LOII, *f.* 36, *op.* 1, *d.* 91/ 102.

ther suspected that something had gone wrong for the British at the Russian court. A more discerning diplomat would have considered the possibility that the empress had already received word about the secret Anglo-Prussian negotiations and that Holdernesse's recent dispatches to him had been seen by the Russians. All this would certainly have been sufficient cause for a delay in the ratifications. But Williams speculated on none of these eventualities even though he had been cautioned about them. Lord Chancellor Hardwicke had already warned the British ministry that a rapprochement between Great Britain and Prussia might have an unfortunate effect in St. Petersburg. Accordingly, the whole matter of the Anglo-Prussian negotiation had to be handled with the utmost delicacy at the Russian court. Thus, along with a draft copy of the future Convention of Westminster, Holdernesse sent the following to Williams:

> If the King of Prussia is sincere, the Peace of Germany may undoubtedly, be maintained; as it cannot be imagined, that France will venture to march an army into the Empire, if the King of Prussia is seriously determined to oppose it. But, if (which is not to be supposed) the King of Prussia should have some sinister Meaning in the Overtures He has made; Endeavours may possibly be used, even by Himself, to instill Jealousies at Petersburg, as if We were neglecting the Russian alliance, and entering into secret Measures for defeating it. The very contrary is the Case—the King knows, that the Conclusion of the Treaty with the Empress of Russia is one great Inducement to the King of Prussia's present Way of Thinking; and His Majesty is persuaded that the Czarina's known Magnanimity will be equally satisfied with having greatly contributed to procure Peace and Security to Her Allies, *par un coup de Plume*, as if she had had an opportunity of shewing the Bravery of Her Troops, and the greatness of Her Power in Arms. Her Grandeur and attachment to Her Allies is equally, perhaps more eminently shewn, by procuring Peace without Bloodshed, than by the most fortunate Success of Her Armies.[5]

Because of the sensitivity surrounding the Anglo-Prussian negotiation, Williams was instructed to keep the entire matter an absolute secret even from the anglophile grand chancellor. Williams was further cautioned that the Austrians might try

[5] BMAddMSS 32861/ 443; and PROSP 91/ 61 (Dec. 26, 1755).

to undermine British interests at the Russian court.[6] The British sincerely believed that one alliance did not contradict the other. It was of capital importance that the Russian court should also think so.

The first obvious manifestation that the British plans were afoul at the Russian court took place on December 31, 1755. On that day Williams was summoned to meet with both chancellors. He expected to receive the ratified Anglo-Russian Subsidy Treaty. Instead, Grand Chancellor Bestuzhev-Riumin had a "Paper" read to Williams; Empress Elizabeth wanted him to accept the document and send it to his court. In essence this paper placed a rigid interpretation on the Anglo-Russian Subsidy Treaty—that Russian forces were to be used exclusively against the king of Prussia.

Vice-Chancellor Vorontsov explained to Williams that the only reason for the delay in Elizabeth's ratifying the treaty was her opposition to using her troops against anyone other than Frederick and that the paper was drawn up to explain clearly her position on this point to the British ministry.

Williams told the two men he could neither accept the paper nor enter into any other business until the treaty was ratified. However, the irresponsible Williams told them that "if, after having ratified it, the Empress should wish to change some of her propositions to the King, His Master, he would hope and would himself dare to assume that His British Majesty would yield with pleasure." When the vice-chancellor asked Williams to place all that he had said in the form of a written declaration, Williams refused saying that he could not engage himself "in any *démarche*, before the Convention was actually ratified." Nevertheless, he was still convinced that after the exchange of ratifications, the king of Great Britain would satisfy the desires of Empress Elizabeth.

After Williams left the conference room, Bestuzhev-Riumin's secretary followed him out and told him that the grand chancellor said he "had done very wisely in not receiving the Paper." Williams finally began to suspect that a clandestine affair was being hatched at the Russian court. He did not feel that the grand chancellor had instigated this new development but that

[6] BMAddMSS 32861/ 443–445; and PROSP 91/ 61 (Dec. 26, 1755).

he had been forced to involve himself as a loyal subject of Empress Elizabeth's will.[7]

Weeks passed and still the Russians did not ratify the treaty. Chancellor Bestuzhev-Riumin had everything to lose from this delay, for the Anglo-Russian Subsidy Treaty was an essential element in his foreign policy system. Its failure would rightly be interpreted by everyone both in and out of Russia as the failure of the grand chancellor himself. Thus, Bestuzhev-Riumin made a desperate attempt to gain Elizabeth's approval for Russia's ratification. In a lengthy memoir to the empress dated January 30, 1756, he made a scathing attack on the opponents of ratification, labeling them enemies and saboteurs of Russia's true interests. He reminded Elizabeth that he had been her devoted servant, loyally executing her wishes, and lectured her on the fundamental principles which had governed Russian foreign policy during the past 12 years; a close and friendly relationship with England was basic to this foreign policy, and the Anglo-Russian Subsidy Treaty was its chief instrument. The ratification of the treaty would sustain the glory of her reign and would be a credit to her and to Russia. A primary goal of Russia's policy was to humble Frederick II; and the treaty with England would not only provide an ally, but would also supply Russia with funds to support her troops on the field.

He reminded Elizabeth that the whole affair had begun as early as 1753 when Frederick threatened the peace of Europe. As soon as Russia had made known her intention to curtail his aggressive actions, Frederick had desisted. Now, a similar situation had arisen and Russia was being called on once again to demonstrate that she could save Europe. If Russia did not act as she had in the past, Europe's respect for and fear of Russian power and greatness would, according to Bestuzhev-Riumin, evaporate and all that Elizabeth had accomplished during the past 15 years would collapse. Elizabeth was truly the daughter of Peter the Great, and the great Czar's wealthy, mighty, and respected legacy was in her hands; therefore, her destiny, in Bestuzhev-Riumin's opinion, was to preserve and further the greatness and power of Russia that had been forged by Peter.

[7] AVPR, f. Snosheniia . . . Angliei, 1755, op. 35/ 1, d. 770/ 285, 288–291; and Williams to Holdernesse, Feb. 19, 1756, PROSP 91/ 62.

Bestuzhev-Riumin concluded his memoir with an extremely important recommendation. He suggested that Elizabeth establish an extraordinary commission to organize, centralize, and supervise the mobilization of Russia's military resources for the diversion Russia was to make against Frederick. He called attention to the many administrative sources of authority in Russia, each of which contained sufficient power to make policy. The commander-in-chief of the armed forces could not be expected to execute his responsibilities efficiently and effectively if he must await orders, requisitions, and policy statements from the War College, the College of Foreign Affairs, the Admiralty, the Senate, and other branches of the administrative hierarchy. Furthermore, each branch was not necessarily apprised of what the other had decided, and conceivably contradictory orders might be issued. In May 1753 Elizabeth had established a court conference in Moscow to advise her how to meet the challenge of Frederick's aggressive actions. Empress Elizabeth, according to Bestuzhev-Riumin, should establish another such commission which would be comprised of respected and responsible people chosen by the empress.[8]

It was evident that the grand chancellor had finally decided to move against his opponents at the Russian court. He not only stressed the immediate necessity of ratifying the subsidy treaty, but also accused opponents of this policy of being unpatriotic. He clearly implied that any deviation from the foreign policy he had initiated and directed over the past several years would be in fact a repudiation of him. He did not think for one moment that Empress Elizabeth would turn against a loyal servant of the Russian crown who had gained distinction and honor under her as well as her father, Peter the Great.

Bestuzhev-Riumin cunningly reasoned that, if Empress Elizabeth established the extraordinary commission, he undoubtedly would be chosen, as grand chancellor, to chair its sessions. And even though the council might include some of his enemies, he was convinced that, because he had more talent for debate and oratory, more ability to cabal and convince, and more experience with court in-fighting than any other man or combination

[8] LOII, f. 36, op. 1, d. 142/ 249–263 (Jan. 30, 1756).

of men at court, he would win in the end. Grand Chancellor Bestuzhev-Riumin was 63 years old with two score years of government service behind him, during which time he survived many blood-letting affairs. He had not lost faith in his ability to survive a new crisis.

Finally, on February 12 the ratifications were exchanged.[9] But at the same time Williams was presented with a declaration which stated that Russia would make a diversion only against Prussia, that is to say, if Prussia attacked Great Britain or a British ally. This would change the *casus foederis* of the Anglo-Russian Subsidy Treaty, for it meant that Russian troops could not be requisitioned by Great Britain if she were threatened from another quarter. Although the British ministry believed that France would not act without the support of Prussia, it was quite conceivable that France could threaten the Netherlands or Hanover on her own. In that event, under the terms of the Anglo-Russian Subsidy Treaty, Great Britain might wish to requisition Russian troops. But by Russia's declaration Great Britain's freedom of action was so grossly limited that the treaty would prove to be practically useless. Williams, therefore, declined to accept the declaration.[10]

Admittedly, Great Britain had originally entered into this negotiation because of her fear of Prussia. However, before the Anglo-Russian Subsidy Treaty was concluded, Great Britain had begun *pourparlers* with Prussia culminating in the Convention of Westminster which provided for the security of Hanover and the neutrality of Germany. Unless Frederick broke the Convention of Westminster, no longer would there be any reason for employing Russian troops against Prussia.

Two days later, on February 14, the grand chancellor sent a message to Williams stating that during the whole Anglo-Russian negotiation Empress Elizabeth's opinion had been consistent: the Russian military diversion would be made solely against the king of Prussia. Therefore, the king of England should not take any offense by the declaration. Williams refused to be moved and answered the grand chancellor that, because

---

[9] Williams to Holdernesse, Feb. 14 and 19, 1756, PROSP 91/ 62. See also Williams to Holdernesse, Feb. 10, 1756, *ibid.*

[10] *Ibid.*, Feb. 19, 1756; and LOII, *f.* 36, *op.* 1, *d.* 91/ 103–104.

the declaration would prevent the "frightening of France," he could not accept it.[11]

That same day Williams received a note which, like the declaration, challenged the solidarity of the Anglo-Russian union. Holdernesse's dispatch of January 23 informed him that the Convention of Westminster had been signed on January 16, 1756. Williams was further distressed to learn that the Russian court had received that very day the same information from Prince Michael M. Golitsyn, the Russian ambassador to Great Britain.[12] On the following day Williams declared to the grand chancellor that the Convention of Westminster could offend no one but France and that, because of the grand chancellor's attachment to Great Britain, he would wish to explain this event in the best possible light to the empress. He was asked to convince the empress of the "Innocence, the Utility and Necessity of this Measure, and to prevent Her Imperial Majesty's being misled upon this occasion."[13]

The chancellor assured Williams that Empress Elizabeth would be considerably outraged upon hearing the news of the Anglo-Prussian convention. He was even worried about the reaction of the Austrian court to this new event. Williams quickly replied that if the Austrians "really desired the Continuation of the Peace, they would not possibly say anything against it." When the chancellor hesitated to commit himself any further to support the British and suggested that Great Britain had not kept all her promises to him, Williams reassured him that his 10,000 pounds would be paid directly upon his promise to "serve the King in this last Affair, and prevent any Jealousies that other Courts might stir up in the Empress's Breast." Bestuzhev-Riumin took his cue and, as a manifestation of his continued adherence to the British cause, allowed several comments, dictated by Williams, to be placed in the margins of Golitsyn's report about the Convention of Westminster. This gave Great Britain—which evidently was naïvely unaware of Elizabeth's

[11] LOII, f. 36, op. 1, d. 91/ 104.

[12] Williams to Holdernesse, Feb. 19, 1756; and Holdernesse to Williams, Jan. 23, 1756, PROSP 91/ 62.

[13] Williams to Holdernesse, Feb. 19, 1756, PROSP 91/ 62; and see LOII, f. 36, op. 1, d. 91/ 104 (Feb. 15, 1756).

real aims—the opportunity to explain the meaning and intention of this recent alliance as follows:

> That the Convention at Petersbourg was what had certainly produced these pacifick Inclinations in His Prussian Majesty and obliged him to make those Steps towards the King, which had occasion'd this Treaty; and that therefore the Honour of it was entirely to the Empress, and that is was full as glorious for Her Imperial Majesty to preserve the Peace of Europe by signing her name as to restore it by a Victory; and as this Step of the King of Prussia's was made thro' Fear, the Continuation of His Pacifick Intentions, must depend upon the same motive; and that, as the only Quarrel now in Europe was between the King and His most Christian Majesty, it was very natural for the King to deprive His Enemy of every Assistance, especially so great a one as Prussia.[14]

Hoping that this marginal note would satisfy Empress Elizabeth and Russian foreign policy and save the Anglo-Russian Subsidy Treaty, Williams allowed himself to be drawn into an extraordinary discussion with the grand chancellor on the declaration:

> The Grand Chancellor advised me to send the Declaration above mention'd to Your Lordship; for that Her Imperial Majesty had ordered them to send it to Prince Gallizin [sic], in case I should refuse it; and that if I did absolutely refuse it, He was sure the Empress would take it ill; but that in case I would send it, the Empress would give Prince Gallizin immediate Orders to ask an Audience of His Majesty's wherein He would give the King such Assurances of Her Imperial Majesty's Resolutions to maintain Her Engagements and continue in the strictest Union with the King, as could not but be agreeable to His Majesty; and these Arguments of the Great Chancellor persuaded me to send it to Your Lordship.[15]

Sir Charles Hanbury Williams had again demonstrated his incompetence because, as ambassador of King George, his acceptance of this declaration was tantamount to the nullification

---

[14] Williams to Holdernesse, Feb. 19, 1756, PROSP 91/ 62; and see LOII, *f*. 36, *op*. 1, *d*. 91/ 104 (Feb. 15, 1756).

[15] Williams to Holdernesse, Feb. 19, 1756, PROSP 91/ 62.

of the Anglo-Russian Subsidy Treaty itself. All that the British ministry had worked for was collapsing, and it soon would be shocked to learn what Williams had done. He justified his action to Holdernesse as follows:

> I shall not make any Comments to Your Lordship upon the Declaration. It says too plainly that the Empress will do nothing but keep the King of Prussia in awe, and attack him in case He should attack the King or any of his Allies; and excuses Her from Marching into Flanders or Germany, under false pretenses, or in hopes of obtaining more money.
>
> By the Treaty lately concluded with the King of Prussia, the Russian troops are not to enter into Germany; I hope the positive part of the inclosed Declaration relative to an attack upon the King of Prussia, will answer His Majesty's Purposes and keep the King of Prussia to His Engagements; and I will be bold to say in case His Prussian Majesty should act otherwise, this Court will infallibly attack Him with Vigour, and with a much larger Body of Troops than that stipulated in the Treaty.[16]

Williams had failed to see that Russia wanted to humble Frederick and would use any means to accomplish this—the Anglo-Russian Subsidy Treaty was merely one of them. Although Russia had put her troops up for sale, she was not interested in fighting battles for Great Britain other than against Prussia. If Great Britain no longer wanted to accomplish this aggressive deed, Russia might find other buyers and willing collaborators.

Grand Chancellor Bestuzhev-Riumin had gained essentially nothing from Russia's ratification of the subsidy treaty since it was accompanied by the declaration which nullified it. He no longer deceived himself; he had lost control of the situation at the Russian court and the presentation of the declaration along with the ratification documents was the first public announcement of his descent from power. His decline had begun as early as October 1755, when Empress Elizabeth had allowed some of her closest advisers and ministers to negotiate secretly with Douglas for the reestablishment of a Franco-Russian rapprochement. Chancellor Bestuzhev-Riumin was not informed of

[16] *Ibid.*

Empress Elizabeth's change of heart toward him and his policies. She was sparing her longtime grand chancellor the humiliation and embarrassment of immediate removal from office. Besides, he could still be useful to the Russian empire as a senior bureaucrat who would continue faithfully to execute the will of the empress. His ability to persuade Williams to accept the declaration was an excellent example of his loyalty to her.

The declaration was undoubtedly concocted by the pro-French group at the Russian court as a means of upsetting the Anglo-Russian Subsidy Treaty, defeating the grand chancellor, and preventing the use of Russian troops against France. This interpretation is supported by the fact that the declaration, as Williams later found out, was first drawn up in the apartment of Empress Elizabeth's favorite, Ivan Ivanovich Shuvalov, a strong francophile.[17] It was rumored that before any business could be taken up with the empress, Ivan Shuvalov's favorable disposition usually had to be obtained. Because of his pro-French sympathies, it was natural that Ivan Shuvalov allied himself with Michael Vorontsov. By their activities the francophiles at the Russian court had steadily prepared the way for the return of Douglas to St. Petersburg.

The French court was greatly affected by the news of the Convention of Westminster. Prussia, France's ally, was now also allied to Great Britain, her most dreaded enemy. Frederick's contention that this new association with Great Britain in no way contradicted his alliance with France did not completely convince Louis XV. It would be a while before the confusing relationship between France and Prussia would be clarified. In the meantime, the effect of the conclusion of the Convention of Westminster was to hasten the developing rapprochement between France and Russia. Great Britain had allied herself with the avowed enemy of Russia, and thus, it was more than probable that France would benefit greatly from this new situation. At least one thing was certain: Michael Vorontsov's scheme, as outlined to Douglas in October, for the overthrow of the subsidy treaty and the grand chancellor was closer to fulfillment.

Douglas had arrived in Paris at the end of December 1755

[17]See *ibid.*

and made a full report to both Rouillé and Conti. At the end of
January 1756, instructions were being drafted for Douglas'
return to Russia by both the Ministry of Foreign Affairs and by
those who directed the King's Secret. Subsequently, the ministry instructed Douglas that he was to do everything in his power
to destroy the Anglo-Russian Subsidy Treaty and remove from
power the anglophile grand chancellor who was its primary
advocate. Vorontsov was to be informed that France would
welcome the opportunity to establish formal diplomatic and
commercial relations with Russia. In the event that Douglas
was successful and the Russians raised the question of French
subsidies, he was empowered to promise that France would
grant what she lost from the British. A more delicate task was
outlined for him by the Secret. Douglas was to endeavor to
obtain for Conti a Russian army command and investment as
Duke of Kurland; and finally, he was to work toward placing
Conti on the Polish throne.[18] Douglas left Paris on February 14
under the assumed name of Leonard and did not arrive in St.
Petersburg until April 21.[19]

In the meantime, Rouillé wrote to Vorontsov, "the Person
that your Excellency commissioned to choose you a librarian
and to send you some burgundy wines . . . is charged to witness
my esteem to you."[20]

[18] Rouillé to Douglas, Feb. 9, 1756, BN SM NAF 22009/ 37–39, and
L. Jay Oliva, *Misalliance,* pp. 29–30.
[19] BN SM NAF 22009/ 46, 48–49, 63–64, 87; Rouillé to de-Liatush
[de la Touch], Feb. 11, 1756, TsGADA, *f.* 1261, *op.* 1, *d.* 154/ 1; and
AVPR, *f. Snosheniia . . . Frantsiei,* 1756, *op.* 93/ 1, *d.* 5/4.
[20] BN SM NAF 22009/ 41 (Feb. 9, 1756). See also Oliva, pp. 30–31.

V Russia Plans For War

Despite the continued decline in power of Grand Chancellor Alexis Bestuzhev-Riumin at the Russian court, he was able to initiate a significant change in the administrative system that lasted until the death of Empress Elizabeth in 1762. This administrative invention came to be called simply *Konferentsiia pri vysochaishem dvore*, which may be rendered "Conference at the Imperial Court."[1] Essentially, the Conference was established by Elizabeth on March 25, 1756, to compose and administer a general and systematic plan to reduce the powers of the king of Prussia and to make him no longer dangerous to the Russian Empire.[2] Next to the empress, who at times presided over its sessions, the Conference became the highest authority in the Russian Empire, standing above all other empowered administrative agencies concerned with external and internal affairs of state. A decision of the Conference became a decision of the Russian Empire.

The Conference was created originally by an imprecise decree and its authority was nebulous.[3] Sessions of the Conference were to be held twice weekly, on Mondays and Thursdays; but in practice they convened more or less frequently as circumstances demanded. Because of the enormous number of rescripts, orders, and requisitions issued by the Conference to the Senate and the colleges to implement its commands, a secretariat was

[1] The entire original collection of materials for the Conference are to be found in TsGADA, *f*. 178. Copies of parts of the entire collection may also be found in LOII, *f*. 36, *op*. 1, *d*. 112, 113; SIRIO CXXXVI; and P. J. Bartenev, ed. *Arkhiv Kniazia Vorontsova* [The Archives of Prince Vorontsov] (Moscow, 1870–1895), Vol. III.

[2] TsGADA, *f*. 178, *d*. 1/ 17–18 (No. 1).

[3] *Ibid.*

attached to it. Heading this agency was a former embezzler and once-accused traitor, Dimitri Volkov, the secretary of the College of Foreign Affairs, who for years had been a trusted associate of the grand chancellor.[4] The Conference eventually concerned itself with nearly everything that was directly or indirectly related to the fulfillment of its principal task of warring against Prussia. It attacked large and small, important and incidental matters with almost the same degree of intensity and detail. In diplomatic affairs the Conference argued and decided general principles of alliances as well as the salaries of diplomats. It decided the general export policy of the whole empire, while it also heard the complaints of individual merchants. The Conference appointed the commander-in-chief and other generals of the army who were to lead the military diversion against Prussia and even took the time to rule on promotions of lower-ranking officers, for example, captains to majors. Not only did it debate the debasement of currency with copper, which would affect the entire financial structure of the country, but it also concerned itself with the allocation of funds for Kalmyck soldiers' caftans. When Alexis Bestuzhev-Riumin had argued in his memoir of January 30 to Empress Elizabeth for the establishment of an extraordinary commission to organize, centralize, and supervise the mobilization of Russia's military resources for the attack on Frederick II, he probably never dreamed that the authority of such a commission would be so pervasive and ubiquitous.

Surely, the grand chancellor's lingering influence was not strong enough in itself to persuade Empress Elizabeth to establish the Conference; his idea was implemented only when it became dramatically clear to her that circumstances required such action. The weeks following the grand chancellor's submission of the memoir were exceedingly troublesome for her. The official and rumored reports about the changing European situation demanded sophisticated discussion and immediate decision by the Russian court. The ailing empress was neither capable of undertaking such tasks herself nor willing to entrust them any longer solely to one man, especially the grand chancellor

[4] For information on D. Volkov's past activities, see SIRIO, CXLVIII, *passim.*

whose policies of late had proved disappointing and embarrassing to Russia. Facing the empress was the ratified Anglo-
Russian Subsidy Treaty which Great Britain and Russia understood differently. Compounding the confusion was the recent
announcement of the conclusion of the Convention of Westminster which could readily be interpreted as negating the
Anglo-Russian Subsidy Treaty or, at least, sufficiently under-
mining it to make it useless for the aims and purposes of Russian
foreign policy. There were also reports that Frederick was attempting to mediate the Anglo-French crisis which, if successful, would remove the circumstances that might allow Russia
the opportunity of going to war against Prussia. Furthermore,
Empress Elizabeth learned that Austria and France had been
secretly negotiating a possible rapprochement, the arrangement
of which would significantly affect future Russian foreign policy,
especially since Russia herself was secretly seeking a rapprochement with France.

These problems needed the serious deliberation which one
person or even one or more administrative agencies would not
be really equipped to handle. The situation demanded the attention of several people who were competent in domestic as
well as foreign affairs, who knew the requirements of the army
and the navy, and who also understood the complexities of
commerce and finance. It was essential that these same people
also be able to coordinate their views in such a way that a quick
and final decision could be made in time to meet the challenge
of any emergency. Empress Elizabeth's reason for frustration
was clearly demonstrated only 11 days before she established
the Conference. On March 14 she requested Vice-Chancellor
Michael Vorontsov, on behalf of the College of Foreign Affairs,
to present an opinion on the position Russia should take in the
European political situation. What resulted, however, was not
one paper but two; not one opinion but rather another debate.
Although Vorontsov submitted a recommendation under the
heading of the College of Foreign Affairs, the grand chancellor
could not resist attacking it in a separate paper of his views on
the subject. Despite Empress Elizabeth's partiality for Vorontsov, she could not deny the merits of the cogently written argument presented by the grand chancellor. An issue this important

could not be resolved in that manner; it had to await the convocation of the Conference.

Empress Elizabeth designated as members of the Conference people who had long occupied celebrated and respected positions at the Russian court and on whose judgment she could rely. Thus, in addition to both chancellors, the Conference was highlighted by names as distinguished as Golitsyn, Trubetskoi, Buturlin, and Shuvalov. It is debatable whether the Grand Duke Peter should be considered a regular member. Despite his name being appended to the document establishing the Conference, his signature appears only twice more during the following year of sessions.[5] Grand Duke Peter was Empress Elizabeth's officially designated successor, and therefore, she would want his name added to the establishing document as a guarantee of the continuation of the Conference in the future. For Empress Elizabeth it was really a false measure of security, since Grand Duke Peter was known to idolize Frederick II. Undoubtedly, he signed the protocol against his will but judged such a compromise absolutely necessary. He was not yet in a position where he could make his personal wishes the policy of the Russian court. Shortly after Empress Elizabeth's death, however, the Conference was dissolved; and Peter, then Emperor, subsequently effected a rapprochement between the Russian and the Prussian courts.

An enormous amount of work went into the first session of the Conference, which convened on March 25. Empress Elizabeth presided and explained the several problems which needed the wise counsel and decision of the Conference. She firmly stated that the Convention of Westminster destroyed the Anglo-Russian Subsidy Treaty. She had conceived of the treaty as a means of giving Russia the opportunity to attack the king of Prussia, but these hopes were dashed by Great Britain's treachery. Empress Elizabeth declared that she still wanted to attack the king of Prussia and curtail his powers, and she wanted the

[5] The other members were: President of the War College, Field-Marshal General Stepan F. Apraksin; Count Michael P. Bestuzhev-Riumin; Senator and President of the Admiralty College, Admiral Prince Michael M. Golitsyn; Field-Marshal General Count Alexander Iv. Shuvalov; General Grand Master of Ordinance, Count Peter Iv. Shuvalov; and General-Procurator Nikita Iu. Trubetskoi.

Conference to recommend the best way of accomplishing this.

Other dangers loomed on the horizon. The empress had received reports that Frederick was attempting to mediate the crisis between France and Great Britain; if he was successful Russia's plans would be totally upset. Russia had to find a way to disrupt that mediation. Moreover, she asked the Conference to suggest a course of action for Russia in the event that rumors proved true that Austria was seeking a union with France.[6]

The Conference examined several important foreign policy documents in the hope of arriving at some fundamental conclusions.[7] Of particular interest were the opinions already submitted on March 14 by both chancellors on the European situation. Vice-Chancellor Michael Vorontsov's paper vigorously attacked the recent policies of Great Britain as well as those of Prussia. In a cursory review of the past few years, Vorontsov stated that Frederick had made himself exceedingly dangerous to the Russian and Austrian courts. Russia and Austria had thus united in a common policy to curtail his might and reduce his territories to their previous limits. In 1746, a treaty had been concluded between Austria and Russia providing that, if the king of Prussia disturbed the peace, Austria and Russia would join forces to attack him and also to regain Silesia for Maria Theresa. Great Britain, continued Vorontsov, was not of the same mind as Austria and Russia. Great Britain had not only confirmed Frederick's possession of Silesia, but also when she acceded to the treaty of 1746 she had not subscribed to the provisions concerning a future attack against Prussia. Nevertheless, when subsequent events indicated the possibility of an attack on Hanover by the king of Prussia, Great Britain was quick to enter into negotiations with Russia to prevent it. But according to Vorontsov, Great Britain "did not desire to irritate the King of Prussia entirely" and she secretly concluded with him a convention which destroyed the subsidy treaty. Russia therefore should not accept payment of the subsidy if it were offered. Her acceptance would merely oblige her to maintain 55,000 troops and 40 to 50 galleys on her frontiers for a period

[6] TsGADA, f. 178, d. 1/ 73–74 (No. 2).
[7] Ibid., d. 1/ 20–53, 55–60, 64–70 (No. 1), 71–72 (No. 2). See also, AVPR, f. Snosheniia . . . Angliei, 1756, op. 35/ 1, d. 776/ 29–33, 35–44.

of four years, subject to periodic examination by the British. This would mean that Russia would not be free to use those troops and galleys for other purposes whenever circumstances demanded. Moreover, there was no assurance that the declaration given to Williams would have the effect of making the British refuse to pay the subsidy. Therefore, Empress Elizabeth should now declare to the English court that she did not desire to fulfill her obligations under this treaty, because the kings of Great Britain and Prussia made it impossible for her to do so.

Concerning the mediation attempts of Frederick, Vorontsov believed that the recently concluded Convention of Westminster would change the effect of the king's endeavors. Vorontsov also stated that rumors of secret negotiations between Austria and France had to be verified before any concrete action could be taken by the Russian court. However, Vorontsov logically assumed that the conclusion of the Convention of Westminster would make France turn to Austria for friendship, and that some kind of action against the king of Prussia would be discussed, probably including the return of Silesia to Maria Theresa.[8]

Grand Chancellor Bestuzhev-Riumin agreed to many of the recommendations submitted by the College of Foreign Affairs. He also professed: "No one can dispute that the conclusion of the treaty in London with the King of Prussia destroys the view of the convention here [i.e., in relation to the subsidy treaty], namely to attack the King of Prussia with common forces, and that the conduct of the English in this event is not praiseworthy and least resembles allied friendship." Despite this the grand chancellor argued, there was nothing in the Convention of Westminster that was directed against the Russian Empire. Moreover, Russia could not immediately go to war against Frederick, since she would first have to agree with Austria in a joint policy which would take some time to arrange. Therefore, the grand chancellor recommended that Russia not reject the existing Anglo-Russian Subsidy Treaty but merely use it to disguise her secret military preparations against the king of Prussia. Russia would thus be able to attack him when he would least expect it, for Frederick would always think that Great Britain controlled

[8] TsGADA, f. 178, d. 1/ 55–60 (No. 1).

the Russian troops close to his frontiers. Russia should try little by little to separate England from Prussia and direct her back to the former system. In the meantime, Russia should collaborate with Austria to curtail the powers of the king of Prussia. Regarding the payment of the subsidy from England, the grand chancellor suggested that Russia not solicit it but if England wished to pay it "then accept it with indifference."[9]

The division of opinion between Bestuzhev-Riumin and Vorontsov was clear, and a compromise was hardly possible. When the question whether Empress Elizabeth should openly declare to Great Britain that she could not consider the subsidy treaty as binding was posed, a heated debate ensued. While the Conference documents are silent about the course of this discussion, Williams does provide an account of what happened:

When the Council met, the Question was actually proposed to break the Convention with England; and the new Treaty with Prussia given as the Reason for so doing. The Great Chancellor opposed this with all his Power, and declared that there was nothing in it against the Engagements subsisting between the King and Her Imperial Majesty; and therefore, this Court had no reason to complain against it directly, but that this Treaty might have Consequences.... But in His Speech He said some things so strong that the Empress was offended and reprimanded him herself in very strong Terms; Upon which the Chancellor's Brother and the Vice Chancellor, encouraged by what the Empress had said, accused him of his constant Partiallity for England, and endeavoured to answer all He had said. To all this the Chancellor reply'd with great Submission to the Empress, and with great Dignity to his Opposers; and after he had exposed Their Arguments, He told the Empress that He had served Her and Her Father as Minister for near Forty Year; That He had never had but one System which He never would depart from; but as to the present Question, He would not only vote against it, but protest against it, and even give in his Protestation in writing; But to this He added, that if His sentiments and Opinion were to be treated in the manner they had been in that Council, He should for the future be as silent as possible. Soon after this, when another Point arose, the Great Chancellor said only that He was for it; Upon which, when the Empress desired him to give his

[9] Ibid., d. 1/ 64–70 (No. 1).

Reasons, he remain'd still Silent, and at last the Empress came
into the best humour with him and took all the Pains imaginable
to make him speak, which at last He did much to the Empress's
Satisfaction.

All that He said had a great Effect, and the Great Duke and the
Schuvalovs joined in his Opinion. At last the Council was divided.
The Six persons against the Question were, the Great Duke, the
Great Chancellor, the two Schuvalovs . . . General Apraxin [sic],
and Admiral Gallitzen.

The Four that supported the Question were, the Vice Chancellor, Count Michael Bestoucheff [sic], Brother to the Chancellor,
Prince Trubetskoi, and General Butterlin [sic].[10]

Williams' report is supported by the subsequent policy followed by the Russian court in this matter. The grand chancellor
had shown that in debate he was still a man to be dealt with
but, more important, the argument he presented was far more
intelligent and practical than the vice-chancellor's. This latter
consideration was surely the reason why the grand chancellor
was able to carry the Conference that day.

On the following day, March 26, the Conference made a
momentous decision, which, with subsequent minor word and
stylistic changes, was formally approved by Empress Elizabeth
on April 10, 1756. The Conference formulated the general and
systematic state plan. It was a lengthy proposal which explained
more elaborately than ever before the foreign policy aims of
Russia and, at the same time, indicated the means by which
she hoped to achieve them. There were five major objectives
that the Russian court set for itself. First, Russia announced
that she wanted "to begin the business of the curtailment of
the powers of the King of Prussia," but she did not want to do
this by herself. Therefore, the Russian court would "endeavor
with all the convenient means possible to incline the Vienna
court to do the same on its part, at the same time and to the
same degree." Thirdly, in order to prevent the Vienna court
from declining this collaboration because of fears that France
might make a diversion against it, France must be mollified.
France must be made to "look calmly upon the curtailing of
the powers of the King of Prussia and not hinder the Vienna

[10] Williams to Holdernesse, April 11, 1756, PROSP 91/ 62.

court." Fourthly, a favorable situation must gradually be prepared in Poland "in order that she not only not hinder the passage of troops from here for the attack on Prussia, but even look
willingly upon it." Finally, every endeavor must be made to
keep the Turks and the Swedes "silent and inactive."

Since it would be a while before an agreement could be
reached with Maria Theresa on joint action, it was further
decided that additional dragoon, cuirassier, and grenadier regiments be formed and that all military units be mobilized and
ready to march. Thus, in the event of an agreement with Austria
to go to war against Frederick, he could be attacked immediately. The Vienna court was to be informed that Russia intended
to use not less than 80,000 troops against Prussia and that Maria
Theresa had the opportunity of regaining the territories which
she had lost in the War of the Austrian Succession. Maria
Theresa should be encouraged not to fear a French diversion
in the event of an attack on Prussia. She had not interfered in
the Anglo-French struggle and had not given any assistance to
England, and therefore the French court should likewise not
interfere in the forthcoming struggle between Maria Theresa
and Frederick. In an attempt to lessen the tension that might
arise between Versailles and Vienna, Russia should instruct all
her diplomats to "treat the French affectionately."

A special envoy should be dispatched to Poland to persuade
the Poles to remain tranquil while Russian troops passed
through their country to invade Prussia. He was to promise
them that Empress Elizabeth "does not intend and does not
want to make any acquisitions for herself in Prussia." The Poles
should be told that, if Russia were to conquer East Prussia, she
would do this to reduce "the unrestricted powers of the King
of Prussia." And by the same token Empress Elizabeth would
demonstrate to the Poles her generous intentions by giving
East Prussia to Poland, since it once belonged to them. By this
act Poland would enjoy an extension of territory as well as the
acquisition of important towns and harbors which would facilitate her commerce. In exchange Russia should then be given
Kurland and several regions lying on the Polish side of the
common frontier. These areas would provide Russia with "the
means to unite the commerce of the Baltic with the Black Sea

and through that have in our hands almost all the Levant Commerce."[11]

Russia now prepared for war.

[11] TsGADA, *f.* 178, *d.* 1/ 75–78 (No. 3); and 80–81 (No. 5), 86–87 (No. 8), 90–95 (No. 10).

VI Russian Mobilization

Empress Elizabeth had resolutely decided to go to war against the King of Prussia, and with equal determination she began to mobilize Russia's military and political resources. She prepared for war with the knowledge that she had a total land army of approximately 330,000 men, of which about two-thirds would be able to engage in offensive operations.[1] Russia had the largest army in Europe, exceeding Prussia's by a ratio of more than two to one.[2]

During the months of April and May the Conference issued dozens of orders to the Senate and the various colleges to bring Russia's military establishment into readiness for the attack on Prussia. In the areas of Riga, Kurland, and along the Dvina River, 28 infantry regiments totaling 73,132 men were to be stationed. Cuirassier and hussar regiments and several thousand Cossacks were to assemble along the Dvina toward Pskov. Regiments of horse grenadiers and dragoons as well as several units of Cossacks, Tartars, Kalmyks, and Bashkirs were deployed from Chernigov to Smolensk. The sum of these troops

[1] The total land army was apportioned in the following manner: field forces, 172,440; garrisons, 74,548; land militia, 27,758; artillery and engineering, 12,937; and irregular troops, 43,739. See War College report of August 2, 1755, in AVPR, f. Snosheniia . . . Angliei, 1755, op. 35/ 1, d. 770/ 157–164; and N. Korobkov, Semiletniaia voina (deistviia rossii v 1756–1762 gg.) [The Seven Years' War: Operations of Russia, 1756–1762] (Moscow, 1940), p. 59.

[2] According to figures compiled by foreign agents for Grand Chancellor Alexis Bestuzhev-Riumin in 1755 the number of men in armies of other European states was as follows: France, 211,753; Prussia, 142,000–145,000; Austria (without Imperial and feudal armies), 139,000; England, 91,179; Holland, 39,637; Denmark, 33,946; Saxony, 18,000; Poland, 16,-837. See Korobkov, p. 53.

amounted to 111,563 men. Moreover, in Reval galleys were to
be manned by three infantry regiments and Don Cossacks together numbering more than 8,000. No fewer than 10,000 troops
from northern Russian areas were to move into Kurland when
the main army was ordered to advance toward the frontier, and
these troops were to act as a reserve corps and were to keep the
lines of communication open. The number of Russian troops
designated for the future campaign against Prussia totaled
129,966 men. Orders were issued for the provisioning of these
troops; maps were to be drawn up of the regions lying near
the frontiers showing the best roads and means of travel for
future troop movements. Spies disguised as couriers were to
be sent to Dresden, Hamburg, and Gdańsk to reconnoiter Prussian military operations. At the same time the Conference su-
pervised the coordination of movements between Russia's land
forces and the Russian fleet. Flagships, galleys, frigates and
other vessels were to be provisioned and stationed in Riga and
Reval ready for the attack.[3]

The Conference had succeeded in launching Russia on the
road toward total military mobilization. On the political front
Empress Elizabeth moved quickly to have Maria Theresa join
in the offensive against Prussia. During the first two weeks of
April, several hurried meetings were held between the Austrian
ambassador Nicholas Esterhazy, the two chancellors, and the
empress herself. The role that France might play in the forthcoming campaign against Frederick was a principal topic of
discussion. Ambassador Esterhazy informed Elizabeth that his

[3] TsGADA, f. 178, d. 1/ 96–97 (No. 11, April 12, 1756); 108–123,
(No. 15, April 15–17, 1756); 126–129 (No. 16, April 23, 1756); 133
(No. 18, April 29, 1756); 134–155 (No. 19, April 29, 1756); 158–159
(No. 20, May 24, 1756); 162–163 (No. 22, May 31, 1756); 164–165
(No. 23, May 31, 1756). TsGADA, f. 1263, op. 1, d. 57/ 2–10 (Nos. 5–42,
April 8–May 26, 1756); d. 8369/ 1–61 (Nos. 1–29, April 9–May 30,
1756). TsGVIA, f. VUA, d. 1655/ 4–8 (May 2, 1756). Williams described
the Russian fleet as follows: 21 ships of the line, 15 of which are at
Kronstadt and 6 at Reval (1 has 99 guns, 3 have 80 guns each, 14 have
66 guns each, and 3 have 54 guns each); 6 of the largest ships are in dock
and were being repaired; 6 frigates of 32 guns each were located in Reval
(2) and Kronstadt (4). The Conference also decided to check the reported activities of Prussian agents who were spying on Russian military
activities in Kurland. See TsGADA, f. 178, d. 1/ 85 (No. 7, April 8, 1756);
and LOII, f. 36, op. 1, d. 104/ 292 (April 17, 1756).

court was very much interested in separating France from Prussia and had been carrying on secret negotiations with France for that purpose. It was hoped in Vienna that Louis XV could be persuaded to conclude a neutrality and defensive treaty with Maria Theresa, to which Empress Elizabeth would accede. As soon as positive word came from either Versailles or Vienna on this matter, Esterhazy promised he would inform Elizabeth. Furthermore, the Vienna court was anxious to discuss the terms of an Austro-Russian offensive alliance for a joint attack on Prussia, for which Maria Theresa was prepared to use no less than 80,000 of her troops.[4]

These Austrian proposals fitted nicely into the Russian plans of March 26. Empress Elizabeth replied to Esterhazy through her chancellors on April 20; she indicated she was willing to accede to the projected Austro-French agreement.[5] The chancellors also spoke of Elizabeth's desire to conclude an offensive alliance with Maria Theresa, and they submitted several preliminary points to serve as the basis for the treaty. First, each court would utilize 80,000 regular troops against Frederick and would attack him simultaneously. Second, in order to organize and coordinate the attack, a liaison should be established between the general staffs of the two courts. Third, one court alone was neither to conclude a separate peace nor to negotiate with the enemy without informing the other court. Peace negotiations were not to be undertaken until Maria Theresa regained Silesia and Glatz from the king of Prussia and Empress Elizabeth conquered East Prussia. Fourth, Russia did not intend to keep East Prussia for her own but intended to give it to Poland in exchange for the duchies of Kurland and Semigalia and some regions on the Polish side of the Polish-Russian frontier. Fifth, after the invasion had begun both imperial courts would invite Sweden and Saxony to join in the attack. The reward for Sweden would be in Pomerania, and Saxony would obtain Magdeburg.

Esterhazy was then informed of the general orders concerning the number, organization, and deployment of Russian troops. Both courts would subsequently decide on a schedule

[4] AVPR, f. Snosheniia . . . Avstriei, 1756, op. 32/ 1, d. 6/ 1, 3, 7–12, 16, 26–34; and see also d. 2/ 94–95.
[5] Ibid., d. 6/ 35–36.

for troop movements and the actual time of the joint attack.[6]

The Russian court did not anticipate any difficulties in arranging an offensive alliance with Austria, but it could not predict when it would be concluded. In the meantime, Empress Elizabeth had to take care that her neighbors would not be overly disturbed by her military preparations. She could not afford to allow anything to happen that might precipitate a Turkish attack on Russia either as a purely independent act of aggression or as an act sponsored and supported by a third power. Thus, Prussia's influence at the Porte had to be counteracted at all costs. It must have delighted the Russian court to learn from its envoy at Constantinople that the Turks were astonished by the Convention of Westminster. The Turks reportedly sympathized with the French and feared negotiating any future engagements with Frederick, since he obviously could not be trusted.[7] The Porte's disappointment in Frederick was not enough to set Russia at ease. Friendly gestures on the part of the empress were also needed. The first step in this direction was the decision of the Conference to suspend the construction of the fortress of St. Elizabeth in New Serbia which, by its proximity to the frontier of the Ottoman Empire, had for some time strained Russo-Turkish relations.[8]

The position of the Polish-Lithuanian Commonwealth presented a different problem for Russian foreign policy. Empress Elizabeth did not fear anything so fanciful as a Polish invasion of her territory; she feared Polish opposition to the advance of her own troops toward Prussia. Fortunately, Russia could always count on the dissensions among the Poles to provide her with the opportunity to insert herself into commonwealth politics to suit her own advantage. Moreover, the Russian court usually had at its disposal a group of influential nobles, the wealthy and powerful Czartoryski family, to act as its agents in the commonwealth itself. The patriarch of that family,

[6] *Ibid.*, d. 6/ 37–38; and LOII, f. 36, *op.* 1, d. 1070/ 273–275. See also LOII, f. 36, *op.* 1, d. 137/ 16.

[7] Obreskov to Golitsyn, March 16, 1756, TsGADA, f. 1263, *op.* 1, d. 2485/ 5–6.

[8] TsGADA, f. 178, d. 1/ 80–81 (No. 5, April 1, 1756); 100 (No. 13, April 15–17, 1756).

Michał, held the office of chancellor of Lithuania, while his younger brother August was governor of Ruthenia. Through family ties and political alliances, some of the highest posts in the church, the military, and the civil authority were controlled by the Czartoryskis.

At this crucial moment, the Russian court took measures to safeguard its interest in the commonwealth. The Conference decided to send Quartermaster Lieutenant-General Weimarn with instructions and money to support the Czartoryskis in their domestic politics and to sway the Poles against Frederick. His mission was to induce the Poles to allow the passage of Russian troops across their territory in order to attack Prussia.[9] The Conference also decided to replace the Russian envoy Gross by a "distinguished person" as ambassador to the king of Poland, adding luster to the Russian embassy. This replacement also reflected the changes that were taking place within the Russian court. Gross was reputedly a close associate of Grand Chancellor Alexis Bestuzhev-Riumin, while the secretary of the embassy in Warsaw, Rzhichevski, was in the camp of Vice-Chancellor Michael Vorontsov. The Conference further recommended the appointment of Count Michael Bestuzhev-Riumin, the estranged brother of the grand chancellor and a member of the pro-French Vorontsov group, as the new ambassador to the commonwealth; such an appointment would place the Russian embassy in the complete control of Vorontsov.[10]

The importance of this intended change cannot be emphasized enough, since the French had worked industriously for several years against the further increase of Russian influence in the commonwealth. The recent negotiations undertaken by the pro-French group at the Russian court for a rapprochement between France and Russia, however, raised the possibility of changing all this. If the French in the commonwealth were to abate in their criticism of the Russians, the Poles might be dis-

[9] *Ibid.*, d. 1/ 82–84 (No. 6, April 6, 1756); 88–89 (No. 9, April 10, 1756).

[10] *Ibid.*, d. 1/ 79 (No. 4, March 29, 1756). The Conference also requested the recall of Marcellis de Swart, the Dutch envoy and confidant of Bestuzhev-Riumin, from Russia. See *ibid.*, d. 1/ 71 (Nov. 2, March 25, 1756).

inclined to oppose the intended march of the Russian army through the commonwealth.[11]

With Alexander Mackenzie Douglas' arrival in St. Petersburg on April 21[12] the rapprochement between France and Russia was a foregone conclusion. His return was anticipated by the pro-French group several weeks before he actually arrived. On behalf of the pro-French group Vorontsov made it clear to Douglas that he was indeed welcome.[13] To prevent any difficulties and facilitate Douglas' speedy and comfortable journey to St. Petersburg, Empress Elizabeth issued a decree to the vice-governor of Riga, Lieutenant-General Voeikov, "that all kindnesses are to be given him, to greet him with distinction and great courtesy and tenderness."[14]

Douglas' movements did not go unnoticed by his rival Williams in St. Petersburg. Furthermore, when Williams asked Bestuzhev-Riumin about the imminent arrival of Douglas, the grand chancellor declared that he was ignorant of the whole affair and considered it an insult personally. Williams was later told that Vorontsov was responsible for Douglas' coming to St. Petersburg.[15]

On April 23, two days after his arrival, Douglas submitted a memoir to Vorontsov which contained the principal points of his instructions from the French Ministry of Foreign Affairs. The memoir stated explicitly that King Louis's intention in sending Douglas to Vorontsov was to explain that, "if Her Im-

[11] At this time the Russian court was sending circular notes to its envoys at other courts instructing them to placate and live on good terms with their French counterparts there. See AVPR, *f. Snosheniia . . . Angliei,* 1756, *op.* 35/ 1, *d.* 776/ 71; and *f. Snosheniia . . . Avstriei,* 1756, *op.* 32/ 1, *d.* 2/ 111.

[12] AVPR, *f. Snosheniia . . . Frantsiei,* 1756, *op.* 93/ 1, *d.* 5/ 1–2, and BN SM NAF 22009/ 87. *Cf.* LOII, *f.* 36, *op.* 1, *d.* 101/ 32 (April 20, 1756).

[13] Vorontsov to Douglas, BN SM NAF 22009/ 50. See also Vorontsov to Douglas, March 9, 1756, *ibid.,* 54.

[14] Ukaze of Empress Elizabeth, March 30, 1756, in Vorontsov to Voeikov, March 31, 1756, TsGADA, *f.* 1261, *op.* 1, *d.* 156/ 1.

[15] Corry to Williams, March 18 and April 16, 1756, CHW 64–10911/ 130–131, 140–141, respectively; and Williams to Holdernesse, March 30 and April 17, 20, 24, 27 and May 4, 1756, PROSP 91/ 62. See also Douglas to Rouillé, May 24, 1756, BN SM NAF 22009/ 121–122; and Combe to Williams, May 28, 1756, CHW 64–10911/ 148–149.

perial Majesty is truly disposed, as assuredly is the King, to the reunion with him, His Majesty will see with pleasure the re-establishment of a friendly harmony between the two courts which because of mutual interests will never be interrupted." But there was "a great obstacle to a reunion"—the Anglo-Russian Subsidy Treaty. The memoir explained that that treaty was directly contrary to the glory of Empress Elizabeth and the true interests of Russia. By hiring out her troops, the empress "excites the jealousy of her neighbors and of the other powers of Europe." When the English had proposed the treaty, they were merely thinking of their own interests and their own am-bitions and not of the welfare of the Russian Empire. The king of France, however, hoped that the empress would avoid "the execution of an onerous treaty" which is to be used in "making war on France." Despite this treaty "the confidence which the King has in the sentiments and probity" of Vorontsov impelled him to send Douglas to St. Petersburg. Douglas was authorized to assure Empress Elizabeth that, as soon as she designated an envoy to serve her at the French court, Louis would reciprocate by naming someone of similar rank and character to serve him at the Russian court. When these envoys were exchanged they would initiate commercial relations between the two countries. Louis was, moreover, inclined to name a consul to St. Peters-burg "to take care of the affairs of commerce" and to stimulate individual French subjects to negotiate directly with Russia. Once these commercial relations proved promising, it would be necessary "to agree immediately to a treaty of commerce which will be equally advantageous to the two nations." The memoir firmly stated that Vorontsov could assure his court "that all the demands it will make on this subject will receive sym-pathetic consideration in France."[16]

Vorontsov's reply to Douglas was made on May 18, and it

[16] BN SM NAF 22009/ 107–109 (April 23, 1756); and AVPR, f. Snosheniia . . . Frantsiei, 1756, op. 93/ 1, d. 5/ 7–8 (April 23, 1756). See also BN SM NAF 22009/ 83, 97–98, 109–114; and LOII, f. 36, op. 1, d. 101/ 32. Count Esterhazy was no doubt taken into Vorontsov's con-fidence and told about Douglas' meeting with him since a copy of the memoir is found among his reports to the Vienna court. See VA, RussBer, karton 38/ 86–87. Douglas had an audience with Empress Elizabeth on May 6, 1756. See BN SM NAF 22009/ 88–89, 95–96.

satisfied French wishes in all regards. Douglas was informed that Empress Elizabeth had for some time waited for the "favorable occasion" when she could agree with the king of France on reestablishing harmony between the two countries. She consented "with pleasure to sending reciprocal ministers invested in the character of ambassador" and said that the person she would choose would be "one of birth and rank agreeable to that which His Majesty will have chosen." Furthermore, she believed that the ambassadors should be named at the same time and as soon as possible. In order to facilitate this and as an expression of her sincere intentions, the empress would name, in reciprocation of Douglas' mission, a person in whom she had complete confidence to travel immediately with a letter to the chief minister of the king of France. The person designated for this mission was a longtime loyal servitor to Vorontsov, Feodor Bekhteev. Moreover, Empress Elizabeth desired that Douglas be appointed as the French chargé d'affaires at the Russian court, and in the meantime, "he will, however, be treated with distinction and received with special favor as a person actually sent to Petersburg on the part of the King."[17]

Empress Elizabeth's promise was kept. During the first weeks of his stay in St. Petersburg, attention was lavished upon Douglas by the Shuvalovs, Razumovskis, Narishkins, Golitsyns, Sheremetovs, Chernishevs, Generals Buturlin and Apraksin, and Michael Bestuzhev-Riumin, as well as Vice-Chancellor Vorontsov. All of them worked to convince Douglas that they were devoted to furthering the interests of France at the Russian court and fervently supported the speedy reestablishment of Franco-Russian diplomatic relations.[18] As a renegade Scotsman working for the French in Russia, he was made to feel important and needed.

The memoir that Douglas gave Vorontsov underscored the extremely valuable service that Louis believed the vice-chan-

[17] AVPR, f. Snosheniia . . . Frantsiei, 1756, op. 93/ 1, d. 5/ 11–12; BN SM NAF 22009/ 98–99 and 109–111; VA, RussBer, karton 38/ 88–89; and LOII, f. 36, op. 1, d. 101/ 32–33. There is some inconsistency in the documents on dating this reply to Douglas, since the old and new style of dating was not always adjusted. See also Vorontsov to Rouillé, May 1, 1756, LOII, f. 36, op. 2, d. 693/ 1–4.
[18] Douglas to Rouillé, May 23, 1756, BN SM NAF 22009/ 112–117.

cellor could do for France. In Louis' opinion Vorontsov was the key to the reestablishment of Franco-Russian diplomatic relations and the person to be relied on for breaking the Anglo-Russian Subsidy Treaty. The latter object was for all practical purposes already accomplished and the former was now on the verge of success. It is significant, too, that the memoir emphasized Louis's concern to establish firm commercial relations between Russia and France. Vorontsov was to be essential to this enterprise as well, and he might be rewarded for his endeavors.

For years Great Britain had been the dominant country in Russian commerce. Thus, France had everything to gain by opening substantial commercial relations with Russia. Despite the considerable trade that France had built up in northern Europe, she did not profit from it as much as she could have. For example, nearly all the French trade that passed through the port of St. Petersburg in 1756 was carried by ships other than French. A report issued about this problem announced, "It is apparent . . . that of the fifteen hundred ships which frequent the ports of the Baltic every year, one sees hardly five or six that are French."[19] And conversely, only three Russian ships out of 50 thousand vessels had entered French ports during the years 1755–1757.[20]

There were, however, a few independent French merchants who ventured their fortunes in Russian commerce. One of them was Michel de Rouen, the secretary and close associate of Vorontsov. In 1747 Michel de Rouen attempted unsuccessfully to establish a solid enterprise in Franco-Russian commerce. During the following years he had to content himself with small personal ventures. With the possible resumption of diplomatic relations between France and Russia and with Vorontsov playing a key role, Michel de Rouen held hopes for what he believed his just reward for serving the pro-French group at the Russian court. He thought he might soon enjoy a position of prominence similar to that which British merchants had achieved in Rus-

[19]Quoted in Oliva, *Misalliance*, p. 125.
[20] Oliva, p. 125. See also Walther Kirchner, "Relations économiques entre la France et La Russie au XVIIIe siècle," *Revue d'histoire économique et sociale*, XXXIX: 2 (1961), 158–197; and Paul W. Bamford, *Forests and French Sea Power, 1660–1789* (Toronto, 1956).

sian commerce.[21] Undoubtedly, the pro-French group at the
Russian court, especially Vorontsov and the Shuvalovs who had
considerable economic interests, would share in the benefits
that would accrue to Russia with the establishment of official
Franco-Russian commercial relations.[22]

By the end of May 1756, the Russian court had accomplished
a great deal toward the successful completion of its preparations for war. Orders for military mobilization had been issued; negotiations for an alliance with the Austrian court had
been initiated; efforts had been made to pacify the Turks and
to persuade the Poles to look favorably on future Russian undertakings; and the first steps in reestablishing diplomatic relations with France had been taken. Empress Elizabeth could
compliment herself on not having made a false start or an
improper *démarche*. Yet there were many other items of business with which she had to concern herself, in particular, the
rationalization of the position with respect to the unhappily
concluded Anglo-Russian Subsidy Treaty and Russia's position
vis-à-vis the impending union between France and Austria.

[21] Oliva, pp. 125–126.
[22] See "Mémoire" of May 10, 1756 and letter of Garde to Rouillé, May
17, 1756, BN SM NAF 22009/ 77, 80, respectively, for an example of
Peter Shuvalov's recent French commercial venture; and Douglas to
Rouillé, May 23, 1756, *ibid.*, 115–120, for Douglas' comments on Michael
Vorontsov's and Peter Shuvalov's capabilities and interests in commercial
affairs.

VII Toward the Formation of Alliances

"The Satisfaction His Majesty received from the Account you sent, that the Ratification of the Russian Treaty were at last, after so many Delays, exchanged, was diminished by the extraordinary Declaration put into Your Hands, at the same Time this great Work was compleated." The king of Great Britain and the British ministry were appalled that Williams had accepted the declaration which fixed the *casus foederis* singly in case of an attack by Frederick on Great Britain or a British ally.[1]

The declaration was sent back to Williams with instructions to return it to both chancellors; and he was also to explain to them that the king of Great Britain did not think that any qualification of the recently concluded treaty was either necessary or expedient. Moreover, the chancellors were to be told that the king of Great Britain did not doubt that Empress Elizabeth would fulfill her obligations pursuant to the treaty as would the king, but that in any event the king wanted the declaration returned. Williams was informed that "the Declaration in Question is of so delicate a Nature, and would so justly give Offense to His Prussian Majesty, were it to become publick, That the King thinks the less That is said of it the better."[2]

The British ministry was further upset by reports of negotiations taking place between Vienna and Versailles. The British suspected that one of the purposes behind these negotiations was to devise a plan by which France was to attack the king of

[1] Holderness to Williams, March 30, 1756, PROSP 91/ 62.
[2] *Ibid.* See also TsGADA, *f.* 178, *d.* 1/ 130–132 (No. 17, April 29, 1756); Vorontsov to Golitsyn, April 17, 1756, TsGADA, *f.* 1263, *op.* 1, *d.* 794/ 4–5.

England in Hanover and the king of Prussia in the Duchy of Cleves. Austria would supposedly support this attack by invading Prussian Silesia.

The king of Great Britain would have to call upon his allies for assistance, Russia in particular, to defeat such a dangerous enterprise. It was extremely important for the British ministry to know Empress Elizabeth's disposition. Williams was reminded that, despite the attempts of the Russian court to place a very narrow interpretation on the Anglo-Russian Subsidy Treaty, the treaty specifically declared, "If His Majesty is attacked by any Foreign Force whatsoever, the Empress of Russia is engaged to assist His Majesty, by Diversion or otherwise." Williams was instructed to obtain an immediate answer to this important question and to notify London without delay.[3]

The British ministry was asking Russia in no uncertain terms whether she would fulfill the obligations of the treaty. There could not be the slightest doubt that the subsidy treaty was already lost, because the Russians by their declaration had revealed how they chose to interpret it. All the British could hope for was Russia's reconsideration, which was, of course, impossible unless the British broke with Frederick. Great Britain had lost the diplomatic game she had set out so cleverly to win—she was in a sense too clever by half.

Williams received these instructions at the beginning of May and on May 8 had a conference with both chancellors at which they reluctantly and with considerable "ill-humour" took back the declaration.[4] At the same time, Williams asked both chancellors what the position of the Russian court would be if France attacked Hanover: "I did not fail upon this Occasion to shew them, not only the Justice of the King's Demands, but the crying Injustice that would be shewn on the part of this Court in case they refused to give the King the stipulated Assistance. I particularly read to them the Fifth Article of the Convention

[3] Holdernesse to Williams, March 30, 1756, PROSP 91/ 62. See also Newcastle to Williams, April 2, 1756, BMAddMSS 32864/ 125–129; TsGADA, f. 178, d. 1/ 130–132 (No. 17, April 29, 1756); Keith to Holdernesse, March 4 and 6, 1756, PROSP 80/ 197; and BMAddMSS 43436, passim.

[4] LOII, f. 36, op. 1, d. 91/ 106–107 (May 8, 1756); and Williams to Holdernesse, May 8, 1756, PROSP 91/ 62.

which makes Hanover so immediately, and so emphatically a Part of the Territories which Her Imperial Majesty was bound to defend."[5] Both chancellors told Williams that they would give him Empress Elizabeth's answer to Great Britain's inquiry. But no less than three weeks passed before Williams received any information on this matter. In fact, Williams was never officially informed about it. He was surprised to learn from the grand chancellor that, when Empress Elizabeth "had anything to say to the Court of London, it should not go thro' me but thro' Prince Gallitzin [sic]." Prince Golitsyn would, therefore, deliver Empress Elizabeth's answer to London, and "particular Care was taken, that [it] should not be communicated to me." It was the grand chancellor who sent word to Williams that the Russian court's decision had been "carry'd by his Enemies" in spite of his opposition. The Russian position on the Anglo-Russian Subsidy Treaty had not changed: "Russian Assistance was to be given only in case His Majesty or any of His Allies were attacked by the King of Prussia."[6]

The issue surrounding the declaration did not, however, end there. Subsequently, on June 17, ambassador Golitsyn in London presented the declaration to Holdernesse who again refused to accept it.[7] But since the Russian court had not yet declared the subsidy treaty null and void, Newcastle still hoped that some arrangement could be made with Russia. Curiously omitting Prussia from his consideration, Newcastle distressingly confessed that "Russia must be had, or we shall not have one Ally in Europe, or America." At the same time he argued that to gain Russia would be an expensive venture, "a dear Bargain," and as he ambivalently wrote to Lord Chancellor Hardwicke, "Of which I see both the Impropriety and the Danger."[8]

[5] Williams to Holdernesse, June 5, 1756, PROSP 91/ 63; and LOII, f. 36, op. 1, d. 91/ 106–107 (May 8, 1756).

[6] Williams to Holdernesse, June 5, 1756, PROSP 91/ 63; and Bestuzhev-Riumin and Vorontsov to A. Golitsyn, AVPR, f. Snosheniia . . . Angliei, 1756, op. 35/ 1, d. 776/ 87-91.

[7] BMEg 3426/ 134; BMAddMSS 32996/ 446–447; and Holdernesse to Keith, June 21, 1756, PROSP 80/ 197.

[8] BMAddMSS 32865/ 278 (June 12, 1756). See also Newcastle to Yorke, June 11, 1756, ibid., 258–262. Joseph Yorke, British ambassador at The Hague, wrote to Newcastle on June 18 explaining the way he would use money to buy the Russians: "this is the Case at least of Russia; & if ten thousand and, nay if twenty thousand Pounds were given to the Min-

At the June 17 meeting of the ministry a proposal was discussed to accept a modified version of the first part of the declaration. Were Russian troops to march into a neutral country to assist the king of England or his allies, the British would consider making an additional allowance of funds for their subsistance.[9] The probability of this proposal succeeding with the Russians was rather small. Williams candidly wrote Holdernesse that there was already talk at the Russian court that Great Britain had forfeited the treaty by not forwarding to Empress Elizabeth the 100,000 pounds promised as the first installment of the subsidy on the exchange of the ratifications. Furthermore, he said, there could be no guarantee that Russia would fulfill her treaty obligations even if the initial sum were paid. Therefore, considering "the present Behaviour of Russia, it must be entirely left to His Majesty's Wisdom, to determine, how far it will be proper or improper to advance that sum, or to make an Offer of immediate paying it upon Condition of this Courts declaring that they will act up to their Engagements."[10]

The position of the British at the Russian court was becoming more and more embarrassing. The British ministry declared that long ago the stipulated 100,000 pounds had been sent to St. Petersburg and assumed that it had already been paid to Empress Elizabeth,[11] but it was only on June 17 that Williams had been informed that the money was in St. Petersburg.[12] Two days later Williams was struck with a fever which prevented his doing any work at all.[13] The British ministry now seriously

---

isters there, to make them act with us, it would be well bestowed; I mean that it should be us'd to buy off the Great Chancellor's Brother & Woranzow [sic], & not be given away by Sir Charles W., only for the encouragement of our friends; To do this effectually it seems clear that we must either send a Proper Person thither on purpose to distribute our Bounty, unless Wolff might be made use of, which I don't know, or even the Dutch Minister, who has certainly more influence with the Great Chancellor than any body & might at least point out good Channels; without one of these methods, I see no other but trusting the King of Prussia to do it; for it is very likely after what has past that these People won't even take money of Sir Charles." Ibid., 35436/ 68.

[9] Ibid., 32996/ 446–447.

[10] PROSP 91/ 63, (June 5, 1756); and Williams to Holdernesse, June 12, 1756, ibid.

[11] See Holdernesse to Williams, June 25, 1756, ibid.

[12] Williams to Holdernesse, June 19, 1756, ibid.

[13] Rineking to Wallace, June 22, 1756, ibid.

considered recalling Sir Charles Hanbury Williams from St. Petersburg.[14]

Great Britain's political credit completely evaporated at the Austrian court as well. Newcastle had been absolutely convinced that Maria Theresa would not do "any mischief" against the Convention of Westminster.[15] According to the British ministry there was no reason why Austria should cause trouble. Great Britain took pains to point out to the Austrians that the Convention of Westminster was "inoffensive to any Power whatsoever; and will probably, be the Means of maintaining Peace in the Empire, whatever may be the Consequences of the present Dispute between His Majesty and the Court of France; which cannot but be very agreeable to Their Imperial Majesties." Robert Keith, the British ambassador at the Austrian court, was to explain "how absolutely necessary it was for the King, to look out for the means of reconciling the King of Prussia sincerely and heartily to Himself, and, if possible, to His Allies." Since Maria Theresa had repeatedly declared that unless she were secure against an attack by Prussia she would not send her troops to the Netherlands or Hanover, there were only two alternatives open to the king of England. He could either financially support the maintenance of the troops of both Maria Theresa and Elizabeth, or he could find the means "to induce the King of Prussia to see His true and lasting Interests; and shewing Him, That He might rest in secure and quiet possession of His late acquisitions, by contracting new Engagements with, or under, the Influence of Great Britain." Great Britain had chosen the latter course of action because it was easily the best one "for the general good of the Common Cause."[16]

The British ministry went one step further in clarifying its foreign policy position, which was so contrary to the one held by the Austrian court that there was no hope for a reconciliation between them. Keith was given instructions to explain that,

if the Court of Vienna (which however, His Majesty will not sup-

[14] See Holdernesse to Newcastle, June 23, 1756, BMAddMSS 32865/ 397.

[15] Newcastle to Devonshire, March 13, 1756, *ibid.*, 32863/ 274.

[16] Holdernesse to Keith, March 23, 1756, PROSP 80/ 197.

pose to be the case) ever did entertain Hopes, that His Majesty
would have joined in so wild and extravagent a View, as that of
making the Destruction of the King of Prussia's Power, the Condition, upon which the House of Austria would have afforded
their assistance to the Maritime Powers against France, It is high
time they should be undeceived; and be convinced, that no Consideration could ever oblige His Majesty to enter into so imprac-
tical and so unjust a Project. Yet in order to be provided against
all Events, and to be enabled to defeat such schemes, as the King
of Prussia might, possibly, have entered into, in conjunction with
France, The King took those Measures with the Court of Russia,
which are now publickly known to the whole world; but which
were never meant to be put in Execution offensively, unless Necessity should oblige the King to It. . . . It is not difficult to conceive,
that the Court of Vienna might have had other hopes from the
Russian Treaty; But, had any other Use been made of It, it would
have been no longer a pacifick, or a preventive Measure; but, on
the contrary, have immediately drawn on a most dangerous War,
which, if successful, might, indeed, have been beneficial to the
House of Austria, but could never have produced any solid Advantage to His Majesty or, at least, not such, as could have been,
in any Ways adequate to the immense Expence and Hazard of
such an Undertaking.[17]

During the troubled months of 1755 Great Britain had been
unable either to guide or even to influence the direction of
Austrian foreign policy. She was now to experience the same
ineffectiveness. Early in May, Keith had an audience with
Maria Theresa at which they discussed the British position in
European affairs. Maria Theresa made it clear to the British
ambassador that it was not Austria but Great Britain who had
abandoned the old system of alliances. The conclusion of the
Convention of Westminster had struck Maria Theresa "like a
fit of apoplexy." Despite all the rumors about the Anglo-
Prussian negotiations, she could not believe that they had been
undertaken. "But now that it was certain, she considered the
old System to exist no longer." Thus, she felt that there was no
reason why Great Britain should be surprised or upset to learn

[17] *Ibid.*

that Austria had been conducting talks with the French. She was merely following the example of the English.[18]

Maria Theresa provided only general clues to the intricate designs that were being put into effect by mid-1756. All the reports that both Great Britain and Russia had received about Austria's having undertaken secret negotiations with France were true, even though some of the suspicions about their contents were not. From the Austrian side negotiation was begun with the hope that Maria Theresa would be able at least to separate Louis XV from Frederick II. Although the course of these negotiations was punctuated with difficulties, one of the greatest impulses to success was the conclusion of the Convention of Westminster. That event alienated France from Prussia and Austria from Great Britain. A subsequent rapprochement between France and Austria led eventually to the conclusion of the Treaty of Versailles on May 1, 1756.

This treaty consisted of two separate parts. There was first a provision requiring Austria to remain neutral in the event of an Anglo-French war. On her part France agreed not to attack any territories belonging to the empress-queen. Thus, Austria promised France not to do something that she had every intention of not doing anyway—refusing to assist Great Britain in a war in Europe. In return Austria achieved the protection of the Austrian Netherlands, which were exceptionally vulnerable to French attack. This agreement gave France the security of knowing that she would not have to fight on two fronts; therefore, she could conceivably concentrate on the sea and colonial battles with England. But in the event of an attack on the European possessions of either Louis XV or Maria Theresa, the second part of the Treaty of Versailles would go into effect, and the aggrieved party could demand from the other 24,000 troops in assistance. Appended to the body of the treaty were several secret articles, the first providing for the *casus foederis* arising for Austria if France were attacked by one of Great Britain's allies. This was of the utmost importance for France if she de-

[18] Keith to Holdernesse, May 16, 1756, *ibid.*; and "Precis de la Reponse . . ." of Kaunitz to Keith, May 9, 1756, AVPR, *f. Snosheniia . . . Avstriei*, 1756, *op.* 32/ 1, *d.* 6/ 101.

cided to invade Hanover. Prussia would then be obliged to assist Great Britain under the terms of the Convention of Westminster and go to war against France. In that event, France could call on Austria for help. Austria would be delighted to assist since she could then attack Prussia in Silesia and attempt to reconquer that territory.

The advantages gained by France and Austria by this treaty were obvious. But what effect would the treaty have on the formulation and conduct of Russian foreign policy? One could argue that it would definitely be positive. Russia was already allied to Austria by the defensive treaty of 1746 and was in the process of arranging an offensive alliance with Austria directed against Frederick. At the same time, she was negotiating secretly with France for the reestablishment of diplomatic relations which might lead to a political alliance, although the conditions had not yet been stated explicitly. At the minimum, however, Russia would want France to stand idle while she invaded Prussia and also to cause no difficulties in Poland, Turkey, or Sweden. Thus, the very fact that an ally of Russia had united herself to her potential ally should naturally be looked on as a good omen at the Russian court.

Notwithstanding the merits of such an alliance for Russia, there were also long-range disadvantages which lay subtly beneath the surface. Russia had announced war aims that Austria and France could neither jointly nor individually wish to see accomplished. While Austria sought to regain Silesia and Glatz from Frederick and could with clear conscience declare that they belonged to her, she could not at the same time be pleased to see East Prussia seized by Russia. That Russia had indicated she did not want to keep East Prussia for herself and wished to exchange it with Poland for Kurland and other territories did not lessen the danger of continued Russian expansion. Although Russian influence in the Polish-Lithuanian Commonwealth fluctuated from time to time, it was always present and persistent. In the event that the commonwealth acquired East Prussia, it would not necessarily diminish Russia's influence. Moreover, the clear-cut incorporation of Kurland into the Russian Empire would only serve to strengthen Russia in that area as well as to provide her with greater access to the Baltic. In a word, a decrease of Prussian power and territory to the point where Russian power was immeasurably increased was not an exchange that Maria Theresa could look upon with a generous heart.

Louis XV could argue the same point. France had not yet declared her interest in a war against Prussia. But aside from that consideration, France, like Austria, would naturally be opposed to the increase of Russia's power in Poland and the Baltic area. While France might not oppose a war against the king of Prussia, she might not wish to allow future peace negotiations that would result in too great a dismemberment of his territories —that is, beyond Austria's reincorporation of Silesia and Glatz. Thus, France and Austria, separately or together, could easily decide to thwart the achievement of Russian war aims. This was not only possible; it was a basis of their future politics. Russia, by the Versailles Treaty, could lose as much as she might gain.

The news of the conclusion of the Treaty of Versailles would not reach St. Petersburg for several weeks; it would thus be a while before it would affect the formulation of Russian foreign policy. In the meantime, Vorontsov and Douglas continued to further Franco-Russian relations by sending Michel de Rouen and Feodor Bekhteev to Versailles. Michel de Rouen left Russia during the third week of May with instructions to inform Rouillé not to be concerned about Russian troops being employed in Great Britain's service in the future, to find out the details of the eventual union between Austria and France, and to express Empress Elizabeth's wishes to see Douglas accredited at St. Petersburg.[19] Douglas wrote the Versailles court on June 5 that, as soon as his credentials reached the frontiers of the Russian Empire, the Russian court would notify its foreign ministers abroad that a reunion between France and Russia had been effected. Regarding the Anglo-Russian Subsidy Treaty, Douglas declared, "you have nothing to fear from the consequences of the famous treaty of subsidy, which from the moment that it had been proposed has been disapproved by all who are the wisest and most respectable in the council of Her

[19] Douglas to Rouillé, May 23, 1756, BN SM NAF 22009/ 112–114. To keep Michel de Rouen's mission and activities an absolute secret, an elaborate code was devised and used by him in all his letters to Vorontsov during the following year. See LOII, *f.* 36, *op.* 1, *d.* 1071/ 156–170.

Imperial Majesty and in the Empire as the disgraceful work of one person only who sacrifices the glory of this sovereign and the ancestry of his peoples from a mercenary and particular view." Douglas also emphasized that the Anglo-Russian commercial treaty was to expire the following year and that France would have the opportunity of replacing English commercial influence in Russia.[20]

Feodor Bekhteev's mission to Versailles was intended to be the more formal expression of Empress Elizabeth's sincere desire to reciprocate for Douglas' return to St. Petersburg. In the letters to Rouillé from Vorontsov dated June 7, it was implied that the Russian court wished to accredit Bekhteev as its chargé d'affaires as soon as Douglas received his credentials. Furthermore, the Russian court declared its sincere intention to name an ambassador to France, corresponding to a similar and simultaneous French nomination to Russia. September 15 was designated as the date for such an announcement, and the respective ambassadors would take up their posts in January 1757.[21] Subsequently, procedures would be initiated to exchange ambassadors. Douglas was instructed to confide in and confer with the Austrian ambassador Count Esterhazy on all matters, as Bekhteev would with Count Starhemberg, and together they would make known to the Russian court the recently concluded Treaty of Versailles.[22]

Vice-Chancellor Michael Vorontsov's politics were based on

[20] "Mémoire" of Douglas to Tercier, June 5, 1756, BN SM NAF 22009/ 151–154; and *ibid.*, 127–128.

[21] Vorontsov to Rouillé, June 7, 1756, AVPR, *f. Snosheniia . . . Frantsiei*, 1756, *op.* 93/ 1, *d.* 3/ 19; and BN SM NAF 22009/ 123–124, 131, 133. See also VA, RussBer, *karton* 38/ 90.

[22] Rouillé to Douglas, June 7, 1756, BN SM NAF 22009/ 133; Rouillé to Douglas, June 16, 1756, *ibid.*, 134–138, 140–141, 142–143; Rouillé to Bestuzhev-Riumin and Vorontsov, June 18, 1756, AVPR, *f. Snosheniia . . . Frantsiei*, 1756, *op.* 93/ 1, *d.* 5/ 18, 22, respectively; Rouillé to Douglas, June 18, 1756, AVPR, *f. Snosheniia . . . Frantsiei*, 1756, *op.* 93/ 1, *d.* 5/ 13; and TsGADA, *f.* 1261, *op.* 1, *d.* 162/ 1–2. See also LOII, *f.* 36, *op.* 1, *d.* 101/ 33; Michel de Rouen to Vorontsov, June 16 and 25, 1756, LOII, *f.* 36, *op.* 1, *d.* 1071/ 173–176, 169–170, respectively; letters to and from Vorontsov to A. Golovkin to this period, LOII, *f.* 36, *op.* 1, *d.* 1109/ 136–173, *passim*; Vorontsov to Golovkin, May 1, 1756, and Golovkin to Vorontsov, May 10, 1756, AVPR, *f. Snosheniia . . . Frantsiei*, 1756, *op.* 93/ 1, *d.* 2/ 10, 11, respectively; and Vorontsov to Golovkin, June 7, 1756, and Golovkin to Vorontsov, June 25, 1756, AVPR, *f. Snosheniia . . . Frantsiei*, 1756, *op.* 93/ 1, *d.* 3/ 15–16, 17, respectively.

both state and personal interests. He had the cunning of a serpent in his manipulations; at times his shrewdness became offensive to those with whom he had dealings and even endangered the secrecy of his political ventures. Count Alexander Golovkin, the Russian ambassador at The Hague and intermediary of the Russo-French secret correspondence, declared that he had been offered the Russian embassy at the French court. Vorontsov wished to have one of Count Golovkin's sons marry his daughter; and according to Golovkin, the appointment to one of the most important diplomatic posts in Europe was used as a bribe to achieve this family union. Feodor Bekhteev had spent several days at The Hague on his way to Paris, and no doubt had conveyed the vice-chancellor's personal wishes to Golovkin. The latter was enough upset by such propositions to reveal the aim of the secret Franco-Russian negotiations to the British ambassador at The Hague and, thereby, confirmed every suspicion the British and Prussian courts had that Russia was seeking to reestablish diplomatic relations with France.[23]

The secret may have been out, but the success of Vorontsov's politics could not be thwarted. Bekhteev arrived in Paris on July 24, and subsequently met with Rouillé and had an audience with Louis XV. The French court agreed to announce the reciprocal ambassadors on September 15; and it was stipulated that they should take up their posts the following January.[24]

In St. Petersburg Empress Elizabeth decided that it was time to inform Grand Chancellor Alexis Bestuzhev-Riumin about the negotiations that she had been carrying on with the French. By her order and to his delight, Vice-Chancellor Vorontsov went to the grand chancellor early on the morning of July 24 and

[23] Yorke to Holdernesse, July 20, 1756, BMAddMSS 35436/ 83; Vorontsov to Golovkin, May 1, 1756, and Golovkin to Vorontsov, May 10, 1756, AVPR, *f. Snosheniia . . . Frantsiei*, 1756, *op.* 93/ 1, *d.* 2/ 10, 11, respectively; Vorontsov to Golovkin, June 7, 1756, and Golovkin to Vorontsov, June 25, 1756, AVPR, *f. Snosheniia . . . Frantsiei*, 1756, *op.* 93/ 1, *d.* 3/ 15–16, 17, respectively; Vorontsov–Golovkin correspondence in LOII, *f.* 36, *op.* 1, *d.* 1109/ 136–173, *passim*; Frederick to Michell and Knyphausen, June 8, 1756, PC XII/ 7551, 7553/ 389–390, 394–395, respectively; and Frederick to Maltzahn, June 12, 1756, PC XII/ 7562/ 403.

[24] Bekhteev to Vorontsov, July 25, 1756, LOII, *f.* 36, *op.* 1, *d.* 1079/ 103; Rouillé to Douglas, July 25, 1756, BN SM NAF 22009/ 182–185; and Bestuzhev-Riumin and Vorontsov to Bekhteev, July 31, 1756, AVPR, *f. Snosheniia . . . Frantsiei*, 1756, *op.* 93/ 1, *d.* 3/ 6–30.

explained that France and Russia were reestablishing diplomatic relations and it was for this purpose that Douglas had been sent to St. Petersburg and Bekhteev to Paris. The grand chancellor was instructed to accept Douglas' credentials as French chargé d'affaires and also to send Bekhteev his appointment papers to the French court. Douglas arrived and Bestuzhev-Riumin accepted his credentials.[25] Only a few days earlier the grand chancellor had professed to Sir Charles Hanbury Williams "the continuation of his being determined strenuously to oppose all the designs of France at this court . . . you must take patience . . . I am now able and resolved to bring back this court into a right way of thinking, and I have no doubt of doing it in six months at farthest."[26] Time had indeed run out. The diplomatic exchange between him and Douglas announced the formal collapse of more than a decade of Bestuzhev-Riumin's policies regarding France.

In August 1756 the culmination of nearly a year's secret diplomacy between France and Russia was reached. Douglas was informed that he was being sent plenipotentiary powers to accept, jointly with Esterhazy, Russia's accession to the Treaty of Versailles.[27] News arrived in St. Petersburg that the Marquis de l'Hôpital would be named the French ambassador to Russia. The Russian court reciprocated by naming Count Michael Bestuzhev-Riumin. The estranged brother of the grand chan-

[25] Bestuzhev-Riumin and Vorontsov to Rouillé, July 25, 1756, AVPR, f. Snosheniia . . . Frantsiei, 1756, op. 93/ 1, d. 2/ 2, 5, respectively; Bestuzhev-Riumin and Vorontsov to Bekhteev, July 31, 1756, ibid., d. 3/ 6–30; Douglas to Vorontsov, Aug. 15, 1756, ibid., d. 5/ 26–29; Bestuzhev-Riumin and Vorontsov to Keyserling, Aug. 3, 1756, ibid., f. Snosheniia . . . Avstriei, 1756, op. 32/ 1, d. 2/ 221; Bestuzhev-Riumin and Vorontsov to A. Golitsyn, Aug. 3, 1756, ibid., f. Snosheniia . . . Angliei, 1756, op. 35/ 1, d. 776/ 139; Vorontsov to Bekhteev, July 20, 1756, TsGADA, f. 1261, op. 9, d. 25/ 1 and also see 3; LOII, f. 36, op. 1, d. 101/ 33; Bestuzhev-Riumin and Vorontsov to Rouillé, July 25, 1756, BN SM NAF, 22009/ 200, 203, respectively; and Douglas to Rouillé, July 31, 1756, BN SM NAF 22010/ 1–22.

[26] Williams to Holdernesse, July 9, 1756, PROSP 91/ 63.

[27] Rouillé to Douglas and Esterhazy, Aug. 14, 1756, BN SM NAF, 22009/ 222–223, 224–225; Douglas to Rouillé, Aug. 17, 1756, ibid., 22010/ 49–51; Rouillé to Douglas, Aug. 14, and Sept. 4, 1756, AVPR, f. Snosheniia . . . Frantsiei, 1756, op. 93/ 1, d. 5/ 66–68, 88–92, respectively; and Bestuzhev–Riumin and Vorontsov to Bekhteev, Sept. 4, 1756, AVPR, f. Snosheniia . . . Frantsiei, 1756, op. 93/1, d. 3/ 58–63.

cellor had originally been recommended to represent Russia in Poland as a "person of distinction." But now with this new and exceptionally important post opening up and the fact that France held a key position in influencing Polish politics, the advantages gained by appointing a leading member of the pro-French group at the Russian court as ambassador to France were obvious and overrode all previous considerations. The appointment of a Bestuzhev-Riumin to represent Russia in France was, moreover, a symbol of the poetry of Vorontsov's diplomacy.[28]

By the end of the summer of 1756 a future triple entente among Austria, France, and Russia seemed a foregone conclusion.

[28] Rouillé to Douglas and Vorontsov, Aug. 10, 1756, BN SM NAF, 22009/ 211–214, 215–216, respectively; Douglas to Rouillé, Aug. 21 and 24, 1756, *ibid.*, 22010/ 53–56, 57–100, respectively; Vorontsov to l'Hôpital and Rouillé, Sept. 18, 1756, AVPR, *f. Snosheniia . . . Frantsiei,* 1756, *op.* 93/1, *d.* 2/ 14–16, 24–25, respectively; Bestuzhev-Riumin and Vorontsov to Bekhteev, Aug. 24, 1756, AVPR, *f. Snosheniia . . . Frantsiei,* 1756, *op.* 93/1, *d.* 3/31; and Rouillé to Douglas and Vorontsov, Aug. 10, 1756, AVPR, *f. Snosheniia . . . Frantsiei,* 1756, *op.*93/ 1, *d.* 5/ 45–46, 51–52, respectively.

VIII General Mobilization

Frederick II kept abreast of the recent developments in Versailles, Vienna, and St. Petersburg and was increasingly convinced that the powers surrounding him were bent on his destruction. The politics and military activities of Russia especially agitated him. His reactions were neither consistent nor predictable. At times he demonstrated an almost stupefied calm and an exaggerated confidence, followed by periods of depression, bewilderment, and fear.

The British ministry continually endeavored to bolster Frederick's confidence in Prussia's security. Holdernesse assured him that Austria was gravely mistaken if she imagined herself capable of separating Russia from Great Britain.[1] The Prussian envoy at Vienna wrote Frederick that the British ambassador there said that Russia preferred to do nothing except receive her annual 100,000 pounds from Great Britain.[2] Frederick, however, considered himself better informed than the English about their situation at St. Petersburg. He advised Holdernesse that several important persons at the Russian court opposed the Anglo-Russian Subsidy Treaty and that Empress Elizabeth regretted ratifying it after learning of the Convention of Westminster.[3] Moreover, Frederick was assured that the first pay-

[1] Michell to Frederick, March 23, 1756, PC XII/ 7397/ 236–237. See also Michell to Frederick, March 9, 1756, and Frederick to Klinggraeffen, March 20, 1756, *ibid.*, 7364, 7365/ 203, 208, respectively.

[2] Klinggraeffen to Frederick, Feb. 19, 1756, *ibid.*, 7306/ 149.

[3] Frederick to Michell, April 13, 1756, *ibid.*, 7424/ 261–262. Frederick named Peter and Ivan Shuvalov, Michael Bestuzhev-Riumin, General Buturlin, and Count Chernyshev as opponents of the Anglo-Russian Subsidy Treaty. See also Frederick to Michell, March 6 and 16, 1756, *ibid.*, 7328, 7354/ 172–173, 194, respectively; Frederick to Podewils, March 7, 1756, *ibid.*, 7332/ 176; Frederick to Maltzahn, April 13, 1756, *ibid.*, 7423/ 260; and Frederick to Michell, May 29, 1756, PROSP 100/ 50.

ment of the subsidy had neither been paid nor refused but merely remained in the keeping of the British Resident in St. Petersburg. This situation was hardly one in which Frederick could have confidence.[4]

Frederick troubled Andrew Mitchell, the newly appointed British ambassador to Prussia, about the resuscitation of French influence at the Russian court. He dwelled on the mission of Douglas, who held, he believed, credentials from the king of France as well as letters of credit for a large sum of money. Mitchell attempted to persuade Frederick that he had nothing to fear from the Russians and that Great Britain's position at St. Petersburg was extremely good. Nevertheless, Frederick stressed that "it was of the utmost Consequence that the King's Interest and Influence should be maintained there, that while Russia was secured the Peace of Germany was safe."[5] Profoundly concerned, he more than once queried Mitchell, "are you sure of the Russians?"[6] He, in any case, was not sure of them, but he did not believe war would break out soon. To the contrary he was confident that "Nothing will happen this year, I can answer for it with my Head, but I do not pretend to say what may happen the next."[7]

In the beginning of June, Frederick's view of his predicament worsened. The news of the Treaty of Versailles, Great Britain's declaration of war against France, and Russia's continued mili-

[4] Frederick to Michell, May 18, 1756, PC XII/ 7500/ 336–337.
[5] Mitchell to Holdernesse, May 27, 1756, PROSP 90/ 65. See also Frederick to Michell, May 29, 1756, *ibid.*, 100/ 50; BMAddMSS 33021/ 214 (April 11, 1756); Mitchell to Holdernesse, June 22, 1756, BMAddMSS 32865/ 378–379; and Podewils to Frederick, June 2, 1756, PC XII/ 7541/ 378. Frederick wanted to inform the British ministry of Douglas' mission himself since Mitchell's ignorance of the whole matter was profound. Mitchell demonstrated this in a letter to Holdernesse: "There is reason to believe that the true Name of the Person employed at Petersbourg is *Mackenzie* and not *Douglass*. This Man served the Prince of Waldeck as Aid de Camp the Beginning of the last war, and was afterwards employed by the Dutch to reside at Liege as their Spy. He is from Scotland, a Roman Catholick, a Jacobite, and believed to belong to the Order of Jesuits, tho He never wears the Dress." (PROSP 90/ 65, June 10, 1756.)
[6] Mitchell to Holdernesse, May 14, 1756, PROSP 90/ 65 and PC XII/ 7493/ 327–328.
[7] Mitchell to Holdernesse, May 14, 1756, PROSP 90/ 65; and PC XII/ 7493/ 327 ff.

tary build-up and reports that she might soon bind herself by
treaty to France and Austria—all made it absolutely necessary
that Frederick reevaluate his position in European affairs.[8] He
wanted Great Britain to deliver on her promises. "He then repeated what he had often said to me of the importance of securing Russia," Mitchell reported after a conversation with
Frederick, "and added that France was stretching every nerve
to gain Russia, that the court of Vienna joined with France in
endeavouring to seduce Russia into their cabals, that no pains
or expence might be spared to preserve our interests there."[9]

Frederick outlined to Mitchell three "precautionary measures"
which should be employed in the event that Russia were really
lost to Great Britain. He made the reasonable recommendation
that the Turks be encouraged to act against the enemies of
Great Britain and Prussia; but his other two proposals—to precipitate a religious war in Hungary and a revolution in Russia
—were extravagant and suggested that Frederick was too
troubled to think sensibly. He declared he would fulfill all his
commitments to Great Britain but wanted to know "in case Russia turned against us, & attacked Him, whether England could
& would send a Fleet into the Baltick to His assistance."[10] A
British squadron in the Baltic would be helpful but it would
certainly not be enough. Consequently, Frederick began to

[8] Frederick to Knyphausen, May 24, and June 5 and 8, 1756, PC XII/
7519, 7545, 7553/ 355, 381, 394–396, respectively; Frederick to Michell,
May 25, June 1 and 8, 1756, *ibid.*, 7521, 7533, 7551/ 361–362, 371, 389–
393, respectively; Frederick to Klinggraeffen, May 31 and June 12, 1756,
ibid., 7532, 7560/ 370–371, 401, respectively; Frederick to Podewils,
June 1, 1756, *ibid.*, 7535/ 372–373; Frederick to Finckenstein, June 7,
1756, *ibid.*, 7550/ 386–389; Feriet to Frederick, May 25, 1756, *ibid.*,
7535/ 372; Duke of Brunswick to Frederick, May 29, 1756, *ibid.*, 7547/
384; Haeseler to Frederick, June 11, 1756, *ibid.*, 7568/ 409; Finckenstein
to Frederick, June 13, 1756, *ibid.*, 75/ 408–409; and Holdernesse to Williams, May 11 and 18, 1756, PROSP 91/ 62.

[9] PC XII/ 7569/ 385 (June 6, 1756). See also Mitchell to Holdernesse,
June 7, 1756, PROSP 90/ 65.

[10] Mitchell to Holdernesse, June 10, 1756, PROSP 90/ 65. *Cf.* PC XII/
7558/ 399–400 (June 10, 1756). There was considerable unhappiness at
the Prussian court, too, over the lack of success of Sir Charles Hanbury
Williams in Russia, and Mitchell was advised that he should be recalled
and replaced by "a wise man." See Mitchell to Holdernesse, June 3 and
22, 1756, PROSP 90/ 65; and Frederick to Mitchell, May 25, 1756, PC
XII/ 7521/ 362.

take his own military measures when reports about Russian mobilization were coupled with similar ones about Austria. There was a rumor that even Saxony might accede to the Treaty of Verasilles.[11] It now seemed to Frederick that an attack on his territories was imminent. Austrian armies would attack him through Bohemia, Saxony, and Silesia, while Russian forces would advance from Smolensk through Poland into Silesia and from Livonia and Kurland into East Prussia.[12]

Despite these odds, Frederick professed confidence in Prussia's ability to withstand and initiate attack. On June 23, 1756, he sent Field Marshal Lehwaldt instructions in the event war broke out. He boastfully assured Lehwaldt that, although the Russians had massed a large number of troops in Livonia and Kurland, at the beginning of hostilities he would be able to crush the Russian army. Frederick viewed the Russian general staff as weak and had a particularly low opinion of General Stepan Apraksin. Lehwaldt was told that, if he defeated the Russians before Frederick himself had been able to decimate the Austrians, Lehwaldt could make peace with the Russians, provided they would remain neutral in the future. However, if Frederick were victorious over the Austrians at the time that Lehwaldt was conducting peace talks with the Russians, then Lehwaldt was to demand rewards for Prussia. Polish Prussia in its entirety, or at least Elbląg (Elbing), Chełmno (Kulm), and Toruń

---

[11] See Klinggraeffen to Frederick, June 2 and 19, 1756, PC XII/ 7560, 7625/ 401, 478–479; Schlabrendorff to Frederick, June 15, 1756, *ibid.*, 7592/ 438; Maltzahn to Frederick, June 18, 1756, *ibid.*, 7608/ 460–461; Finckenstein to Frederick, June 26, 1756, *ibid.*, 7618/ 468–469; Frederick to Klinggraeffen, March 2, and June 22 and 29, 1756, *ibid.*, 7318, 7595, 7625/ 165, 441, 479, respectively; Frederick to Knyphausen, March 6, 1756, *ibid.*, 7315/ 171; Frederick to Schlabrendorff and Kyau, June 19, 1756, *ibid.*, 7587, 7588/ 432–433, 433–434, respectively; Frederick to Quadt and Finckenstein, June 21, 1756, *ibid.*, 7590, 7592/ 434, 436–437, respectively; Frederick to Maltzahn, June 25 and 30, 1756, *ibid.*, 7608, 7629/ 461, 485, respectively; Frederick to Field Marshal Keith, June 23, 1756, *ibid.*, 7602/ 457; "Circulaireordre," June 23, 24, and 25, 1756, *ibid.*, 7603, 7606, 7610/ 457, 459, 463, respectively; Frederick to Finckenstein, June 24, 1756, *ibid.*, 7607/ 459–460; Frederick to the Prince of Brunswick, June 25, 1756, *ibid.*, 7609/ 463; PROSP 90/ 65, *passim*; and Mitchell to Holdernesse, June 22, 24, 26, and 29, 1756, PROSP 90/ 65.

[12] Frederick to Knyphausen, June 19, 1756, PC XII/ 7586/ 431–432; Frederick to Finckenstein, June 21, 1756, *ibid.*, 7592/ 436–437; and Mitchell to Holdernesse, June 22, 1756, BMAddMSS 32865/ 379–380.

(Thorn), were to go to Prussia, and the Russians themselves were to arrange the cession with the Polish-Lithuanian Commonwealth.[13]

Frederick was given a reprieve of sorts. Ironically, it was Austria, the country Russia had for so long counted on to assist her in striking a death blow to Frederick, that called for a delay in the attack on Prussia. This gave Frederick more time to continue his military mobilization and also to plan the defensive and offensive measures he believed necessary to protect Prussia.

Count Esterhazy reported to the Russian court on June 9 that, although Austria would happily join Russia in the venture against Prussia, it was absolutely necessary that France should agree beforehand not to prevent its execution. Austria was endeavoring to obtain France's agreement on this matter; but until she did, it was impossible to begin hostilities that summer.[14]

Russia reluctantly agreed to Austria's request. She had no alternative. On June 10 the Conference called an immediate halt to the movement of Russian forces toward the frontiers. Although all land and sea forces were to remain essentially where they were at that time, they were to be ready to move at a moment's notice to their previously appointed rendezvous. The invasion of Prussia, however, was not to take place before the spring of 1757.[15]

The Russian court had difficulty in concealing its frustration and disappointment. The Conference on June 15 resolved to inform the Vienna court that Empress Elizabeth in her desire to please Maria Theresa had ordered her troops not to advance any further; nevertheless it wished to make known that those troops would be reinforced and prepared when Austria decided to join Russia in the attack. Because there was always the possibility of a reconciliation between France and Great Britain, Austria was cautioned not to delay entering into an offensive alliance with Russia. Count Esterhazy was to be informed that Empress Eliza-

---

[13] PC XII/ 7601/ 448–457. See also Mitchell to Holdernesse, June 24, 1756, BMAddMSS 32865/ 406.

[14] TsGADA, f. 178, d. 1/ 166–170 (No. 24); and Kaunitz to Esterhazy, May 22, 1756, PPS LXXIV/ 99/ 367–370.

[15] TsGADA, f. 178, d. 1/ 166–170 (No. 24).

beth would like very much to be invited to accede to the Treaty of Versailles.[16]

Undoubtedly, France played a vital role in determining the Austrian court's decision; however, there were other reasons for her decision to delay the invasion. She was faced with the unhappy realization that she was unprepared militarily for the enormous responsibility of going to war. As early as May 16 Maria Theresa was so informed by her cabinet secretary Baron von Koch, who stated in a note to her that Austria would have no more than 67,000 regular troops available to undertake military operations in 1756. In his opinion this number was insufficient if Maria Theresa hoped to gain a victory over Frederick, and he recommended that at least another 40,000 to 50,000 troops be recruited into a second army. The summer of 1756 should be used for this end, and Austrian military preparations could be completed in the winter. By the spring of 1757 Austria could be ready to launch her attack together with France and Russia, with whom she should have concluded all the necessary offensive and defensive arrangements.[17]

Austria had originally mobilized her military forces and begun deploying them throughout Habsburg dominions because she wanted to go to war against Prussia jointly with Russia and not solely because Frederick had by the beginning of the summer shown signs of mobilization. Moreover, several months before Frederick or Maria Theresa decided to launch their respective military mobilizations, Russia had had a sufficient number of troops on her frontiers and had mobilized tens of thousands more, which had forced Frederick to undertake defensive measures. He believed the conclusion of the Convention of Westminster might be sufficient to keep the Russians from moving against him. But as he subsequently found out, Great Britain's influence at the Russian court was fading and he had to plan to defend himself militarily. At Austria's request, Russia merely stopped her movement of troops without reducing the

[16] *Ibid.*, *d.* 1/ 174–184 (No. 27). See also AVPR, *f. Snosheniia* . . . *Avstriei*, 1756, *op.* 32/ 1, *d.* 4/ 120–122, 125–130, 132–142.

[17] PPS LXXIV/ 102/ 376–382; and Baron Koch to Kaunitz, May 26, 1756, *ibid.*, 102*a*/383.

potential threat to Prussia's safety which they posed. Austria
wanted France to commit herself to an aggressive program
which would produce an invasion of Frederick's territories and
the restoration of Silesia and Glatz to the Habsburgs. At the
same time she wanted to be prepared militarily to back up her
political designs and assure success. Both her military and political activities further intensified Frederick's fears that the
house of Hohenzollern was in mortal danger.

Not unnaturally, the Austrian court chose to interpret any
military movement taking place in Frederick's territories as
indicative of aggressive intent. Whereupon the Austrians as-
serted that they had the right to defend themselves in the event
of an attack by Frederick; this assertion, however, was merely
a diplomatic cloak to cover their own mobilization efforts. The
slow but steady pace of Austrian preparations, from the pro-
curement of horses and ammunition to the actual deployment
of regiments in Bohemia, Moravia, and Hungary, was definitely quickened after the establishment on July 9 of the
Rüstungscommission.[18]

Austria attempted to keep these troop movements secret, but
Frederick learned of them. According to his intelligence reports, regiments were in a constant state of movement in Bohemia, Moravia, and Hungary. Others were expected from
Italy momentarily.[19] The news that Russia had halted the movement of her troops,[20] which might have calmed Frederick's
nerves, was quickly overshadowed by Mitchell's news of the
declaration Russia wanted to add to the subsidy treaty. If he
had not suspected it before, Frederick now knew that the Rus-

[18] *Hofkriegsrathsprotokoll,* May 29–July 7, 1756, PPS LXXIV/ 106–
107, 122, 124–126, 132, 135–136, 138–139, 145, 149–150, 153–155/393,
419–421, 433, 437, 439, 453, 456–457, 458–459, respectively; *Hofkriegsrath* to Maria Theresa, F. M. L. von Bohn, and F. M. L. Baron von And-
lau, June 4 and 9, and July 6, 1756, *ibid.,* 110, 113, 148/ 394–395, 408–
409, 455–456, respectively; Lichtenstein and Browne to *Hofkriegsrath,*
June 9, and 24, 1756, *ibid.,* 114, 127/ 409, 421–422, respectively; and
Protokoll . . . Rüstungscommission, July 9, 1756, *ibid.,* 156/ 460–465,
et seq.
[19] See Klinggraeffen to Frederick, June 23, 1756, PC XIII/ 7648/ 11;
Frederick to Klinggraeffen, July 3, 1756, *ibid.,* 7648/ 12; Eichel to Finckenstein, July 4, 1756, *ibid.,* 7650/ 13–14.
[20] Eichel to Finckenstein, July 4, 1756, *ibid.,* 7650/ 15.

sian military diversion, of which the British were supposed to be the masters, would under any and all circumstances be made only against Prussia.[21] Subsequently, Frederick received word from The Hague that Russia intended to supply 150,000 troops and Austria 80,000 for an attack on Prussia. The only saving grace would be that the attack not take place until the following year because—as Frederick was informed—of a lack of sufficient forces at the disposal of Austria and Russia.[22]

On July 18 Frederick instructed his envoy at Vienna to demand an audience with Maria Theresa and to inquire whether her recent military activities were for the purpose of attacking him. If Maria Theresa replied that the only reason for her military mobilization was to emulate Frederick's, the Prussian envoy was to say that Frederick had moved troops to Pomerania solely to protect that territory from the menace of 70,000 Russian troops stationed on the frontier. Maria Theresa was to be told that Frederick had not made any changes on the borders of Silesia and had not given one order that might induce her to become alarmed.[23]

Empress Elizabeth still held the principal position. She had set in motion the almost uncontrollable machinery of military mobilization in both Austria and Prussia. She was considerably irritated over having to keep her troops waiting until Austria was ready. On July 20 it was decided to inform Count Esterhazy that the slowness of Austria's preparations had disturbed Empress Elizabeth and had created an unfavorable situation for the future invasion of Prussian territories. The delay provided Frederick not only with the time to undertake defensive measures, but with the opportunity to conclude new political alliances. Esterhazy was to be told that in any case Elizabeth's

---

[21] Mitchell to Holdernesse, July 9, 1756, PROSP 90/ 65. See also Maltzahn to Frederick, June 18 and 25, 1756, PC XII/ 7608, 7629/ 460–461, 484, respectively.

[22] Frederick to Klinggraeffen, July 24, 1756, PC XIII/ 7747/ 114.

[23] Frederick to Klinggraeffen, *ibid.*, 7722/ 90–91. Robert Keith, the British ambassador at Vienna, reported that the Austrians claimed that they were not the aggressors, but that the "motions made by the Prussian troops and the camps, which His Prussian Majesty intends to form in their neighborhood, oblige them to put themselves in a Posture of Readiness and Defence." (Keith to Holdernesse, July 9, 1756, PROSP 80/ 197.)

interests and inclinations made her union with Maria Theresa indissoluble. Consequently, she had chosen to enter into the closest agreement with France; but the mere reestablishment of diplomatic relations would not be sufficient if it were not supported by other, more fundamental measures. Russia stood to lose a large sum of money by breaking with Great Britain. Recently, however, Great Britain had shown a desire to satisfy the Russian court in all matters. Esterhazy was to be told that, if Russia was expected to reject such beneficial rewards from Great Britain, France, as a reciprocal sacrifice on her part, should abandon Prussia.[24]

Disconcerting reports circulated at European courts that any further military buildup by Austria or Prussia might lead to war. Holdernesse informed Mitchell that Frederick's warlike preparations were exciting his neighbors, especially Austria.[25] From Dresden the Russian envoy Gross informed his court of fears that Frederick's armies would pass through Saxony when he invaded Bohemia and Moravia; and the Saxon court wanted to know what Russia would do in that event.[26] Stormont, the British ambassador to the king of Poland, suggested to Gross that Frederick's military operations might be "only to prevent an Alliance being formed against him." Gross sarcastically brushed this aside: "prevent it? No, My Lord; on the contrary if there is any such Design, This step the King of Prussia undertakes will only forward it."[27]

When the British ambassador Andrew Mitchell discussed with Frederick the delicate question of Prussia's military mobilization and asked whether he intended to undertake any aggressive measures against his neighbors, Frederick pleaded innocence. He declared that he had no intention of invading Bohemia or Moravia and really desired only peace. All he had done was to march 11 or 12 battalions into Pomerania because

[24] TsGADA, f. 178, d. 1/ 203–206 (No. 35).

[25] Holdernesse to Mitchell, July 13, 1756, PROSP 90/ 65.

[26] TsGADA, f. 178, d. 1/ 198–202 (No. 34, July 19, 1756).

[27] Stormont to Holdernesse, July 21, 1756, PROSP 88/ 78. Sometime earlier Gross had the audacity to tell Stormont that "The Encampment of Fifty thousand Men which he [Frederick] is making in Pomerania, made it very probable that he meant to attack Russia." (Stormont to Holdernesse, July 4, 1756, ibid.)

he feared a Russian attack in that area. That, Frederick said, should not offend Maria Theresa since he was not supposed to be disturbed over her sending troops into Florence. Until mid-July Frederick claimed "not a single man had been sent into Silesia and all He had yet done was to order the Palisades to be placed and the Canons to be mounted in the fortified Places in that Country." Mitchell was not convinced by these assurances. He wrote Holdernesse that he believed Frederick had taken precautions so that within 14 days he could send 40,000 troops into Silesia and raise the number of men there to 90,000.[28]

The French court was concerned enough to have its envoy to Prussia, Marquis Valory, present Frederick with a declaration on July 26 stating that, if Frederick attacked Maria Theresa, Louis XV would assist her under the provisions of the Treaty of Versailles. Frederick replied that his armament was merely defensive and was undertaken in order to prevent a Russian invasion of his territory. His strengthening of his fortresses in Silesia, however, was done solely in view of the dangerous actions taken by Maria Theresa; in a word, he had not initiated these military *démarches* but had responded to threats made by other countries.[29]

The mobilization politics of the great powers had their repercussions in Sweden and Denmark. Those courts viewed a disruption of peace on the European continent as dangerous to their own security. The flurry of negotiations and conventions between the great powers during the first half of 1756 had intensified the anxiety of Swedish and Danish diplomats.

[28] Mitchell to Holdernesse, July 17 and 23, 1756, *ibid.*, 90/ 65. For Frederick's military preparations see Frederick to Klinggraeffen, June 29, 1756, PC XII/ 7625/ 479–480; Frederick to the Prince of Darmstadt, July 2, 1756, PC XIII/ 7638/ 5; Frederick to Lattorff and Kalsow, July 4, 1756, PC XIII/ 7651/ 16–23; Puebla to Kaunitz, June 26 and 29, and July 1, 3, 5, and 6, 1756, PPS LXXIV/ 131, 131a, 131b, 134, 141, 143, 146, 151/ 431–432, 432–433, 435–437, 440–441, 442, 454–455, 457, respectively; Puebla to Kaunitz, June 26 and 29, and July 1, 5, 9, and 27, 1756, AVPR, f. Snosheniia . . . Avstriei, 1756, op. 32/ 1, d. 6/ 187–189, 123–125, 121, 119–120, 184–185, 244–245, respectively; Mitchell to Holdernesse, July 3, 1756, PROSP 90/ 65; Corry to Holdernesse, July 17, 1756, PROSP 91/ 63; and LOII, f. 36, op. 1, d. 104/ 292.

[29] PC XIII/ 7763/ 133–134; Puebla to Kaunitz, July 28 and 30, 1756, f. 36, op. 1, d. 1070/ 282–286, 287–291, respectively; AVPR, f. Snosheniia . . . Avstriei, 1756, op. 32/ 1, d. 6/ 238, 239–240, 242–243.

They, therefore, initiated negotiations between each other to strengthen their defenses and consolidate their armed forces. By July the news that the fleets of Denmark and Sweden had been joined for the defense of their commerce became public and was widely discussed. The possible implications of this act for Great Britain, France, Prussia, and Russia were obvious. The Danes and Swedes were now in a superb position to police the Baltic Sea, which could seriously affect the commercial and military activities of one or more powers.[30]

"From day to day I see myself on the verge of being attacked by Austria and Russia," Frederick despondently wrote his sister, the Queen of Sweden, at the beginning of July.[31] His mood did not change in the days that followed. Frederick speculated that he might be saved if he attacked first. When he intimated this to Podewils on July 21, his minister of state disagreed: to act aggressively would only accelerate the as yet incomplete union among France, Austria, and Russia. Rather than attempt to combat all three powers at once, it would be better, Podewils argued, for Prussia to continue to strengthen herself militarily and politically during the next ten months and even to endeavor to reestablish the peace between France and Great Britain. Frederick recklessly dismissed his minister with: "Adieu, Monsieur de la timide politique."[32]

[30] Korff to Golitsyn, March 20, May 8, June 5 and 26, July 24 and 31, 1756, TsGADA, *f.* 1263, *op.* 1, *d.* 1764/ 8, 11–12 and 16, 18, 27–28, 31, 35, respectively; Panin to Golitsyn, April 6 and Aug. 3, 1756, *ibid., d.* 2652/ 9–12, 26–32, respectively; LOII, *f.* 36, *op.* 1, *d.* 97/ 54–55 (May 15, 1756); TsGADA, *f.* 178, *d.* 1/ 71 (No. 2, March 26, 1756), 1/ 193–195 (No. 32, July 12, 1756); Frederick to Michell, April 3, 1756, PC XII/ 7397/ 239; Williams to Holdernesse, March 9 and 16, and May 4, 11, and 15, 1756, PROSP 91/ 62; Williams to Holdernesse, July 9, 13, and 31, 1756, PROSP 91/ 63; and Holdernesse to Williams, April 2, 1756, PROSP 91/ 62.

[31] PC XIII/ 7645/ 10 (July 3, 1756).

[32] Podewils to Eichel, July 22, 1756, *ibid.,* 7735/ 104–107.

IX Frederick Precipitates Hostilities

Although Empress Elizabeth may have hoped that her preparations to invade Prussia would create a situation so critical that Frederick would initiate hostilities, still his invasion of Saxony could not have been predicted. Russia had wanted for a long time to go to war against Prussia. She tried to enlist her allies for a direct attack on Frederick's territories in the spring of 1756, but circumstances beyond her control demanded a postponement until the following spring.

As early as May 8 and later on August 31, Empress Elizabeth announced in a circular letter to her ministers abroad that Russia would aid her allies if any one of them were attacked. Between the first note and the second, Elizabeth observed that Prussia had begun arming herself and was thus "kindling the flames of a great war." According to the Russian empress, Frederick had no intention of preserving the peace but was planning "some madness" to destroy it.[1] Meanwhile, Russia sought to reinforce her troops and keep them in readiness for striking Prussia.[2]

There is enough evidence to support the view that, despite his menacing military activities, Frederick wanted neither to be forced into war nor to declare it. Frederick aptly characterized his precarious situation when he stated that a nation "which is forced in spite of her wish to begin the first hostilities, so that she may not have her hands and feet tied and be slaughtered with impunity, is acting only from self defense."[3]

[1] AVPR, f. Snosheniia . . . Avstriei, 1756, op. 32/ 1, d. 4/ 176–179.
[2] TsGADA, f. 178, d. 1/ 215–216, 241–242, 243, 244, 254–257, 258–261, 262 (Nos. 40, 47, 48, 49, 51, 52, 53, Aug. 16 and 30, Sept. 2 and 8, 1756), respectively. Also, TsGADA, f. 1263, op. 1, d. 57/ 14–17; and d. 8369/ 103–108, 117–125, 135.
[3] Frederick to Knyphausen, Aug. 16, 1756, PC XIII/ 7859/ 225.

Both before and after his invasion of Saxony, Frederick on more than one occasion expressed his desire for peace to Maria Theresa and Elizabeth.

Before invading Saxony Frederick had several times sent instructions to his envoy in Vienna to obtain Maria Theresa's declaration that she had no present or future intentions, alone or in collaboration with Elizabeth, of making war against him. The first of these fruitless endeavors had been undertaken on July 26, when Klinggraeffen, the Prussian envoy at Vienna, inquired about the meaning of Austria's mobilization. A prepared statement was read to him which explained that Austria merely had taken military measures for her own security in view of the critical state of European politics; no harm to anyone was intended.[4]

On August 2 Frederick learned of this reply and instructed Klinggraeffen once again to present his views to the Vienna court. This time Frederick was more specific, if less diplomatic. Maria Theresa was to be informed of Frederick's awareness that she and Empress Elizabeth had concluded in the beginning of 1756 an offensive alliance against him with the intention of striking him by surprise, Russia with 120,000 troops and Austria with 80,000. Frederick had also learned that, because Russia lacked recruits, the attack was put off until the spring of 1757. What he wanted—and this request was submitted in the form of a demand—was Maria Theresa's promise that she had no intention of attacking him that year or the next. He wanted her to decide for peace or war.[5]

Klinggraeffen presented Frederick's requests on August 20, and within 24 hours Chancellor Kaunitz gave a stinging reply: Frederick's information that Russia and Austria had concluded an offensive alliance was not only false but seemingly invented.[6]

Couriers moved swiftly during those last peaceful days of August 1756. The Austrian court's reply was in Frederick's hands on the twenty-fifth, and on the following day another instruction was on its way to the Prussian envoy in Vienna. For the fourth time he futilely beseeched the empress-queen to act

---

[4] Klinggraeffen to Frederick, July 27, 1756, ibid., 7795/ 163.
[5] Ibid., 163–165.
[6] Ibid., 7923/ 285–291.

peaceably. Not convinced by the earlier protestations of Austria, Frederick declared that he was being forced to take severe measures in defense of his territories. He would recall his armies only if Maria Theresa announced that she did not intend to attack him that year or the next.[7]

To each Prussian request, the Vienna court reacted in accordance with its previous commitment to Russia. Each time the Prussian envoy was given a vague and haughty answer which only confirmed Frederick's suspicions that an understanding had been reached between the two imperial courts.

Since no official diplomatic relations existed between Prussia and Russia, Frederick had to operate in a different and less direct manner with Empress Elizabeth in order to avert a full-scale war. Weeks before he had received the discouraging reports from Vienna and before he invaded Saxony at the end of August, Frederick sent out "feelers" (through ambassadors Mitchell and Williams) to the Russian court to the effect that he wanted very much to reestablish friendly relations with Empress Elizabeth and that his military preparations were not to be interpreted as an indication of aggressive intent toward Russia.[8] Frederick explicitly stated to Mitchell that he was willing not only to send "a minister to Petersburg, if there was a proper Opening on the Part of the Czarina, but that He would even accept Her Mediation . . . to make up the Differences between Him and the Empress Queen."[9]

This mediation proposal was presented to Vice-Chancellor Vorontsov on September 9 by ambassador Williams. Elizabeth's reply left nothing in doubt:

> Her Majesty is indeed offended by the King of Prussia and, finding herself at the same time in the most intimate liaison with Her Majesty the Empress Queen, it does not agree with Her magnanimity and Her justice to charge herself with the said mediation. Her Imperial Majesty leaves it to the two courts to reconcile

[7] Frederick to Klinggraeffen, Aug. 26, 1756, *ibid.*, 7914/ 278–279.
[8] See Mitchell to Holdernesse, July 9, 1756; Holdernesse to Mitchell, July 13, 1756; Mitchell to Williams, July 30, 1756, PROSP 90/ 65. Williams to Holdernesse, Aug. 10, 1756, *ibid.*, 91/ 63; and Williams to Catherine, Aug. 11, 1756, ICC, p. 27.
[9] See Mitchell to Holdernesse, Aug. 30, 1756, *ibid.*, 90/ 65.

their differences, which were created by Berlin. The Empress will content herself to fulfill punctually and religiously the engagements that she has with Her Majesty the Empress Queen.[10]

It was in Elizabeth's power to call a halt to the ever closer outbreak of a European war, but she chose not to. This, of course, was not a surprise. To do anything else would have been to abandon the major tenets of her foreign policy as well as her expensive and protracted military preparations.

Contemporaries assumed that as soon as Frederick invaded Saxony the emerging union between Russia, Austria, and France would coalesce quickly. This did not prove true. Whereas the public announcement on September 15 that the Marquis de l'Hôpital and Michael Bestuzhev-Riumin had been designated ambassadors to Russia and France, respectively, may have given credence to the prophecy, it was merely a formality which had been planned long before Frederick's invasion of Saxony.[11] Moreover, on the following day, l'Hôpital wrote Michel de Rouen that, because of his ill health, the extreme cold, and the indirect route to St. Petersburg necessitated by the invasion of Saxony, he would not be able to depart until the following April or May.[12] Michael Bestuzhev-Riumin was subsequently delayed in his journey to France. Thus, neither ambassador would assume his position in January 1757, as previously agreed.

Far more important obstacles to the speedy consolidation of the Franco-Russian union were to be found in the negotiations for Russia's accession to the Treaty of Versailles and her march across the Polish-Lithuanian Commonwealth. The peculiarities of the commonwealth's history in the eighteenth century allowed other European powers to interest themselves in both the internal and external policies of that complex country. For years both France and Russia had contributed considerable amounts of money and arms to maintain and advance their in-

[10] AVPR, f. Snosheniia . . . Avstriei, 1756, op. 32/ 1, d. 6/ 292. See also, ibid., d. 4/ 201–202 (Sept. 17, 1756); and VA, RussBer, karton 38/ 272–274, 276.
[11] See TsGADA, f. 178, d. 1/ 220, 221–224 (Nos. 42 and 43, Aug. 23, 1756). LOII, f. 36, op. 1, d. 101/ 34–35 (Sept. 10, 1756); and op. 2, d. 693/ 6 (Sept. 18, 1756). Also, BN SM NAF, 22010/ 125–127, 132 (Sept. 18, 1756).
[12] AVPR, f. Snosheniia . . . Frantsiei, 1756, op. 93/ 1, d. 5/ 122–123. See also LOII, f. 36, op. 1, d. 101/ 39.

fluence in the commonwealth. Whereas Russia chose to act without disguise, France operated in Poland through two agencies, the Ministry of Foreign Affairs and the "King's Secret." This dual machinery tended not only to confuse French policy, but also to nullify it. The debate over the question of Russian troops marching through the commonwealth created such a situation.

The ostensible reason for Empress Elizabeth's desire to cross Polish-Lithuanian territory with her armies was military. In order to aid Austria and Saxony and defeat Frederick, Russian armies could approach Frederick's territories from two directions, across the Baltic Sea and through the commonwealth. It was improbable that an effective invasion could be launched solely by way of the Baltic; Russia did not have sufficient transport for the tens of thousands of troops she wished to use in the invasion, and success was more promising if Russian armies could attack Frederick from different points.

Moving troops across the commonwealth, however, posed important political questions. Could Russian troops be trusted to act in a disciplined manner, not causing strife in and damage to the countryside and not interfering in Polish domestic politics? Would the Russian armies return home when the battles with Frederick had ceased and not be quartered in the commonwealth? Earlier experience had shown that there was no guarantee against the first danger. The events of the 1760s justified apprehensions concerning the latter.

The Russian court, anticipating possible opposition, sent Quartermaster Lieutenant-General Weimarn to the commonwealth early in the summer on a special mission. He carried with him letters from Elizabeth to the great nobles pronouncing her friendship for the commonwealth and money to be spent on behalf of Russian interests there. His arrival coincided with the preparations for elections to the dietines and the national Diet, and he met with Prince Radziwiłł, the Grand General of Lithuania, and other equally important Polish magnates.[13]

All this disconcerted Heinrich Brühl, the chief minister of Augustus III, King of Poland. Brühl regarded Weimarn's activi-

[13] See TsGADA, f. 178, d. 1/ 82–84 (No. 6, April 6, 1756), 88–89 (No. 9, April 10, 1756); Radziwiłł to Bestuzhev-Riumin, Aug. 1, 1756, AVPR, f. Snosheniia . . . Pol'shei, 1756, op. 79/ 1, d. 3/ 1, 5, 13–14; and Brühl to Bestuzhev-Riumin, Aug. 18, 1756, AVPR, f. Snosheniia . . . Pol'shei, 1756, op. 79/ 1, d. 3/ 9–11.

ties as subversive. In a letter to Chancellor Bestuzhev-Riumin, he protested that, if "the unique and principal object of the extraordinary mission of M. Weimarn in Poland is only to re-affirm the authority of the King and of the laws of the Kingdom of his subjects, . . . it would have been necessary to take other means." If anything, Brühl pointed out, the Russian court's action would create an effect opposite the one desired.[14]

The march of Prussian soldiers into Saxony added to the confusion over maintaining the integrity of the Polish-Lithuanian Commonwealth. As Elector of Saxony and King of Poland, Augustus III could not easily divide his loyalties or responsibilities. He could not justify the saving of one country with the loss of the other. Saxony was in deep trouble, and soon Austria would be in the same predicament. The most powerful available armed force he could call on to aid his besieged Saxony was Russia. But could he count on Empress Elizabeth's lending her assistance without at the same time endangering the laws and liberties of the commonwealth?

The situation was further complicated because of the strong commitment that France had in the commonwealth. French policy had hitherto been to prevent Russia from dominating the country. However, with friendship developing between France and Russia, could France be expected to maintain a sustained opposition to Russian armies crossing the commonwealth?

The complexity of this dilemma was clearly reflected in the instructions subsequently sent to Douglas. Count de Broglie, the French ambassador to the Saxon court and a highly placed member of the "King's Secret," wrote Douglas on September 7 requesting him to impress on the Russian ministry Louis XV's desire that Russia not send her armies through Poland when she attacked Prussia. France's good will toward Poland was not to be sacrificed for the sake of a Franco-Russian alliance.[15]

Two weeks later, Durand, the French Resident stationed in Warsaw, wrote Douglas that, if Empress Elizabeth intended to pass troops through the commonwealth, she should request permission from the Polish government. At the same time she

---

[14] AVPR, f. Snosheniia . . . Pol'shei, 1756, op. 79/ 1, d. 3/ 9–11 (Aug. 18, 1756).

[15] AVPR, f. Snosheniia . . . Frantsiei, 1756, op. 93/ 1, d. 5/ 79.

should assure that these troops would observe a strict discipline during their march, and that payment for their maintenance would be made in an acceptable currency.[16]

A mixture of the same views was announced by Rouillé from Versailles. He stressed the French court's desire that if at all possible Russia should ship her armies to Prussia and thereby by-pass Polish territory proper; he also argued that Russia should consult with the government of the commonwealth before taking any action affecting that country.[17] It was the French hope that, if asked, the commonwealth would refuse to allow the march. In a conversation held on September 26 with the primate of Poland, Durand said: "His Most Christian Majesty desired, that the Republick would give all possible opposition to such a march."[18]

Before these messages had been communicated to Elizabeth and before she had learned of Frederick's invasion of Saxony, she had taken measures that not only anticipated but also undermined opposition to her plans. Her intentions were spelled out in a note of September 13 to Gross, her envoy at the Saxon court:

> The Russian court hopes that the King of Poland and the Republic would, if the unjust act of Frederick took place, allow and even assist Russian troops to cross the Republic in order to aid the Austrian court. Every assurance will be given that every man down to the last of 30,000 troops will conduct himself in a disciplined manner and his [maintenance] will be paid for. Russia will always guarantee the laws, welfare, and liberties of the Polish state. If it would be pleasing to the Poles that a formal request for the passage of Russian troops be made, it would be done.[19]

Upon learning of the invasion of Saxony, Empress Elizabeth decided to give King Augustus 100,000 roubles as well as military aid. Gross was to receive 10,000 roubles for expenses, which

---

[16] Durand to Douglas, Sept. 20, 1756, AVPR, *f. Snosheniia . . . Avstriei,* 1756, *op.* 32/ 1, *d.* 4/ 357; and BN SM NAF, 22011/ 24–25.

[17] Rouillé to Douglas, Sept. 23, 1756, BN SM NAF, 22010/ 74–79; and AVPR, *f. Snosheniia . . . Frantsiei,* 1756, *op.* 93/ 1, *d.* 5/ 132–136.

[18] Quoted in Williams to Holdernesse, Oct. 9, 1756, PROSP 91/ 64.

[19] AVPR, *f. Snosheniia . . . Avstriei,* 1756, *op.* 32/ 1, *d.* 4/ 193–194. See also *ibid., d.* 5b/ 39.

would no doubt be used to win adherents to the Russian cause.[20]

The French court received its answer when Douglas was informed in the beginning of October that it was "absolutely impossible" for Russian armies to avoid passing through the commonwealth to attack Frederick. Nevertheless, the Russian court assured the French that it would not abuse the hospitality of the Poles. Some unwise Poles might cause trouble over the march, but if the French envoy in the commonwealth cooperated with his Russian counterpart, no serious difficulties should arise.[21]

Before Russia could go to war against Frederick and the Franco-Russian union could be realized, the Polish question would have to be solved.

On October 4 Douglas and Esterhazy presented a formal invitation to chancellors Bestuzhev-Riumin and Vorontsov for Empress Elizabeth's accession to the Treaty of Versailles.[22] No immediate reply was forthcoming; what might have been a simple procedure, especially after Frederick had precipitated hostilities, became a complex affair. During the following weeks, confusion reigned. No one seemed to know whether it was France or Austria who was to provide Russia with a subsidy of two million florins.[23] Estimates of Turkish reaction to Russia's accession to the treaty frightened some observers and delighted others; to some the Ottoman Porte was not alarmed, and to others it was massing troops on the frontiers and intended to conclude a treaty with Prussia.[24]

Douglas assumed that Russia saw in the negotiations for her accession to the Treaty of Versailles an opportunity to link France to a broader Russian foreign policy commitment. Rus-

[20] TsGADA, f. 178, d. 1/ 287–290 (No. 65, Sept. 24, 1756). See also LOII, f. 36, op. 1, d. 101/ 35–36; and AVPR, f. Snosheniia . . . Frantsiei, 1756, op. 93/ 1, d. 5/ 61–62.

[21] Bestuzhev-Riumin and Vorontsov to Bekhteev, Oct. 11, 1756, AVPR, f. Snosheniia . . . Frantsiei, op. 93/ 1, d. 3/ 112–117; and VA, RussBer, karton 38/ 57–64.

[22] LOII, f. 36, op. 1, d. 101/ 39; and AVPR, f. Snosheniia . . . Frantsiei, 1756, op. 93/ 1, d. 5/ 98–115.

[23] See Douglas to Rouillé, Oct. 18 and 26, 1756, BN SM NAF 22011/ 7–19, 44–55, respectively.

[24] See Williams to Holdernesse, Oct. 5, 1756, PROSP 91/64; Douglas to Rouillé, Oct. 26, 1756, BN SM NAF, 22011/ 36–55. Also AVPR, f. Snosheniia . . . Frantsiei, 1756, op. 93/ 1, d. 3/ 76–83 and d. 5/ 172–174; and f. Snosheniia . . . Avstriei, 1756, op. 32/ 1, d. 4/ 189–190.

sia, in his view, sought to gain French support against the Ottoman Empire. He supported his argument with what the grand chancellor—still a good friend of England—had told him about making the exclusion of any attack on Hanover a condition of Empress Elizabeth's accession to the treaty. Douglas conjectured that the Russian court would not insist on this condition if France would commit herself to going to Russia's aid in the event of a Turkish attack. By this act France would undoubtedly alienate the Porte and thus serve Russia's long-term interests.[25]

Austro-Russian relations suffered as well. Despite the many declarations of Empress Elizabeth that she would aid Maria Theresa with a large military force, nothing had happened even though Frederick was threatening Bohemia. Empress Elizabeth's delay in acceding to the Treaty of Versailles was no argument for her inaction, since she was already obliged to send aid to Maria Theresa under the treaty of 1746.

Maria Theresa's position was made clear in a lengthy communication to Esterhazy on October 19. She wanted Russia to open a second front and engage Frederick's army that winter. Empress Elizabeth was reminded of her obligation under the fourth secret article of the treaty of 1746 to assist Austria with 60,000 men. To coordinate their future operations, Maria Theresa was sending Elizabeth her military plans.

The empress-queen all but apologized for not having acted sooner in concluding the offensive treaty suggested by Empress Elizabeth in April, which would have made it possible to bring Russia's forces into operation earlier. But at that time the Austrian court could not reconcile its negotiation for a defensive treaty with France with an offensive one with Russia. Moreover, the French and Austrian courts were extremely considerate of the sacrifice Russia had made in not accepting Great Britain's subsidy treaty and would not allow her to suffer because of it. France and Austria had already agreed to arrange a subsidy of their own for Russia, and it would be provided for in the forthcoming Austro-Russian treaty.

Maria Theresa explained that France had expressed a desire to break off relations with Prussia and support Austria's claims

[25] Douglas to Rouillé, Oct. 9 and 26, 1756, BN SM NAF, 22011/ 3–5, 36–55, respectively.

for the reunification of Silesia and Glatz. However, France was not inclined to a further weakening of the king of Prussia, for this might disturb the balance of power in Europe. It was hoped that Empress Elizabeth would unite with both France and Austria by acceding to the Treaty of Versailles.[26]

In a sophisticated manner Maria Theresa presented a forceful foreign policy statement to the Russian court. While carefully disclaiming responsibility for not having earlier arranged the offensive treaty which would have provided her with the assistance of tens of thousand of Russian troops, she called attention to Russia's obligation to supply essentially the same aid under a previous treaty. Encouraging Russia to act in unison with France and Austria, Maria Theresa held out the promise of a subsidy which would take the place of that of Great Britain—almost naïvely suggesting that a subsidy was almost all that concerned Russia. But what she really wanted to impress on the Russian court was that acting with France and Austria was the only way she should or could act. This was clear in Maria Theresa's explanation of French policy toward Prussia which supported Austrian territorial claims against that state but explicitly refused to agree to any further dismemberment. It was an indirect way of telling Russia that she, too, would not countenance Russia's desire to detach East Prussia from Frederick even ostensibly to exchange it for Polish land.

There was a flaw in Maria Theresa's calculations; for now that war had actually broken out, she was more dependent on Russia than Russia on her. The recognition of this important fact explains in part Russia's reluctance to engage in military operations during the winter of 1756–1757. Russia would have remained hesitant to assist Austria until she had received a firm commitment in support of Russian war aims. Nevertheless, without this obstacle there are other reasons why Russia could not have aided Austria that winter. These reasons also delayed the conclusion of harmonious relations between Russia and France. They can best be explained by examining the stress under which the Russian court was operating at this time.

[26] TsGADA, f. 1261, op. 1, d. 169/ 1–12.

X Crisis at the Russian Court

"Elle est une des plus grandes beautés de nôtre Siècle," an anonymous contemporary wrote of Empress Elizabeth.[1] In the autumn of 1756, however, she was seriously ill. Far more talented in poetically describing people at the Russian court than in mastering the political decisions made by them, Sir Charles Hanbury Williams noted the physical deterioration of Elizabeth: "Her Imperial Majesty is at that time of life when it ceases to be with Her after the ways of Women—Her losses of blood upon this occasion are very great." In addition to this unfortunate menopausal condition it was believed that she also suffered from dropsy and asthma. No longer able to negotiate the stairs easily, she was provided with a machine which carried her from one floor to another.[2]

Toward the end of 1756 her health worsened to the point that her death was expected at any moment. The political significance of such an eventuality can be imagined in light of what happened when she actually died in January 1762: One of the first acts of her successor Peter III was to effect a rapprochement between the Russian and Prussian courts eventuating in an armistice and treaty between them which took Russia out of the Seven Years' War. Peter would undoubtedly have undertaken that policy sooner had Elizabeth not recovered in the winter of 1756–1757 and had he succeeded to the Russian throne.

Grand Duke Peter was a Holsteiner, a Lutheran by birth who did not take his conversion to Orthodoxy very seriously; nor

---

[1] TsGADA, f. 1261, op. 1, d. 2812/ 1.
[2] Williams to Holdernesse, Oct. 2, 1755, PROSP 91/ 61.

did he fondly embrace Russian culture and traditions. Frederick II was his idol, and Peter conspicuously manifested his predilection for things Prussian by frequently dressing in that uniform. He was also violently anti-French and never missed an opportunity to state his opinion on the subject. This was clearly shown on one occasion in 1756 when Alexander Shuvalov brought a memorandum for him to sign declaring that an exchange of ambassadors between France and Russia was necessary in the existing situation. Peter refused to sign because of French intrigues in Sweden which conflicted with his personal interests. "I am not sufficiently pleased either with the Vice Chancellor," he said, "or with Douglas, with whose plots I am fully conversant, to grant them this pleasure." Despite the endeavors of Shuvalov, Peter was obstinate and declared that an alliance with France must not be allowed. He said he would not sign anything which he knew in his heart to be wrong. When told that the negotiation was already too far advanced for withdrawal, Peter exclaimed, "So much the worse if my opinion is asked after a thing is done, I refuse to sign."[3]

The matter did not end there. Grand Duchess Catherine was approached with a suggestion that she convince her husband to sign and not cause Empress Elizabeth any further frustration, since the issue would be settled in any event. Alexander Shuvalov explained to her why it was important to have a French ambassador in St. Petersburg. The Russian court feared that the sending of troops across Polish territory might offend the Turks and give them a pretext to act aggressively against Russia; since the French had considerable influence at the Porte, they might be able to prevent any future trouble from arising there to the detriment of Russia. Catherine feigned ignorance of the complicated business of politics but told Shuvalov that she could "only see one more intriguer in one more Minister." Shuvalov slyly answered that "Powers which are anything but friendly place them at one another's courts, and why should we not do the same?" General Stepan Apraksin, the President of the War College and future Commander-in-Chief

---

[3] As quoted in, Catherine to Williams, Aug. 16, 1756, ICC, pp. 36–37.

of the Russian armies against Prussia, added his weight to the argument. He told the grand duke that if he did not sign, "the blame for it will fall on the Grand Chancellor and me."[4]

The conclusion of this affair was predictable, but that is not what is significant about it. The efforts made to gain Peter's signature reflected the desire of Empress Elizabeth to see that her policies should not be interrupted after her death. At the same time, the play of the argument clearly revealed the desire of several leading members of the Russian court to keep on good terms with Peter, the legally designated successor to the imperial throne. Peter's views on foreign policy were diametrically opposed to those of Elizabeth, and in the event of her death everyone assumed that her policy would be scuttled. A jettisoning of those responsible for initiating Elizabeth's policy and implementing it was also probable. The realignment of associations became more pronounced as Elizabeth's health rapidly declined.

In this political whirlpool, the grand duchess became one of the central figures. It was not solely because she was the woman Peter had married, but more importantly because of the kind of woman she was. Comparisons were not infrequently made between her and Peter. Williams characterized Peter as "a Prince of a weak Constitution and as weak an Understanding Unfit either to govern an Empire, or to furnish a Succession. The Great Dutchess certainly is proper for both; The first She will do Hereafter, the last She has already done, without the assistance of her Husband."[5] Even Peter reportedly professed his deference to Catherine: "his confidence in the Great Dutchess is so great, that sometimes he tells people, that tho' he does not understand things himself, yet His wife understands everything."[6]

Catherine had a captivating personality and a quick mind;

[4] As quoted in, Catherine to Williams, Aug. 19, 1756, ICC, pp. 40–41. See also Williams to Catherine, Aug. 21, 1756, ICC, pp. 47–51. Grand Duke Peter signed the memorandum on August 23, 1756. Catherine to Williams, Aug. 23, 1756, ICC, p. 53.
[5] Williams to Holdernesse, July 4, 1755, BMEg 3463/ 34.
[6] Williams to Holdernesse, Oct. 2, 1755, PROSP 91/ 61.

and according to the Grand Chancellor, she demonstrated "more steadiness and resolution" than anyone else.[7] She was passionate for political power as well as men and sought to conquer both in her apartments, where she plotted her succession to the throne of Russia. While she may not have loved her husband, she never denied his usefulness to her. He was only needed in the present so that he might be discarded in the future. There could be no question of her desire for the Russian throne, as her letter to Williams of August 29 demonstrates:

You have allowed me to call you my friend. Your title awes me, but as my designs are in no way criminal, I make so bold as to communicate to you and to ask your advice upon the thoughts forced upon my mind by the increased indisposition of certain persons during the last twenty-four hours. This is my dream. After being informed of her death, and being certain that there is no mistake, I shall go straight to my son's room. If I meet or can quickly get hold of the Grand Master of the Hunt [Alexis Razumovski], I shall leave him with him and the men under his command. If not, I shall carry him off to my room. I shall also send a man that I can trust to warn five officers of the Guards of whom I am sure, who will each bring me fifty soldiers. . . . I shall send orders to the Chancellor, Apraksin and Lieven to come to me, and meanwhile I shall enter the death chamber, where I shall summon the captain of the guard, and shall make him take the oath and retain him at my side. It appears to me that it would be better and safer if the two Grand Dukes were together, than if only one went with me; also that the rendezvous for my followers should be my ante-chamber. If I see the slightest signs of commotion, I shall secure, either with my own people or with those of the captain of the guard, the Shuvalov and the adjutant-general of the day. Besides, the lower grade officers of the bodyguard are trustworthy; and, though I have had no communication with all of them, I can count sufficiently on two or three, and on having enough means at my disposal to make myself obeyed by everyone who is not bought.

As my friend, correct me and point out any defect in my views and anything that I have not foreseen. Much will depend on the

[7] See *ibid.*

general aspect, or on the view which I shall take of things. Pray
Heaven to give me a clear head. The extreme hatred for the
Shuvalov, which all those who do not belong to them feel, the
justice of my cause, as well as the easy sequence of everything
which runs its natural course, make me hope for a happy issue.[8]

Catherine's foreign policy was determined by her ambition
for the throne. She was anti-French and pro-English. She ab-
horred the conduct of Austria toward Great Britain and had
mixed feelings about Prussia. To champion all things Russian
she symbolically denied her German heritage by seeking to
humble the king of Prussia whom she held in contempt, speak-
ing of him as "the natural and formidable enemy to Russia,"
believing him "the worst in the world."[9] Nevertheless, she also
saw the utility of having a Prussian envoy in St. Petersburg to
counter the influence of the French.[10] Catherine envisaged a
"Northern System" which became her policy after she took the
throne. According to Williams, Catherine said that "nothing
can save Europe but an alliance between England, Russia, Prussia, & Holland, to which some of the German Princes might be
invited to accede, and declared She will attempt it—the Day
She is in a Situation to do it."[11]

The English ambassador was her confidant and acted as her
broker, providing her not only with personal subsidies but also
a lover in Stanislas Poniatowski, the future king of Poland. Williams still hoped that Russia would accept the first payment of
the Anglo-Russian Subsidy Treaty, or at least in some way guarantee the security of Hanover, and he sought the assistance of
Catherine and the grand chancellor in this matter. While he
was subsequently reprimanded by his court for it, Williams
went so far as to tell Vorontsov that the acceptance of the
100,000 pounds sterling would not place Empress Elizabeth

[8] ICC, pp. 59–60.
[9] See Williams to Holdernesse, Oct. 2, 1755, PROSP 91/ 61.
[10] Catherine to Williams, Aug. 20, 1756, ICC, p. 46.
[11] Williams to Holdernesse, Sept. 28, 1756, PROSP 91/ 64. See also
K. Rahbek Schmidt, "Wie ist Panins Plan zu einem Nordischen System
enstaden?" *Zeitschrift für Slawistik*, II:3 (Berlin, 1957), 406–422.

under any "new obligation, or be any tye upon Her Imperial Majesty."[12]

Catherine's "secret" relationship with Poniatowski had the convenient support of the grand chancellor. This was not the first time that Bestuzhev-Riumin performed this service for the grand duchess. He had arranged her affair with Sergei Saltykov earlier and had kept the issue of that relationship, Grand Duke Paul, from becoming a court scandal.[13]

[12] See Williams to Holdernesse, Aug. 21 and 24, Sept. 4 and 28, 1756, PROSP 91/ 63, 64, respectively; Williams to Mitchell, Sept. 28, 1756, *ibid.*, 90/ 66; Holdernesse to Williams, Sept. 24, 1756, LOII, *f.* 36, *op.* 1, *d.* 117/ 7–10 (Aug. 23, 1756); TsGADA, *f.* 178, *d.* 1/ 235–240 (No. 46, Aug. 28, 1756); AVPR, *f. Snosheniia . . . Angliei*, 1756, *op.* 35/ 1, *d.* 776/ 171–173, 178–181 (Sept. 9 and 26, 1756, respectively); Williams to Catherine, Aug. 30 and 31, Sept. 2, 3, 4, 8, 17, 19, 20, 22, 24, and Oct. 3, 1756, and letter of November (n.d.), 1756, ICC, pp. 64, 64–68, 72–75, 77–83, 83–84, 92–95, 110–113, 115–117, 122–124, 130–133, 133–136, 141–144, 216, respectively; and Catherine to Williams, Sept. 1, 3, 7, 15, 19, 22, 25 and Oct. 2 and 4, 1756, ICC, pp. 70–72, 75–77, 87–92, 108–109, 117–119, 127–129, 136–137, 140–141, 144–145, respectively.

[13] Williams presents a glowing report of the Saltykov business in a "very secret" letter to Holdernesse of July 4, 1755 (BMEg 3463/ 34–35). Catherine wanted an heir and was convinced that "The Grand Duke's assistance was not sufficient to provide one." Her designs were at first frustrated because she was closely watched at the court. "She therefore began by applying to the Schuwalows, who are the reigning Favorites at this Court, to assist her in her Necessitys; but the fear of incurring the Empress's Displeasure, in case the affair was found out, made them Excuse themselves." What followed was a secret "amorous correspondence" with Hetman Razumovsky and the letters were carried by Sergei Saltykov. But, alas "before the affairs were ripe, the Hetman was obliged to leave this place, and go into the Ukraine. Upon which Soltikoff, upon the strength of the Secret He had been trusted with, began to speak for himself; He was her Chamberlain, She lik'd his figure, and He was much younger than Rosamovski; in short she fell desperately in love with him." This did not solve her problems, however, and it was owing to the "Great Chancellor who kindly took compassion of her Sufferings, facilitated her seeing Soltikoff in private, and by these means provided an Heir for the Russian Empire." The course of true love never runs smoothly and so it was with Catherine and Saltykov. "After Her Imperial Highness had lain in, Her love for her Gallant grew every day more and more violent, and Soltikoff's Vainity began to turn his head." The grand chancellor thus intervened to prevent a court scandal which might have proven as fatal to him as to the lovers. He sent Saltykov to Stockholm as an imperial messenger carrying the news of Grand Duke Paul's birth. When Saltykov returned he was given a post as Resident at Hamburg which kept him away from the court and Catherine. (For the grand chancellor's involvement with the "Ponia-

In both cases the grand chancellor satisfied the "violence of the Great Dutchess Passion" and "the warmth of Her own Constitution,"[14] while being rewarded with Catherine's political influence and friendship. He was shrewd enough to work for the goodwill of the wife of the future emperor. He communicated with her on confidential matters at court, avowed his friendship for Great Britain, and gave Catherine the impression that he would serve her interests faithfully. The loathing of Peter and Catherine for all things French coincided with and added strength to Bestuzhev-Riumin's continuing struggle against the party of Vorontsov.[15]

The grand chancellor maintained a pragmatic relationship with the English ambassador, which brought him to the point of denying his previous anti-Prussian policy. It is from Williams' letter of September 28 to Mitchell that we first hear of this extraordinary *volte-face*:

> I write you this very secret Letter to beg you would inform the King of Prussia, how far I succeeded here with the Great Chancellor. I found Him for the two or three first Times inflexible, but the broader my Hints grew about the Sum, the more He Yielded. In my last Conversation, He . . . turned short upon me and said, "Would what you propose please your 'Master?' and do you speak by His Order or at last by His Approbation?" I replied, I speak by Authority, You know by Experience that you may de-

---

towski affair" see, Williams to Catherine, Sept. 2, 8, 17, 19, 20, 22, and Oct. 3, 1756, ICC, pp. 72–75, 92–95, 110–113, 115–117, 122–124, 130–133, 141–144 respectively; and Catherine to Williams, Sept. 3, 15, 19, 22, 25, and Oct. 2, and 4, 1756, ICC, pp. 75–77, 108–109, 117–119, 127–129, 136–137, 140–141, 144–145, respectively.

[14] Just before one of the court balls began, Catherine pretended that she was ill and desired to remain in bed. "But as soon as She heard that every Body was gone to Court and the Ball was begun, She got up, dress'd her self, and went in a Hackney Coach to Soltikoff's Lodging. The Lover thank'd Her three times for the Honor She had done him, & She got safely back to her own Apartments, before the Ball was finish'd." See Williams to Holdernesse, July 4, 1755, BMEg 3463/ 34–35.

[15] See Catherine to Williams, Sept. 3, 7, 9, 15, 19, and Oct. 4, 5, 9, and 11, 1756, ICC, pp. 75–77, 87–92, 95–96, 108–109, 117–119, 144–145, 146–147, 158–160, 161–162, respectively; Williams to Catherine, Sept. 2, 3, 8, 20, 22, 24, and Oct. 4, 7, and 12, 1756, ICC, pp. 72–75, 77–83, 92–95, 122–124, 130–133, 133–136, 145–146, 147–152, 162–163, respectively; and Williams to Holdernesse, Oct. 16, 1756, PROSP 91/ 64.

pend upon me. He then said I can refuse The King of England
Nothing, and will serve His Prussian Majesty. Tell me what I am
to do? for though I am willing the Task is difficult. I replyed you
must begin by declaring to me, that you are no longer the King
of Prussia's enemy. He then gave me His Hand and said—from
this Hour I am His Friend, but I do not see how I can serve Him
at present; had I known this two Months ago, much might have
been done but He has begun a War, and nothing can hinder the
Empress from assisting the House of Austria; Everything is already determined. It is true He has taken Us a little unprepared;
and you know Our Motions are slow. I cannot promise to do any
thing at present because it is not in my Power, But you may assure
The King of Prussia . . . that I am willing to do Service to His
Prussian Majesty. He then went on by saying. "The War is begun, we may probably soon hear of a Battle, and therefore we
must wait for what the Chapter of Accidents may produce; and
depend upon it, that on the first Occasion that offers, I will consult
with, and join myself to you, to assist the King of Prussia at this
Court." He concluded by saying, "That He hoped this Change
and Declaration of His, might be kept as the greatest Secret for
some Time at least."[16]

The grand chancellor was not the only one at the Russian
court during these turbulent months to suggest that he had
second thoughts about previously declared policies. Nikita Trubetskoi, General-Procurator of the Senate and member of the
powerful Conference, hinted to Catherine that he would attempt to thwart Russia's accession to the Treaty of Versailles
and serve her in other matters as well.[17] General Apraksin was
already acting as a liaison between the grand duke and duchess
and other members of the court; he also obtained valuable information for Peter and Catherine about Conference proceed-
ings.[18] General Alexander Buturlin offered his vote in the Conference to Catherine and declared he would follow her wishes

[16] PROSP 90/ 66. See also Mitchell to Holdernesse, Oct. 21, 1756, and
Mitchell to Williams, Oct. 24, 1756, ibid.
[17] See Catherine to Williams, Aug. 30, Sept. 1, and Oct. 9 and 11, 1756,
ICC, pp. 60–62, 70–72, 158–160, 161–162, respectively; and Williams to
Catherine, Oct. 12, 1756, ICC, pp. 162–163.
[18] See Catherine to Williams, Sept. 1, 3, 7, 1756, ICC, pp. 70–72, 75–77,
87–92, respectively.

"blindly."[19] There was even speculation at the court that Vice Chancellor Michael Vorontsov was becoming less enthusiastic about the French and more sympathic toward the English.[20]

Others reflected in their actions a different attitude toward persons, if not policies. With Elizabeth's declining health, the Shuvalovs anxiously sought a reconciliation with Peter and Catherine from whom they were estranged because of their favored position with the empress. However, Peter and Catherine, who despised the French for their activities in Sweden and saw in their reestablishment at the Russian court a band of intriguers scheming to prevent them from taking the throne, disliked the Shuvalovs even more for their continued support of the French cause.[21]

Nevertheless, when they extended their friendship to the grand duke and duchess, the Shuvalovs also made efforts to convince them of the necessity of having the French in Russia. Ivan Betskoi, a man of letters and friend to both sides, acted as mediator. His personal interests notwithstanding, he argued that "the French, if assured of protection, would establish themselves here and would cultivate the arts and sciences. To introduce these the Ambassador would be useful." Catherine mocked him, "will he give public lectures?" "If the advantage is not great on the exchange of goods," she said, "we shall anyhow have bales of wit to our credit." Betskoi deplored the emphasis on money, but Catherine would not let him rest. "Our dandies will profit most; they will have someone to set the fash-

[19] Catherine to Williams, Sept. 11, 1756, ICC, pp. 101–103.

[20] Catherine to Williams, Aug. 22, 1756, and Williams to Catherine, Sept. 2, 1756, ICC, pp. 51–52, 72–75, respectively. See also Williams to Holdernesse, Sept. 28, 1756, PROSP 91/ 64.

[21] Despite the closeness of the Shuvalovs to Empress Elizabeth, their criticism of Catherine and Peter did not always hit its mark. Williams relates an interesting piece of court gossip: "Madame Shuwalow, who is the Czarina's Favorite, and who is in the Secret of all her Amours, held the Young Prince in her arms, and said (out of Malice to the Great Duchess) who is He like? Like the Father said the Empress; that cant be, said Shuwalow, for He is very brown, & the Father is fair; Well then said the Czarina He is like his Grandfather: Not at all, repl'd Shuwalow, which answer put the Empress in a passion, and made her say, Hold your Tongue you B— I know what you mean, you want to insinuate He is a Bastard, but if He is, He is not the first that has been in my Family." Williams to Holdernesse, July, 4, 1755, BMEg 3463/ 36.

ions for them." Betskoi could not compete with her and laughingly stated, "I am a bad politician."[22]

Catherine was a serious woman and calculated her political strength wisely. To her the French ambassador was "an enemy, armed from head to foot," and his friends could not be hers. She informed Ivan Ivanovich Shuvalov, the favorite, "that it will be a proof of his devotion to the Grand Duke if he prevents the arrival of a French Ambassador." She was, however, a realist and knew that this offer would not be accepted, but she wanted to serve him notice. The Shuvalovs were too much involved to withdraw and as an excuse for their action would say that it was Elizabeth's wish and, therefore, they could do nothing.[23]

The Conference still remained the most powerful institution for deciding Russian policy. It was there, according to Bestuzhev-Riumin, that Peter and Catherine were at a distinct disadvantage. The grand chancellor earnestly believed that, if Elizabeth permitted the grand duke to attend all its meetings and express his opinions openly, its members would be "frightened" and not take positions to which he objected.[24] The grand chancellor also reported that it was Peter Shuvalov who stubbornly refused to accept the first installment of the subsidy or provide for the protection of the Electorate of Hanover.[25]

There was no reason for despair. If Empress Elizabeth's illness could effect changes in political and personal alignments, the newly formed associations would undoubtedly have an impact on policy. Catherine had faith that they would. Williams had despondently written to her that he expected the Russian court to decide in favor of France and not Great Britain; and he thought that Hanover would not even be given any guarantees.[26] Catherine answered him prophetically and intuitively: "Let us build a few castles in the air, as they call them. If the

[22] As quoted in, Catherine to Williams, Aug. 14, 1756, ICC, pp. 28–32. See also Catherine to Williams, Aug. 16 and 31, and Sept. 10 and 11, 1756, ICC, pp. 36–37, 68–70, 100–101, 101–103, respectively; and Williams to Catherine, Aug. 15, 1756, ICC, pp. 32–36.

[23] Catherine to Williams, Aug. 20, 1756, ICC, pp. 45–46.

[24] As quoted in, Catherine to Williams, Sept. 7, 1756, ICC, p. 89.

[25] Williams to Catherine, Sept. 8, 1756, ICC, p. 94.

[26] Williams to Catherine, Sept. 2, 1756, ICC, p. 73.

Chancellor, the Vice-Chancellor, Apraksin, Troubetskoi, and perhaps Buturlin, are on your side, what unfavorable answer can you expect? Do not swear about the guarantees; it might still come to pass, though you will not believe it."[27] When Bestuzhev-Riumin told Douglas that Russia would wish to have Hanover excluded from attack or insult during the present war and that this would be made part of Empress Elizabeth's accession to the Treaty of Versailles, Catherine's optimism seemed to be borne out.

The severity of Elizabeth's illness created such uncertainty at the court that it affected Russia's military operations. General Apraksin, the Commander-in-Chief of the Russian army against Prussia—who was often characterized as having a lack of experience and ability and as being a coward—was a rather shrewd general who timed his political role well. To lead Russian forces against Prussia at a time when Elizabeth was on the verge of dying seemed to him political suicide. To be away from the capital at that crucial moment was serious enough, but to engage in battle with a monarch who was the idol of the legal successor to the Russian throne was to court disaster. As a liaison and mediator among the powerful politicians at the court, Apraksin served the grand duke and duchess admirably; but he chose to go one step further despite his responsibility to Elizabeth. His delay in leaving for Riga to set up his headquarters drew upon him the disapproval of every section of St. Petersburg society; also he was ready to allow Peter and Catherine to control his actions and impede Russian participation in the war against Frederick.[28] Catherine relates that Apraksin, two days after Elizabeth suffered a collapse, "sent to ask me whether under present circumstances I gave him orders to leave or to remain, and said that he would delay or hasten his departure

[27] Catherine to Williams, Sept. 3, 1756, ICC, p. 76.

[28] TsGADA, f. 178, d. 1/ 273–276 (No. 59, Sept. 20, 1756); Williams to Holdernesse, Sept. 21 and Oct. 9, 12, 17, and 26, 1756, PROSP 91/ 64; Williams to Stormont, Oct. 2, 16, and 19, 1756, CHW 22–10885/ 433–438, 441–451, 453–463, respectively; N. Korobkov, Semiletniaia voina (deistviia rossi v 1756–1762 gg.), pp. 88–90; and S. M. Solov'ev, Istoriia rossii s drevneishikh vremën [History of Russia from the oldest times] (Moscow, 1959–1966), XXIX, 377–380.

according to my command, I sent him word in reply . . . that I
desired him most strongly to remain, and that it would be a
mark of loyalty to me."[29]

Russian military inaction, coming when the Austrian army
had already suffered a significant defeat before the Prussians
and when the Saxon army was being put into Frederick's service, considerably distressed the Austrian ambassador, Nicholas
Esterhazy. His complaints to the grand chancellor about the
slowness of the Russian troop movement brought him no satisfaction. The grand chancellor declared that it was Vienna's
fault that Russia had not moved her forces against Frederick
earlier.[30]

The situation pleased the grand chancellor. Russia's inability
to satisfy her chief ally with military assistance and to frustrate
a potential one by not signing the accession to the Treaty of
Versailles inhibited the success of a policy which he neither
supported nor directed. In fact, he encouraged its failure. Concerning General Apraksin's delay in departing from St. Petersburg, the grand chancellor told Williams that "he had contrived
this delay and would contrive many more."[31] He was confident
also that "Russian troops would not march this year."[32] He based
this not merely on his own ability to hold them back but on
a more fundamental diagnosis of the situation. The Russian
army recruitment had not been fulfilled according to plan and
many regiments were yet incomplete; of the last 60,000 recruits
called up, not more than half had reported for duty.[33] This situation worsened during the following months and was one of the
major causes for the protracted delay of the Russian military
offensive against Frederick.

Meanwhile, Elizabeth was fighting for her life. On October
11 Catherine wrote, "The Empress did not go out yesterday,
because she finds difficulty in lacing her dress from the pains
in her body. . . . She has similar pains in her legs, and her cough

[29] Catherine to Williams, Oct. 28, 1756, ICC, p. 182.
[30] See Williams to Holdernesse, Oct. 19, 1756, PROSP 91/ 64; and
Williams to Stormont, Oct. 16 and 19, 1756, CHW 22–10885/ 443–444,
453–455, respectively.
[31] Williams to Stormont, Oct. 19, 1756, CHW 22–10885/ 460–463.
[32] Williams to Catherine, Oct. 29, 1756, ICC, p. 184.
[33] See Williams to Stormont, Oct. 16, 1756, CHW 22–10885/ 441–447.

is worse again. She drags herself to meals, nevertheless, so that it may be said that she has been seen, but she must in reality be very ill."[34] Breathlessness accompanied severe pains in her abdomen. Cancer was suspected.[35]

On October 26 Empress Elizabeth collapsed. "The fingers of her hands were bent back, her feet and arms were cold as ice, her eyes sightless," was Catherine's graphic description. "They drew much blood from her; and sight and feeling returned. . . . To-day she is being purged."[36] Her pathetic condition was characterized by giddiness, fainting, and weeping. "There are moments when she forgets where she is and does not recognize those around her. My surgeon," Catherine reported, "a man of great experience and good sense, expects an apoplectic seizure, which would certainly carry her off."[37]

Catherine and the others at the court waited.

[34] Catherine to Williams, ICC, p. 161.
[35] Catherine to Williams, Oct. 15, 1756, ICC, p. 167.
[36] Catherine to Williams, Oct. 26, 1756, ICC, p. 180.
[37] Catherine to Williams, Oct. 28, 1756, ICC, pp. 182–183.

XI Ebb and Flow

Elizabeth did not die that winter, and most probably the course of Russian history was cheated of dramatic change. The health of the Russian Empress determined Russia's participation in the beginning as well as the end of the Seven Years' War.

Field Marshal Apraksin had no choice but to leave St. Petersburg on November 10 for Riga where he was to establish his military headquarters and direct operations against Prussia. These were his instructions, but he could not execute them as quickly as Elizabeth had wished. The principal reason for Russian military inaction was not the fierce Russian winter. The task of maintaining the army in peak condition for nearly one year was tremendous and had failed. Regiments were still incomplete, morale was low, and supplies were insufficient. Apraksin had complained of these matters before he left St. Petersburg, and Empress Elizabeth was as much suprised as she was disconcerted by his comments. At this late date, there could not be any guarantee that Russia would be ready to invade Prussia before the spring of 1757.[1]

[1] TsGADA, f. 178, d. 1/ 263, 264–269, 270, 271, 272, 282–283, 291–293, 296–301, 302–305, 319–324, 327–348, 350–364, 365, 367–368, 369–371, 372, 377, 388, 391–393, 431–432, 459–460, 463–464, 471–472 (Nos. 54, 55, 56, 57, 58, 63, 66, 69, 70, 73, 75, 77, 78, 80, 81, 82, 86, 91, 94, 109, 119, 121, 125; Sept. 11, 13, 23, 28; Oct. 4, 7, 9, 14, 16, 18, 31; Nov. 9, 23, 25, 29; and Dec. 1, 1756), respectively; f. 276, op. 1, d. 1393/ 1–4; f. 1263, op. 1, d. 57/ 17–24 and d. 8369/ 125, 135–143, 153–161, 171–178, 185–191, 198. Apraksin to Elizabeth, Nov. 28, 1756, TsGVIA, f. VUA, d. 1655/ I, 28–35; LOII, f. 36, op. 1, d. 105/ 68; AVPR, f. Snosheniia ... Frantsiei, 1756, op. 93/ 1, d. 3/ 150–151; Catherine to Williams, Sept. 17, 1756, ICC, p. 110; Williams to Holdernesse, Sept. 7, 18, Oct. 5, 23, 30, Dec. 9, 1756, PROSP 91/ 64, respectively; Stormont to Holdernesse, Nov. 14, 1756, PROSP 88/ 79; Williams to Stormont, Nov. 6, 1756, CHW 22–10885/ 465–477; and N. Korobkov, Semiletniaia voina (deistviia rossi v 1756–1762, g.g.), pp. 59, 67–68, 88, 90–91.

Russia, however, enjoyed greater success that winter in her diplomatic affairs. The Poles found themselves caught in the web of European politics which strangled the political opposition of some and permitted others the opportunity to bring the commonwealth under the sway of Russian influence. During the Seven Years' War, Poland played no role except as a battlefield—a fate she had suffered many times before.

By October Augustus III, Elector of Saxony and King of Poland, was desperate. Frederick the Great had successfully overrun his electorate, ransacked his archives, and occupied Dresden. Although Augustus contemplated it, resistance with the meager forces available to him seemed a fruitless endeavor. On October 6, as in the months that followed, he requested speedy and forceful assistance from Empress Elizabeth.[2] Polish territory would have to be violated if Saxony were to be aided.

The French continued to argue and work against the passage of Russian troops through the commonwealth. Both from Poland and France instructions were sent to Douglas urging him to influence the Russian court to decide against the passage. If this could not be achieved, then at least Russian troops should conduct themselves with exemplary dignity while also taking the shortest route possible.[3]

The Russians did not take kindly to Douglas' repeated and insistent recommendations. Nor were they pleased by the clandestine attempts of Broglie and Durand to stir up the Poles and the Turks against the march of Russian troops through the commonwealth. In a note of October 18 to Douglas detailing their irritation, the Russians blistered the French for their opposition and went so far as to suggest that the union beween the two courts was in jeopardy.[4]

Seeking to avoid violent conflict, the Russian court made use of every channel to encourage the Poles to support Russian political and military policies. Michael Bestuzhev-Riumin, the newly appointed ambassador to France, was instructed that during his trip through the commonwealth to Versailles he

[2] LOII, f. 36, op. 1, d. 105/ 309.
[3] See Rouillé to Douglas, Oct. 11, 1756, AVPR, f. Snosheniia . . . Frantsiei, 1756, op. 93/ 1, d. 5/ 161–163.
[4] Ibid., d. 5/ 126–128; and LOII, f. 36, op. 1, d. 101/ 39.

should excite the Poles against the king of Prussia.[5] At the same time Elizabeth added strength to her contingent of envoys in the commonwealth and Saxony by appointing Major-General Michael Volkonsky envoy plenipotentiary to Warsaw to assist Russian officials in convincing the Poles not to oppose Russian designs.[6] Count Ivan Chernyshev was entrusted with delivering Empress Elizabeth's gift of 100,000 roubles to the king of Poland and 20,000 roubles to his wife.[7]

At this crucial moment, the Austrians were more interested in defending themselves than in protecting the commonwealth's integrity against encroachment by the Russians. The Austrians desperately sought military assistance from the Russians, and the passage of Russian troops through Poland seemed a *sine qua non* for the speedy delivery of that aid. Russia utilized the mediation of Esterhazy, the Austrian ambassador in St. Petersburg, in an attempt to reduce French opposition. He wrote to the Austrian ambassador at the French court, explaining Russia's position on the passage of her troops through Poland. In Esterhazy's opinion, the king of France would be aiding his future ally if he would not oppose this march and would not encourage the Poles to confederate against it or call on the Turks to protest it.[8]

The Russians also dealt directly with the Poles. In a circular letter of November 25 to the Polish nobility, Empress Elizabeth announced her solemn intention to right the wrongs committed against Augustus III and Maria Theresa with a large military force which would of necessity be obliged to cross the territory of Poland.[9]

By the turn of the year Russia had scored a diplomatic victory. The kings of Poland and France both agreed to allow the Rus-

[5] See AVPR, *f. Snosheniia . . . Frantsiei*, 1756, *op.* 93/ 1, *d.* 9/ 72–74 (Nov. 17, 1756).
[6] See TsGADA, *f.* 178, *d.* 1/ 415–417 (No. 103, Nov. 19, 1756); and LOII, *f.* 36, *op.* 1, *d.* 105/ 310.
[7] See LOII, *f.* 36, *op.* 1, *d.* 105/ 310–311 (Nov. 21, 1756); and TsGADA, *f.* 178, *d.* 1/ 433–434 (No. 110, Nov. 23, 1756).
[8] Esterhazy to Starhemberg, Nov. 24, 1756, *f. Snosheniia . . . Avstriei*, 1756, *op.* 32/ 1, *d.* 5a/ 95–99. See also Maria Theresa to Esterhazy, Nov. 13, 1756, TsGADA, *f.* 1261, *op.* 1, *d.* 169/ 13–19.
[9] BN SM NAF 22011/ 87–92.

sians their march.[10] When the new Polish envoy to Russia Stanislas Poniatowski arrived in St. Petersburg in January 1757, he
communicated the commonwealth's permission and the conditions under which the march would take place. Russian troops
were to observe the strictest discipline and pay for all supplies
used as well as all damages incurred during their sojourn. The
Russian court promptly agreed.[11]

Russia was not as successful as she had hoped in the negotiation for her accession to the Treaty of Versailles. What had at
first seemed an easy arrangement to conclude bogged down
owing to protocol delays and Russian demands which were not
part of the treaty and were quite contrary to the policies of the
cosignor, France. Austria, the other signatory, was not as deeply
involved as France in this diplomatic exchange; and although
Austria supported the French position at the Russian court,
Douglas believed Esterhazy was partial to Russian interests in
this affair.[12]

The Ottoman Empire had not been mentioned in the Treaty of
Versailles; but in connection with her accession to the treaty,
Elizabeth sought to gain France's support in the event that the
Ottoman Empire attacked the Russian Empire. Russia was very
much concerned over what the Porte's policy would be once
Russian troops were committed to campaigns in Western Europe. Although the empress had been given assurances that she
had nothing to fear from the Ottoman Empire, she also was
aware that both Great Britain and Prussia were attempting to
influence the Porte against her.[13] The negotiation for her acces-

---

[10] Brühl to Bestuzhev-Riumin, Dec 5, 1756 (communicated to the Russian court on Jan. 16, 1757), AVPR, *f. Snosheniia . . . Pol'shei*, 1756, *op.*
79/ 1, *d.* 3/ 36–37; and Rouillé to Douglas, Nov. 20, 1756 (communicated
to the Russian court on Dec. 28, 1756), *f. Snosheniia . . . Frantsiei*, 1756,
op. 93/ 1, *d.* 5/ 198–205.

[11] See LOII, *f.* 36, *op.* 1, *d.* 105/ 311; VA, RussBer, *karton* 39/ 46–47,
173, 174.

[12] Maria Theresa to Esterhazy, Nov. 13, 1756, TsGADA, *f.* 1261, *op.*
1, *d.* 169/ 13–19; and Douglas to Rouillé, Dec. 3, 1756, BN SM NAF
22011/ 94–105.

[13] See Rescripts to Obreskov, Nov. 23, 1756, VA, RussBer, *karton* 38/
315–324; and Dec. 3, 1756, AVPR, *f. Snosheniia . . . Avstriei*, 1756, *op.* 32/
1, d. 5a/ 264–274. See also TsGADA, *f.* 178, *d.* 1/ 398–399 (No. 97, Nov.
13, 1756).

sion to the Treaty of Varsailles was a perfect opportunity to weaken Franco-Turkish relations.

Russia had produced a rather shrewd diplomatic gambit. It was not so much that Russia underestimated French staying power in this case; rather Russia chose to test it and had nothing to lose if she failed in her endeavor.

The Versailles court would have none of Russia's proposals. In instructions to Douglas on November 20 and 27, the court committed itself more forcefully than it had on the Polish question. France was, moreover, aided by the wording of the Treaty of Versailles itself. Since the Ottoman Empire was not part of the treaty, France claimed that there was no reason or right to introduce her into it. It was "absolutely indispensable" that the Ottoman Empire be excluded from it. In answering the remarks of Bestuzhev-Riumin to Douglas about protecting Hanover from insult or invasion during the present war, the French court argued that the treaty did not require France's allies to participate in her war with Great Britain; thus, they would not be asked to send their troops into Hanover. In any case, since France was at war with Great Britain, she could under no circumstances be expected not to invade Hanover if she believed it to be in her best military and political interests.[14]

Before these instructions arrived in St. Petersburg, the Russians had already made up their minds on the issue of their accession to the Treaty of Versailles. Early in December Douglas had complained to the French court that he was confused about the accession negotiation and wanted orders on that matter. More and more, he said, he found himself following the advice of Esterhazy who wanted to see the whole affair speedily concluded.[15] By the third week in December, drafts of the accession documents were being drawn up and their contents rumored at the Russian court.[16] On December 27 Douglas was informed

[14] See AVPR, f. Snosheniia . . . Frantsiei, 1756, op. 93/ 1, d. 5/ 230–233; LOII, f. 36, op. 1, d. 101/ 43; and TsGADA, f. 1261, op. 9, d. 29/ 1–4 (communicated to Grand Chancellor on Dec. 31, 1756).

[15] See BN SM NAF 22011/ 94–105 (Dec. 3, 1756).

[16] See Williams to Holdernesse, Dec. 9, 18, and 25, 1756, PROSP 91/ 64; Catherine to Williams, Dec. 24, 1756, ICC, p. 248; and TsGADA, f. 178, d. 1/ 406, 483, 493–494 (Nos. 100, 132, 139; Nov. 18, Dec. 10 and 22, 1756).

that Elizabeth's accession to the treaty would be accompanied by a secret declaration.[17]

It seemed for a moment that Douglas would be overwhelmed by the play of events in St. Petersburg. But with the arrival of his instructions, he could no longer be confused about France's intentions; when he communicated them to Bestuzhev-Riumin on December 31, the Russian court could have no doubts about the French position on Turkey and Hanover. Nevertheless, the French were not totally successful in St. Petersburg because of Douglas' inability and immaturity in formal diplomatic affairs. On January 11, 1757, he signed and accepted on behalf of France not only Russia's accession to the Treaty of Versailles but also a secret declaration which seriously undermined its spirit and contents.[18]

By this declaration the king of France promised that, if the Ottoman Empire threatened to attack Russia, he would employ all his efforts to deter it. However, if he was unsuccessful and the Ottoman Empire attacked Russia, then the king of France would for the duration of the war supply Russia with a monthly monetary subsidy as a substitute for 24,000 troops. In return, the empress of Russia would aid the king of France with 24,000 troops or their financial equivalent in the event that his possessions in Europe should be attacked by Great Britain, excepting the present war and a war in the colonies. The secret declaration was to have the same force and effect as if it were inserted in the act of accession itself.[19]

Hanover was not mentioned in the secret declaration. The explanation for its exclusion may be found in the origins of the proposal itself. As we have already noted, Bestuzhev-Riumin's stipulation to Douglas that Russia wanted to exclude Hanover from invasion during the present war was undoubtedly made to satisfy the pro-English forces at the Russian court which had

[17] See LOII, f. 36, op. 1, d. 101/ 43; AVPR, f. Snosheniia . . . Frantsiei, 1756, op. 93/ 1, d. 5/ 219–220; and TsGADA, f. 178, d. 1/ 504–505 (No. 142).

[18] Esterhazy signed and accepted only the accession on behalf of Austria. LOII, f. 36, op. 1, d. 101/ 44; AVPR, f. Snosheniia . . . Frantsiei, 1757, op. 93/ 1, d. 3/ 8–11; and TsGADA, f. 178, d. 2/2.

[19] AVPR, f. Snosheniia . . . Frantsiei, 1756, op. 93/ 1, d. 5/ 223–228. See also LOII, f. 36, op. 1, d. 101/ 44.

gained increased influence when Elizabeth had become dangerously ill. As soon as Elizabeth was out of the crisis, the influence of the anglophiles rapidly declined. There was no longer any reason for supporting their demands, especially in view of the forceful position taken on this issue by the French.

The victory the Russians may have thought they had gained in St. Petersburg by securing Douglas' signature to the secret declaration was quickly turned into defeat in Versailles, when the French chose not to accept the declaration as binding upon them. Douglas had acted very much as Williams had done during the negotiation of the Anglo-Russian Subsidy Treaty, and he was repudiated by his court. Louis XV took matters into his own hands by writing to Empress Elizabeth on February 19, saying that while he was very happy to ratify the act of accession he could not ratify the declaration for this would have him enter into "two absolutely contrary engagements at the same time."[20]

Empress Elizabeth had no alternative but to accept Louis's position on the declaration. She had no way of forcing her will on him. She had not made her accession to the Treaty of Versailles conditional upon his acceptance of the declaration; and even if she had, she would have probably not been successful. On March 25 Empress Elizabeth wrote the king of France that she had "without the least delay" ratified the act of her accession to the treaty.[21] The matter of the declaration ended there. Franco-Russian relations did not suffer from the outcome of this part of their negotiations. Rather, both countries understood each other better because of it.

Great Britain suffered the greatest loss from Russia's acces-

---

[20] AVPR, f. Snosheniia . . . Frantsiei, 1757, op. 93/ 1, d. 1/ 1–2 (communicated to the Russian court on March 20); and LOII, f. 36, op. 1, d. 101/ 50 (Mar. 20, 1757). See also L. Jay Oliva, Misalliance. A Study of French Policy in Russia During the Seven Years' War, pp. 58–60; and S. M. Solov'ëv, Istoriia Rossii s drevneishikh vremën, XXIV, 394.

[21] AVPR, f. Snosheniia . . . Frantsiei, 1757, op. 93/ 1, d. 1/ 5–6. See also Bestuzhev-Riumin and Vorontsov to Bekhteev, March 30, 1757, ibid., d. 3/ 60. The formal exchange of ratifications to the act of accession to the Treaty of Versailles took place in St. Petersburg on April 19, 1757. See Williams to Holdernesse, April 23, 1757, PROSP 91/ 65.

sion to the Treaty of Versailles. It formally announced the end
of Bestuzhev-Riumin's political system which had guided Russian foreign policy for more than a decade. It also allowed for
the possibility of a new orientation in Russian commercial policy. Great Britain did not succeed at this time in obtaining a
renewal of her commercial treaty with Russia, and her former
privileged position could be taken by the French. At least, part
of the negotiations between France and Russia during the year
provided for that very thing. France now had a greater opportunity to penetrate a lucrative Russian market. Those who had
commanded the new policy in Russian foreign affairs were also
those interested in establishing a firm commercial tie with
France. This juncture occurred at a critical time for Great Britain—during a war when Russian naval stores were essential
to British sea power.[22]

From the time that Frederick II invaded Saxony, Austria was
singularly interested in having Russian armies attack Prussia.
While Russia was obliged to aid Austria under the terms of the
treaty of 1746, it soon became apparent that she was not going
to fulfill her obligations unless a new treaty was concluded
which provided for Austria's support of Russian war aims.

As the months passed, Austria's determination not to enter
into such an arrangement with Russia weakened. She recognized
that she had already suffered because of her reluctance to come
to terms with Russia and stood to lose much more. In her decision to accommodate Russia, Austria nevertheless demonstrated
that she remained still both cautious and shrewd in her diplomatic undertakings.

On November 13, 1756, the Austrian court sent its ambassador
in St. Petersburg instructions outlining its position on the of-

[22] See Holdernesse to Williams, Aug. 31, 1756, PROSP 91/63; Williams
to Holdernesse, Oct. 26 and Dec. 18, 1756, PROSP 91/ 64; Mitchell to
Holdernesse, Aug. 24, 1756, PROSP 90/ 66; Yorke to Holdernesse, Aug.
24, 1756, BMAddMSS 35436/ 93. BN SM NAF 22009/ 156–173, 209–
210, 218; 22010/ 143–148, 161, 163–189, 191–200; 22011/ 106. LOII, *f*.
36, *op*. 1, *d*. 1095/ 253, 255; *d*. 1124/ 37. TsGADA, *f*. 276, *op*. 1, *d*. 1328,
1329. Oliva, pp. 124–134, provides a good summary and analysis of the
problems besetting the initiation and continuation of Franco-Russian commercial relations during the period of the Seven Years' War.

fensive alliance and drafts of the treaty to be concluded with Russia.[23] These documents contained the essential features of the treaty which was later signed in St. Petersburg on February 2, 1757.[24]

In a sophisticated presentation, the Austrian court in its instructions to Esterhazy briefly described the aggressive activities of Frederick II which led to his seizure of Silesia and Glatz several years before and made the point that other European courts could not object to Austria's "reconquest of them." But when it came to Russia's intended incorporation of Kurland and Semigalia, "it was easy to foresee" how other powers, especially France and the Ottoman Empire, would be opposed to a change in the frontiers of northern Europe, despite the advantages that Poland might gain by her acquisition of East Prussia. Nevertheless, the Austrian court desired to support "as much as possible" the designs of the empress of Russia.

The Austrian court saw the necessity of concluding with Russia a new treaty which would reaffirm that of 1746 and also conform to the proposals made by Russia in April 1756. The purpose of the treaty would be "to make war against the King of Prussia" in order to reconquer Silesia and Glatz and place him in a position whereby he could no longer disturb the peace. Furthermore, the provisions of the treaty should be written in "general terms" so as not to prevent France, Sweden, Denmark, and Saxony from acceding to it at a later date. For their accession these four powers would be rewarded territory, but "these lands would not be specifically designated" until future negotiations could take place. By this means it was hoped that, at the end of the war, both Austria and Russia would have enough power "to control the situation without difficulty." It would allow both Austria and Russia "to exact promises and to incline" those powers, in exchange for their "private advantages, to support the views about Kurland and Semigalia," "that Kurland and

[23] Maria Theresa to Esterhazy, TsGADA, f. 1261, op. 1, d. 169/ 20–26. On drafts of treaty see, ibid., 27–34, and AVPR, f. Snosheniia . . . Avstriei, 1756, op. 32/ 1, d. 6/ 350–358, 370–374, 375, 376.

[24] See F. de Martens, ed. Recueil des traités et conventions, conclus par la Russie avec les puissances étrangères (St. Petersburg, 1871–1909), I, 201–202.

Semigalia would be appropriated by the Russian Empire and East Prussia by the Republic of Poland."[25]

The Austrian court further proposed that the war continue until Silesia and Glatz were safely and peacefully in the possession of Maria Theresa and that this repossession be assured by the future treaty of peace and be guaranteed by the empress of Russia. Neither Russia nor Austria was to conclude a truce or peace with Frederick II without first obtaining the consent of the other. The number of regular troops to be employed by each party was to be increased to 80,000, and Russia was also to use from 15 to 20 vessels of the line. Both sides were to coordinate their military activities by exchanging plans as well as appointing generals to sit in the councils of war of the other party. It was absolutely necessary that Russian armies invade the territories of Frederick as soon as possible. Maria Theresa promised to pay Empress Elizabeth one million roubles annually for the duration of the war, and by this payment Elizabeth would consider Maria Theresa discharged from paying the two million florins stipulated in the fourth separate and secret article of the treaty of 1746. Other powers were to be invited to accede to the new treaty.

By a separate and secret declaration appended to the new treaty, Maria Theresa explained her position on Russia's acquisition of Kurland and Semigalia. She promised that, in the future peace negotiations and in agreement with those powers who would participate in those negotiations, she would support Russia's claims to those territories provided East Prussia was given to the crown of Poland in exchange.[26]

By the spring of 1757 the major alliances and unions which Russia had sought to enter into had been concluded and little more remained to be done than to move Russian armies into the theatre of war. Empress Elizabeth was again disappointed in this matter, because her time-table of military operations was again delayed. Her armies were not prepared to advance that

[25] Maria Theresa to Esterhazy, November 12, 1756, TsGADA, f. 1261, op. 1, d. 169/ 20–26 (communicated to Bestuzhev-Riumin and Vorontsov on December 10, 1756).

[26] Ibid., 27–34; and AVPR, f. Snosheniia . . . Avstriei, 1756, op. 32/ 1, d. 6/ 350–358, 370–374, 375, 376.

spring against Prussia as had been planned. The empress had to wait until the summer before it seemed likely that Prussia would be invaded.

Field Marshal Apraksin had set up his headquarters in Riga and established a war council to supervise and direct the military operations of more than 100,000 men. The Austrian court had sent their advisers to join him and plans were exchanged and deliberated. The tedious detailing of orders to Russian commanders, the deployment of troops, and the coordination of naval operations took months to accomplish. But if judged by results, however slowly they matured, the Russian court could at least be happy with the first reports of Russian military engagements. Memel surrendered in early July and Russian armies won a shattering victory over the Prussians at Gross-Jägersdorf at the end of August.[27]

[27] TsGADA, f. 178, d. 1/ 465–514; d. 2/ 28–531; d. 3/ 29–178. TsGA-DA, f. 1261, op. 1, d. 169/ 35–87; d. 178/ 1–7; d. 179/ 1–2, 5–7; d. 353/ 4–9. TsGADA, f. 1261, op. 9, d. 31/ 1–2. TsGADA, f. 1263, op. 1, d. 29/ 1–173; d. 469/ 6–7, 9–10; d. 576/ 1–2; d. 684/ 1–3; d. 1091/ 1–6; d. 1619/ 26–27; d. 1620/ 8–9; d. 1659/ 1–36; d. 1765/ 23, 26; d. 2653/ 17–18, 22; d. 3106/ 5, 7–8. TsGVIA, f. 48, op. 202, d. 6, 10, 13, 15; f. VUA, d. 1655/ 14, 47–62, d. 1657a/ 18–592, d. 1657 II/ 1–309. AVPR, f. Snosheniia . . . Avstriei, 1756, op. 32/ 1, d. 5b/46; op. 32/ 2, d. 179/ 2–5. AVPR, f. Snosheniia . . . Avstriei, 1757, op. 32/ 1, d. 1/ 9–10; d. 4/ 5–6, 9, 13–15, 26, 34–35. AVPR, f. Snosheniia . . . Frantsiei, 1757, op. 93/ 1, d. 3/ 105–106, 111; d. 7/147, 165–170, 177–189; d. 8/ 162–166. LOII, f. 36, op. 1, d. 97/ 59; d. 101/ 44, 51, 54, 56; d. 103/ 129; d. 1077/ 91–92; d. 1086/ 3, 6, 11; d. 1124/ 5, 26. VA, Vorträge, 1756, faszikel, 124; and 1757, faszikel, 125. PROSP 91/ 65.

Conclusion

Professor Herbert Butterfield in his provocative essay, "The Reconstruction of an Historical Episode: The History of the Enquiry into the Origins of the Seven Years War," argued that in order to gain a clearer understanding of the origins of the Seven Years' War, not only how but why it came about, we must unravel the tangled skein of motivations, policies, and actions of the Russian court.

Indeed, Russia was central to the entire story. From the beginning of 1755 down to the conclusion of the Convention of Westminster, the position Russia occupied in the foreign policies of Austria, Great Britain, and Prussia was of the utmost importance. It was the pivot of George II's foreign policy on the continent as articulated in the Anglo-Russian Subsidy Treaty proposal. The calculation of Russia's enormous military potential was the key to Maria Theresa's understanding of her role in European politics. The fear that dominated Frederick was his belief that his territories would soon be invaded by tens of thousands of Russian troops in the pay of Great Britain. It was that conviction which made him conclude the Convention of Westminster.

At the same time both George and Maria Theresa need not have worked so hard to convince Elizabeth that Frederick was a dangerous *parvenu* who needed to be disciplined by military force if necessary. Elizabeth despised him personally as did others at her court, but she had a *raison d'état* which sufficed to support her war policies: she coveted his territory that bordered on the Baltic and the Polish-Lithuanian Commonwealth. What the dismemberment of East Prussia would do to Frederick and what—if in fact the exchange with the commonwealth was effected—the acquisition of Kurland would do for

Russia would be enough to justify a war which would make Elizabeth the very proud daughter of Peter the Great.

Elizabeth was dismayed by the British refusal to accept her interpretation of the Anglo-Russian Subsidy Treaty, and she was outraged by the Convention of Westminster; but those disappointments did not dampen her aggressive spirit. She plunged ahead with her military mobilization, believing that Austria would soon join her in an offensive alliance dedicated to the destruction of Prussia. When Austria called for a postponement of the scheduled invasion, Elizabeth was disappointed and frustrated; but she did not deviate from her policy to attack Frederick by force even though she might have to wait a year.

In the meantime Elizabeth had mobilized not only Russia's military resources but also Russia's administrative hierarchy. A major reform was the establishment of the Conference, which served as a coordinating body for the colleges and the Senate and was disbanded only after Elizabeth's death. As an administrative organ of the Empress' will, the Conference was, next to Elizabeth, the highest authority in the Empire of Russia. While precedents may be found for this institution in the eighteenth century, the Conference undoubtedly served as the example for Empress Catherine II's council in the following decade. It cannot be emphasized enough how important this reform of the governmental administration was for the history of Russia during the eighteenth century.

If military mobilization is to be construed as a precipitant of war, then Russia, not Austria or Prussia—whose mobilization followed Russia's by months—is culpable. The provocation once made had to be dealt with, and Frederick again reacted to Russia's foreign policy; but this time he contracted for war by invading Saxony. This act was welcomed by Elizabeth as much as if she had attacked him herself. Frederick before and after his invasion of Saxony sent peace feelers out to both Maria Theresa and Elizabeth which were disregarded or rejected altogether.

Elizabeth was successful on the diplomatic front with both France and Austria. After several years of estrangement, Elizabeth and Louis XV reunited, primarily owing to the ambitious undertaking of the clever Vice-Chancellor Michael Vorontsov who saw in a Franco-Russian rapprochement the opportunity to unseat the aging Grand Chancellor Alexis Bestuzhev-Riumin who was as much a francophobe as he was an anglophile. To destroy the Anglo-Russian Subsidy Treaty, which was basic to Bestuzhev-Riumin's foreign policy, was to overthrow the grand chancellor himself. To all this, Elizabeth gave her approval and her blessing. Vorontsov and his pro-French colleagues at the Russian court won the empress over to this new orientation in foreign policy, which not only paved the way for a reduction of French opposition to Russian armies crossing the Polish-Lithuanian Commonwealth, but also created opportunities for the further development of Franco-Russian commercial and cultural relations.

From Maria Theresa, Empress Elizabeth obtained as much support as was possible at that time for Russia's war aims. Elizabeth was, however, confident that the force of her armies would enable her to secure what she had envisaged in her diplomatic bargain with Austria.

Successful as her diplomacy had been, her good health was the most important factor sustaining her policies. Ailing for some time, Elizabeth succumbed to greater illness until it was thought by everyone at the Russian court that she would die at any moment, her armies not yet on the field to strike the death blow to Frederick. Functioning in a theoretically absolute monarchy, royal courtiers were in despair. They correctly perceived that the continuity of policy could not be guaranteed with the succession of Grand Duke Peter to the throne. His policies in foreign affairs were diametrically opposite to those of Elizabeth and the Vorontsov pro-French group. During this crucial period of waiting both Peter and his wife, Catherine, performed their roles as if in dress rehearsal.

Along with Elizabeth's recovery came the acceleration of Russia's military activity after the army had suffered great deprivations from standing idle for almost a year. Once unleashed, the Russian armies in their first campaigns lived up to the expectations of other European powers. It was a legacy well remembered during the second half of the eighteenth century.

Abbreviations
Used in Notes

AVPR   Arkhiv Vneshnei Politiki Rossii [Archives of the Foreign Policy of Russia] (Bibliography, p. 140)

BMAddMSS British Museum, Additional Manuscripts (Bibliography, p. 131)

BMEg   British Museum, Egerton Manuscripts (Bibliography, p. 136)

BN SM NAF Bibliothèque Nationale, Salle des Manuscrits, Nouvelles Acquisitions Françaises (Bibliography, p. 136)

CHW   The Correspondence of Sir Charles Hanbury Williams (owned by Sheldon Wilmarth Lewis) (Bibliography, p. 154)

d.   *delo* (corresponds to catalogue number)

f.   *fond* (individual set of papers or collection of documents)

ICC   Ilchester, the Earl of & Mrs. Langford-Brooke, eds. and trans. Correspondence of Catherine the Great When Grand Duchess with Sir Charles Hanbury-Williams, and Letters from Count Poniatowski (Bibliography, p. 154)

LOII   Leningradskoe Otdelenie Instituta Istorii Akademii Nauk SSSR [Leningrad Division of the Institute of History of the Academy of Sciences of the USSR] (Bibliography, p. 137)

op.   *opis'* [inventory]

PC   Politische Correspondenz Friedrichs des Grossen (Bibliography, p. 154)

PPS   Publicationen aus den K. Preussischen Staatsarchiven (Bibliography, p. 154)

130

PROSP   Public Record Office, State Papers: Foreign (Bibliography, p. 136)

RussBer   Russland II, Berichte (Bibliography, p. 131)

SIRIO   Sbornik imperatorskago russkago istoricheskago obschestva [The Collection of the Imperial Russian Historical Society] (Bibliography, p. 155)

TsGADA   Tsentral'nyi Gosudarstvennyi Arkhiv Drevnikh Aktov [Central State Archives of Ancient Acts] (Bibliography, p. 146)

TsGVIA   Tsentral'nyi Gosudarstvennyi Voenno-Istoricheskii Arkhiv SSSR [Central State Archives of Military History of the USSR] (Bibliography, p. 153)

VA   Vienna Archives (Bibliography, p. 131)

Bibliography

ARCHIVES

[The spellings of the archival manuscript titles are as they appeared in the original.]

Vienna

ÖSTERREICHISCHES STAATSARCHIV HAUS-, HOF-UND STAATSARCHIV (*VA*)
Staatskanzlei
> Vorträge, 1755–1757
> Russland II, Berichte 1755–1757 (RussBer)
> Russland II, Weisungen 1755–1757

London

BRITISH MUSEUM, ADDITIONAL MANUSCRIPTS (*BMAddMSS*)
Cat. No.
> 6804 Mitchell Papers. Vol. I. Copies of Despatches from Mr. Mitchell. 8 May–19 Aug. 1756.
> 6805 Mitchell Papers. Vol. II. Copies of Mr. Mitchell's Despatches. 20 Aug.–5 Oct. 1756.
> 6806 Mitchell Papers. Vol. III. Copies of Mr. Mitchell's Despatches. 14 Oct. 1756–13 Nov. 1757.
> 6807 Mitchell Papers. Vol. IV. Copies of Mr. Mitchell's Despatches. 16 Nov. 1757–1 Oct. 1759.
> 6811 Mitchell Papers. Vol. VIII. Original Despatches from Earl of Holdernesse to Andrew Mitchell during May and June 1756.
> 6823 Mitchell Papers. Vol. XX. Original Letters to Mr. Mitchell. May 1756–Jan. 1771.
> 6824 Mitchell Papers. Vol. XXI. Original Letters from Sir Charles Hanbury Williams. Jan. 1756–July 1757.
> 6825 Mitchell Papers. Vol. XXII. Original Letters to Mr. Mitchell. Dec. 1757–Aug. 1763.

6827   Mitchell Papers. Vol. XXIV. Original Letters from Viscount Stormont and Thomas Wroughton to Mr. Mitchell. Jan. 1757–Aug. 1769.

6829   Mitchell Papers. Vol. XXVI. Original Letters to Mr. Mitchell. June 1756–Dec. 1769.

6831   Mitchell Papers. Vol. XXVIII. Private Correspondence of Mr. Mitchell with Various English Ministers.

6832   Mitchell Papers. Vol. XXIX. Original Letters from the Duke of Newcastle and the Earl of Holdernesse to Mr. Mitchell. May 1756–Mar. 1761.

6833   Mitchell Papers. Vol. XXX. Original Letters to Mr. Mitchell. 1756–April 1766.

6834   Mitchell Papers. Vol. XXXI. Original Letters from Lord Barrington to Mr. Mitchell. June 1756–Jan. 1771.

6835   Mitchell Papers. Vol. XXXII. Original Letters from H.R.H. the Duke of Cumberland to Mr. Mitchell. Apr.–Sept. 1757.

6836   Mitchell Papers. Vol. XXXIII. Original Letters to Mr. Mitchell. May 1756–Apr. 1770.

6837   Mitchell Papers. Vol. XXXIV. Original Letters to Mr. Mitchell. Apr. 1757–Mar. 1758.

6840   Mitchell Papers. Vol. XXXVII. Original Letters to Mr. Mitchell. Oct. 1756–Dec. 1770.

6843   Mitchell Papers. Vol. XL. Original Letters of Frederic II to Mr. Mitchell. 23 July 1756–25 Jan. 1765.

6844   Mitchell Papers. Vol. XLI. Papers Received by Mr. Mitchell from the King of Prussia or His Ministers.

6845   Mitchell Papers. Vol. XLII. Writings of the King of Prussia.

6847   Mitchell Papers. Vol. XLIV. Original Letters from M. Eichel to Mr. Mitchell. Oct. 1756–Sept. 1762.

6848   Mitchell Papers. Vol. XLV. Original Letters from Count Podewils and Count Finckenstein to Mr. Mitchell. July 1756–Sept. 1768.

6849   Mitchell Papers. Vol. XLVI. Original Letters to Mr. Mitchell from Prince Ferdinand of Brunswick. Mar. 1757–Aug. 1759.

6851   Mitchell Papers. Vol. XLVIII. Original Letters from Foreigners of Rank to Mr. Mitchell. 1757–1770.

6852   Mitchell Papers. Vol. XLIX. Original Letters to Mr. Mitchell from General Cornabé and General Donop. Apr. 1756– Dec. 1761.

6856   Mitchell Papers. Vol. LIII. Original Letters to Mr. Mitchell from Countess of Yarmouth, Lord Marischall, Madame Keith, and Mr. Keith. Dec. 1757–June 1763.

6862 Mitchell Papers. Vol. LIX. Original Instructions to Mr. Mitchell. Apr. 1756.

6864 Mitchell Papers. Vol. LXI. Copies of Some Letters to Mr. Mitchell. 1756–1757.

6867 Mitchell Papers. Vol. LXIV. Journals Kept by Mr. Mitchell. 20 Apr. 1757–27 Aug. 1758.

6870 Mitchell Papers. Vol. LXVII. Memoranda of Mr. Mitchell on the State of Europe in 1755.

6871 Mitchell Papers. Vol. LXVIII. Papers Relating to the Revenues, Population, and Statistics of France, Scotland, Prussia, Sweden, and Russia, 1740–1758.

32852 Newcastle Papers. Vol. CLXVII. General Correspondence. Jan.–Feb. 1755.

32853 Newcastle Papers. Vol. CLXVIII. General Correspondence. Mar. 1755.

32854 Newcastle Papers. Vol. CLXIX. General Correspondence. Apr.–16 May 1755.

32855 Newcastle Papers. Vol. CLXX. General Correspondence. 16 May–15 June 1755.

32856 Newcastle Papers. Vol. CLXXI. General Correspondence. 16 June–10 July 1755.

32857 Newcastle Papers. Vol. CLXXII. General Correspondence. 11 July–5 Aug. 1755.

32858 Newcastle Papers. Vol. CLXXIII. General Correspondence. 6 Aug.–5 Sept. 1755.

32859 Newcastle Papers. Vol. CLXXIV. General Correspondence. 6 Sept.–10 Oct. 1755.

32860 Newcastle Papers. Vol. CLXXV. General Correspondence. 11 Oct.–15 Nov. 1755.

32861 Newcastle Papers. Vol. CLXXVI. General Correspondence. 16 Nov.–Dec. 1755.

32862 Newcastle Papers. Vol. CLXXVII. General Correspondence. Jan.–15 Feb. 1756.

32863 Newcastle Papers. Vol. CLXXVIII. General Correspondence. 16 Feb.–25 Mar. 1756.

32864 Newcastle Papers. Vol. CLXXIX. General Correspondence. 26 Mar.–15 May 1756.

32865 Newcastle Papers. Vol. CLXXX. General Correspondence. 16 May–June 1756.

32866   Newcastle Papers. Vol. CLXXXI. General Correspondence. July–20 Aug. 1756.

32867   Newcastle Papers. Vol. CLXXXII. General Correspondence. 21 Aug.–Sept. 1756.

32868   Newcastle Papers. Vol. CLXXXIII. General Correspondence. Oct.–10 Nov. 1756.

32869   Newcastle Papers. Vol. CLXXXIV. General Correspondence. 11 Nov.–Dec. 1756.

32870   Newcastle Papers. Vol. CLXXXV. General Correspondence. Jan.–Apr. 1757.

32871   Newcastle Papers. Vol. CLXXXVI. General Correspondence. May–June 1757.

32996   Newcastle Papers. Vol. IV. Memoranda of the Duke of Newcastle. 1755–June 1756.

32997   Newcastle Papers. Vol. V. Memoranda of the Duke of Newcastle. July 1756–Mar. 1758.

33020   Newcastle Papers. Vol. XVI. Diplomatic Papers. Jan.–July 1755.

33021   Newcastle Papers. Vol. XVII. Diplomatic Papers. Aug. 1755–1756.

33022   Newcastle Papers. Vol. XVIII. Diplomatic Papers. 1757–Mar. 1758.

33046   Newcastle Papers. Vol. I. Papers Relating to the Army and Navy. XVII cent.–1755.

33047   Newcastle Papers. Vol. II. Papers Relating to the Army and Navy. 1756–1759.

35351   Hardwicke Papers. Vol. III. Correspondence of Philip Yorke, Ist Earl of Hardwicke and Lord Chancellor, with His Son Philip, Viscount Royston (1754) and 2nd Earl of Hardwicke (1764–1790). 1731–1757.

35352   Hardwicke Papers. Vol. IV. Correspondence of Philip Yorke, Ist. Earl of Hardwicke and Lord Chancellor, with His Son Philip, Viscount Royston (1754) and 2nd Earl of Hardwicke (1764–1790). 1757–1763.

35357   Hardwicke Papers. Vol. IX. Correspondence of Philip Yorke, Ist. Earl of Hardwicke, with His Son Sir Joseph Yorke, K. B., Successively Aide-de-Camp to the Duke of Cumberland, Minister at Paris, and Minister at the Hague, Created K. B. (1761) and Baron Dover (1788). 1756–1759.

35360   Hardwicke Papers. Vol. XII. Correspondence of Philip Yorke, 2nd Earl of Hardwicke, with His Brother, the Hon. Charles Yorke. 1740–1760.

35364   Hardwicke Papers. Vol. XVI. Correspondence of Philip Yorke, 2nd Earl of Hardwicke, with His Brother, Sir Joseph Yorke. 1754–1758.

35373   Hardwicke Papers. Vol. XXV. Letters from Daniel Laval *alias* Delaval, Secretary to Sir Joseph Yorke at the Hague, to Philip Yorke, 2nd Earl of Hardwicke. 1647–1749 and 1757–1772.

35385   Hardwicke Papers. Vol. XXXVII. Correspondence of the Hon. Charles Yorke with His Brother Sir Joseph Yorke, Consisting Principally of Letters from the Latter at the Hague. 1742–1769.

35415   Hardwicke Papers. Vol. LXVI. Political Correspondence of Philip Yorke with Duke of Newcastle and Others. July 1755–Aug. 1756.

35416   Hardwicke Papers. Vol. LXVII. Political Correspondence of Philip Yorke, Ist. Earl of Hardwicke, with Duke of Newcastle and Others. Sept. 1756–June 1757.

35423   Hardwicke Papers. Vol. LXXV. Political Correspondence of Philip Yorke, Ist. Earl of Hardwicke.

35425   Hardwicke Papers. Vol. LXXVII. Letters to Philip Yorke, 2nd Earl of Hardwicke, from Duke of Newcastle and Others.

35430   Hardwicke Papers. Vol. LXXXII. Political Correspondence of the Hon. Charles Yorke.

35436   Hardwicke Papers. Vol. LXXXVIII. Letter-Books of Sir Joseph Yorke. 14 Oct. 1755–31 May 1757.

35437   Hardwicke Papers. Vol. LXXXIX. Letter-Books of Sir Joseph Yorke. 3 June 1757–31 Jan. 1758.

35440   Hardwicke Papers. Vol. XCII. Letter-Books of Sir Joseph Yorke. 29 July 1755–7 Sept. 1756.

35441   Hardwicke Papers. Vol. XCIII. Letter-Books of Sir Joseph Yorke. 10 Sept. 1756–16 Sept. 1757.

35442   Hardwicke Papers. Vol. XCIV. Letter-Books of Sir Joseph Yorke. 20 Sept. 1757–17 Feb. 1758.

35479   Hardwicke Papers. Vol. CXXXI. Correspondence, Chiefly Diplomatic, of Robert Keith. Feb.–17 June 1755.

35480   Hardwicke Papers. Vol. CXXXII. Correspondence, Chiefly Diplomatic, of Robert Keith. 19 June 1755–16 July 1756.

35481   Hardwicke Papers. Vol. CXXXIII. Correspondence, Chiefly Diplomatic, of Robert Keith. 22 July 1756–July 1757.

35503   Hardwicke Papers. Vol. CLV. Correspondence, Principally Diplomatic, of Sir Robert Murray Keith. 1752–Sept. 1772.

38332 Liverpool Papers. Vol. CXLIII. Official Papers of the Ist. Earl of Liverpool. 1756–1760.

43434 Keene Papers. Vol. XXIII. General Correspondence of Sir Benjamin Keene. Mar.–June 1755.

43435 Keene Papers. Vol. XXIV. General Correspondence of Sir Benjamin Keene. July–28 Aug. 1755.

43436 Keene Papers. Vol. XXV. General Correspondence of Sir Benjamin Keene. 27 Aug. 1755–Mar. 1756.

43437 Keene Papers. Vol. XXVI. General Correspondence of Sir Benjamin Keene. Apr.–June 1756.

43438 Keene Papers. Vol. XXVII. General Correspondence of Sir Benjamin Keene. July–Sept. 1756.

43439 Keene Papers. Vol. XXVIII. General Correspondence of Sir Benjamin Keene. Oct. 1756–Apr. 1757.

BRITISH MUSEUM: EGERTON MANUSCRIPTS (*BMEg*)

3401–3403 Leeds Papers. Vols. LXXVIII–LXXX. D'Arcy Family Papers.

3425–3490 Leeds Papers. Vols. CII–CXLVII. Correspondence and Papers of Lord Holdernesse as Secretary of State.

PUBLIC RECORD OFFICE, STATE PAPERS: FOREIGN (*PROSP*)

80 Germany (Empire) and Hungary, Vols. 195–198.
84 Holland, Vols. 468, 471–475.
88 Poland (and Saxony), Vols. 77–79.
90 Prussia, Vols. 65–69.
91 Russia, Vols. 56–65.
95 Sweden, Vols. 102–103.
97 Turkey, Vols. 38–39.
100 Foreign Ministers in England, Vols. 50, 54.
103 Treaty Papers, Vol. 62.
107 Intercepted Dispatches, Vols. 63–65.
109 German Troop Accounts, Vol. 2.
110 Archives of British Legation, Vol. 6.

Paris

BIBLIOTHÈQUE NATIONALE, SALLE DES MANUSCRITS, NOUVELLES ACQUISITIONS FRANÇAISES (*BN SM NAF*)

22009–22011 Russie, 1756–1757.

23975 Correspondance d'Antoine-Louis de Rouillé, Comte de Jouy, Ministre des Affaires étrangères, principalement relative à la Russie. Février 1756–Janvier 1757.

ARCHIVES DU MINISTÈRE DES AFFAIRES ÉTRANGÈRES, CORRESPONDANCE
POLITIQUE, RUSSIE
Volume 51.
Supplements 7–8.

Leningrad

LENINGRADSKOE OTDELENIE INSTITUTA ISTORII AKADEMII NAUK SSSR
(*LOII*) [*Leningrad Division of the Institute of History of the Academy of Sciences of the USSR*]
f. 36, *op.* 1, VORONTSOVYKH
[*f.* 36, *op.* 1, VORONTSOVS]

Delo

91 Vypiska iz Konferentsii, Memorialov, vzaimnykh Soobshchenii mezhdu Rossiiskimi i Agliiskimi v Rossii byvshimi Ministrami s 25 Noiabria 1741 po 28 Iiunia 1762 [Extracts from Conferences, Memorials, reciprocal Communications between former Russian and English Ministers in Russia from 25 Nov. 1741 to 28 June 1762].

95 Vypiska iz Konferentsii, Memorialov, i vzaimnykh Soobshchenii mezhdu Rossiiskimi i Gollandskikh Statov v Rossii byvshimi Ministrami s 25 Noiabria 1741 po 28 Iiunia 1762 [Extracts from Conferences, Memorials, and reciprocal Communications between former Russian Ministers and Dutch States in Russia from 25 Nov. 1741 to 28 June 1762].

97 Vypiska iz Konferentsii, Memorialov, i vzaimnykh Soobshchenii mezhdu Rossiiskimi i Datskimi v Rossii byvshimi Ministrami s 25 Noiabria 1741 po 28 Iiunia 1762 [Extracts from Conferences, Memorials, and reciprocal Communications between former Russian and Danish Ministers in Russia from 25 Nov. 1741 to 28 June 1762].

101 Vypiska iz Konferentsii, Memorialov, i vzaimnykh Soobshchenii mezhdu Rossiiskimi i Frantsuzskimi v Rossii byvshimi Ministrami s 25 Noiabria 1741 po 28 Iiunia 1762 [Extracts from Conferences, Memorials, and reciprocal Communications between former Russian and French Ministers in Russia from 25 Nov. 1741 to 28 June 1762].

103 Vypiska iz Konferentsii, Memorialov, i vzaimnykh Soobshchenii mezhdu Rossiiskimi i Shvedskimi v Rossii byvshimi Ministrami s 25 Noiabria 1741 po 28 Iiunia 1762 [Extracts from Conferences, Memorials, and reciprocal Communications between former Russian and Swedish Ministers in Russia from 25 Nov. 1741 to 28 June 1762].

104 Sokrashchennoe Izvestie o vzaimnykh mezhdu Rossiiskimi
    Monarkhami i Evropeiskimi Derzhavami Posol'stvakh, Pere-
    piskakh i Dogovorakh, khraniashchikhsia Gosudarstvennoi
    Kollegii Inostrannykh Del v Moskovskom Arkhive s 1485–
    1802 god. Chast' vtoraia [Brief News about reciprocal Em-
    bassies, Correspondence and Agreements between Russian
    Monarchs and European Powers preserved in the State Col-
    lege of Foreign Affairs in the Moscow Archive from 1485 to
    1802. Part II].

105 Sokrashchennoe Izvestie o vzaimnykh mezhdu Rossiiskimi
    Monarkhami i Evropeiskimi Derzhavami Posol'stvakh, Per-
    episkakh i Dogovorakh, khraniashchikhsia Gosudarstvennoi
    Kollegii Inostrannykh Del v Moskovskom Arkhive s 1481–
    1798 god. Chast' 3 [Brief News about reciprocal Embassies,
    Correspondence and Agreements between Russian Monarchs
    and European Powers preserved in the State College of
    Foreign Affairs in the Moscow Archive from 1481 to 1798.
    Part 3].

112 Protokoly Konferentsii v sovremennykh Spiskakh Mart–
    Avgust 1756 [Protocols of the Conference in Contemporary
    Lists, Mar.–Aug. 1756].

113 Protokoly Konferentsii 1756 goda. 2 polovina [Protocols of
    the Conference, 1756. 2nd half].

117 Chernovnyia Zapiski i Doklady Kantslera gr. M.L. Voron-
    tsova o Konferen. s Inostr. Poslami, 1756–1763 g. [Rough
    Notes and Reports of the Chancellor Count M.L. Vorontsov
    about Conferences with Foreign Envoys, 1756–1763].

137 Reestry khraniashchimsia delam v Moskovskom Kollegii
    Inostrannykh Del Arkhive Ministerskoi Korrespondentsii s
    Evropeiskimi Dvorami, v Tsarstvovanie Gosudaryni Imper-
    atritsy Elisavety I. s 25 Noiabria 1741 po 1762 Iiunia [Regis-
    tries to Affairs of Ministerial Correspondence with European
    Courts in the Reign of Empress Elizabeth I from 25 Nov.
    1741 to June 1762 preserved in the Moscow Archive of the
    College of Foreign Affairs].

142 Diplomat. Bumagi [Diplomatic Papers].

145 Bumagi grafov Bestuzhevykh [Papers of Counts Bestuzhev].

160 Perepiska po Delam Pol'shi 1743–1761 [Correspondence on
    Affairs of Poland, 1743–1761].

174 Fragment relatif aux rapports qui ont existé entre la Russie
    et la France, sous le règne de l'Imperatrice Elisabeth. Tiré
    des Mémoires recemment publiés du Comte de la Messelière
    alors Cavalier d'Ambassade à St. Petersbourg.

332 Ukazy s 1740 po 1762 godov [Decrees from 1740 to 1762].

1070 Bumagi grafa M.L. Vorontsova, tom. I [Papers of Count M.L. Vorontsov, Vol. I].

1071 Bumagi grafa M.L. Vorontsova, tom. II [Papers of Count M.L. Vorontsov, Vol. II].

1077 Bumagi grafa M.L. Vorontsova, tom. VIII [Papers of Count M.L. Vorontsov, Vol. VIII].

1079 Arkhiv Kniazia Vorontsova [Archive of Prince Vorontsov].

1080 Arkhiv Kniazia Vorontsova [Archive of Prince Vorontsov].

1084 Perepiska grafa M. I. Vorontsova s grafom Sapegoiu, gr. P.A. Rumiantsevym, gr. Z. G. Chernyshovym, baronom Cherkasovym, Monmartelem, kn. A. M. Golitsynym i Khorvatom [Correspondence of Count M. I. Vorontsov with Count Sapieho, Count P. A. Rumiantsev, Count Z. G. Chernyshev, Baron Cherchaski, Monmartel, Prince A. M. Golitsyn, and Khorvat].

1086 Perepiska grafa M. I. Vorontsova s gr. Kaunitsem, kn. Lubomirskim, gr. Saltykovym i Mardefel'dom [Correspondence of Count M. I. Vorontsov with Count Kaunitz, Prince Lubormirski, Count Saltykov, and Baron Mardefeld].

1092 Pis'ma grafa A. P. Bestuzheva k grafu M. L. Vorontsovu, 1742–1762 [Letters of Count A. P. Bestuzhev to Count M. L. Vorontsov, 1742–1762].

1093 Pis'ma grafa M. P. Bestuzheva-Riumina k grafu M. L. Vorontsovu [Letters of Count M. P. Bestuzhev-Riumin to Count M. L. Vorontsov].

1094 Otvetnyia pis'ma gr. M. L. Vorontsova k gr. M. P. Bestuzhevu 1745–1759 [Replies of Count M. L. Vorontsov to Count M. P. Bestuzhev, 1745–1759].

1109 Perepiska grafa M. L. Vorontsova s grafom A. G. Golovkinym, 1744–1761 [Correspondence of Count M. L. Vorontsov with Count A. G. Golovkin, 1744–1761].

1124 Perepiska gr. M. L. Vorontsova s Kavalerom Makenzi Duglasom, 1756–1759g. [Correspondence of Count M. L. Vorontsov with Chevalier Mackenzie Douglas, 1756–1759].

1136 5 Pisem Sergeia Soltykova k gr. M. L. Vorontsovu, 1755 [Five Letters of Sergei Soltykov to Count M. L. Vorontsov, 1755].

1146 Perepiska Ivana Ivanovicha Shuvalova s grafom Mikhailom Larionovichem Vorontsovym. 1753–1766 [Correspondence of Ivan Ivanovich Shuvalov with Count Mikhail Larionovich Vorontsov, 1753–1766].

f. 36, *op.* 2, VORONTSOVYKH
[*f.* 36, *op.* 2, VORONSTOVS]
693 Perepiska Rul'e s M. L. Vorontsovym [Correspondence of
Rouillé with M. L. Vorontsov].
867 Pis'ma Neizvestnykh-Neizvestnym/bezpodpisei/-XVIIIv.
[Anonymous Letters (without signatures), 18th Century].

Moscow

ARKHIV VNESHNEI POLITIKI ROSSII (*AVPR*) [*Archives of the Foreign
Policy of Russia*]
f. SNOSHENIIA ROSSII S AVSTRIEI
[*f.* RELATIONS OF RUSSIA WITH AUSTRIA]
1755, *op.* 32/1
Delo
1 1755 Genv.–Dek. Otpuski Gramot Imperatritsy Elisavety I
k Rimskomu Imperatoru Frantsu I.i k supruge Ego Rimskoi
Imperatritse Marii Terezii [Jan.–Dec. 1755. Dispatches of
Letters of Empress Elizabeth I to Roman Emperor Francis I.
and to His Wife Roman Empress Maria Theresa].
3 1755 Genv.–Dek. Otpuski Reskriptov i Kantseliarskikh Tsidul
k Chrezvychainomu v Vene Poslu Deistvitel'nomu Tainomu
Sovetnitsu Grafu Keizerlingu i (po otezde ego k vodam)
k Sekretariu Bitneru—tut" zhe i pis'ma k Poslu ot Kantslera
Grafa Bestuzheva Riumina [Jan.–Dec. 1755. Dispatches of
Rescripts and Chancellery Letters to The Extraordinary Ambassador in Vienna, Actual Secret Councilor, Count Keyserling and (on his departure to the waters) to Secretary Bitner
and Letters to the Ambassador from Chancellor Count
Bestuzhev-Riumin].
5 1755 Genv.–Dek. Soobshchenii vzaimnyia, i zapiski Konferentsiiam Rimsko-Imperatorskago v Rossii Chrezvychainago Posla Grafa Estergaziia. Chast' I. [Jan.–Dec. 1755. Reciprocal Communications and Notes to the Conferences of the
Roman-Imperial Extraordinary Ambassador in Russia, Count
Esterhazy. Part I.].
6 [No title given].
11 1755 Genv.–Dek. Otpuski reliatsii posla v Vene . . . tainago
sovetnika grafa Keizerlinga [Jan.–Dec. 1755. Dispatches of
Relations of the Ambassador in Vienna . . . Secret Councilor
Count Keyserling].
1756, *op.* 32/1
1 1756 Genv.–Dek. Gramoty k Imperatritse Elisavete I. ot

Rimskago Imperatora Frantsa I, i ot suprugi EIA Imperatritsy-korolevy Marii Terezii [Jan.–Dec. 1756. Letters to Empress Elizabeth I. from the Roman Emperor Francis I, and from his wife the Empress-Queen Maria Theresa].

2   1756 Genv.–Dek. Otpuski Reskriptov i Kantseliarskikh Tsidul k Chrezvychainomu v Vene Poslu Deistvitel'nomu Tainomu Sovetniku Grafu Keizerlingu—tut zhe i pis'ma k nemu Poslu ot Kantslera Grafa Bestuzheva-Riumina [Jan.–Dec. 1756. Dispatches of Rescripts and Chancellery Letters to the Extraordinary Ambassador in Vienna, Actual Secret Councilor, Count Keyserling—and Letters to the Ambassador from Chancellor Bestuzhev-Riumin].

4   1756 Genv.–Dek. Soobshchenii vzaimnyia i zapiski Konferentsiiam Rimsko-Imperatorskago v Rossii Chrezvychainago Posla Grafa Estergaziia. Chast' I. [Jan.–Dec. 1756. Reciprocal Communications and Notes to the Conferences of the Roman-Imperial Extraordinary Ambassador in Russia, Count Esterhazy. Part I.].

5a 1756 Noiabr.–Dek. Soobshchenii vzaimnyia, i zapiski Konferentsiiam Rimsko-Imperatorskago v Rossii Chrezvychainago Posla Grafa Estergaziia. Chast' II. [Nov.–Dec. 1756. Reciprocal Communications and Notes to Conferences of the Roman-Imperial Extraordinary Ambassador in Russia, Count Esterhazy. Part II.].

5b 1756 Dekabr'. Soobshchenii vzaimnyia, i zapiski Konferentsiiam Rimsko-Imperatorskago v Rossii Chrezvychainago Posla Grafa Estergaziia [Dec. 1756. Reciprocal Communications and Notes to Conferences of the Roman-Imperial Extraordinary Ambassador in Russia, Count Esterhazy].

6   1756 Mart. 22–Dek. Soobshchenii vzaimnyia, i zapiski Konferentsiiam Rimsko-Imperatorskago Posla Grafa Estergaziia, o priniatii mezhdu Rossiiskim, i Venskim dvorami mer protivu Korolia Prusskago. Chast' III. [Mar. 22–Dec. 1756. Reciprocal Communications and Notes to Conferences of the Roman-Imperial Ambassador Count Esterhazy, about Undertaking between the Russian and Vienna Courts Measures Against the King of Prussia. Part III.].

1756, *op.* 32/2

179 1756 Dekabria 18. Gramota Imp: Marii Terezii k Imp: Elisavete I., veruiushchaia prislannomu ot neia dlia soglasheniia o voennykh prigotovleniiakh protiv Prusskago Korolia Baronu Bukovu [Dec. 18, 1756. Letter of Empress Maria

Theresa to Empress Elizabeth I, faithfully sent to Baron Buccow from Her for Agreement about Military Preparations Against the Prussian King].
1757, *op.* 32/1

1 1757 Genv.–Dek. Otpuski Gramot Imperatritsy Elizavety I k Rimskomu Imperatoru Frantsu I i k Rimskoi Imperatritse-Koroleve Marii Terezii [Jan.–Dec. 1757. Dispatches of Letters of Letters of Empress Elizabeth I to Roman Emperor Francis I and to Roman Empress-Queen Maria Theresa].

4 1757 Genv.–Dek. Perepiska Rossiiskikh Ministrov s Avstriisko Imperatorskim Kantslerom Grafom Kaunitsom [Jan.–Dec. 1757. Correspondence of Russian Ministers with Austrian Imperial Chancellor Count Kaunitz].

5 1757 Genv.–Dek. Otpuski Reskriptov i Kantseliarskikh Tsidul k Chrezvychainomu v Vene Poslu Grafu Keizerlingu—tut zhe i pis'ma k nemu ot kantslera Grafa Bestuzheva-Riumina. Pervaia polovina [Jan.–Dec. 1757. Dispatches of Rescripts and Chancellery Letters to the Extraordinary Ambassador in Vienna, Count Keyserling—and Letters to Him from Chancellor Count Bestuzhev-Riumin. First Half].

6 Reliatsii i pis'ma k kantsleru grafu Bestuzhevu ot polnomochnoiu v Vene posla grafa Keizerlinga i (po otëzde ego k tselitel'nym vodam) ot sekretaria posol'stva Bitnera [Relations and Letters to Chancellor Count Bestuzhev from Plenipotentiary Ambassador in Vienna, Count Keyserling and (on his departure to curative waters) from Secretary of the Embassy Bitner].

8 1757 Genv.–Mart. Soobshchenii vzaimnyia i zapiski Konferentsiiam Rimsko-Imperatorskago v Rossii Chrezvychainago Posla Grafa Estergaziia. Pervaia Polovina [Jan.–Mar. 1757. Reciprocal Communications and Notes to Conferences of the Roman-Imperial Extraordinary Ambassador in Russia, Count Esterhazy. First Half.].

f. SNOSHENIIA ROSSII S ANGLIEI
[*f.* RELATIONS OF RUSSIA WITH ENGLAND]
1755, *op.* 35/1

768 1755 Genv.–Dek. Otpuski Reskriptov i Kantslerskikh pisem k chrezvychainym v Anglii 1) Ministru Kamergeru Grafu Chernyshevu po otzyv ego iz Londona i 2) Poslanniku Kantseliarii Sovetniku Kniaz' Aleksandru Mikhailovichu Golitsynu [Jan.–Dec. 1755. Dispatches of Rescripts and Chancellery Letters to Extraordinary Minister Chamberlain Count Chernyshev on His Departure from London and to

Envoy, Chancellery Councilor, Prince Alexander Mikhailovich Golitsyn, in England].
770 1755 Genv.–Dek. Soobshchenii vzaimnyia i Konferentsii
Angliiskikh v Rossii; 1) Chrezvychainago Poslannika Geid-
ekensa po otezd ego iz Rossii; 2) Posla Villiamsa, i 3)
Rezidenta Barona Vol'fa [Jan.–Dec. 1755. Reciprocal Communications and Conferences of the English in Russia: (1)
Extraordinary Envoy Guy Dickens on His Departure from
Russia, (2) Ambassador Williams, and (3) Resident Baron
Wolff].
1755, *op.* 35/2
111 1755 Apr. 10 [10 April 1755].
112 Apr. 10 [April 10].
1756, *op.* 35/1
776 1756 Genv.–Dek. Otpuski Reskriptov i Tsydul k Chrezvychainomu v Anglii Poslanniku Kantseliarii Sovetniku Kniaziu
Aleksandru Golitsynu [Jan.–Dec. 1756. Dispatches of Rescripts and Letters to Extraordinary Envoy in England Chancellery Councilor Prince Alexander Golitsyn].
f. LONDONSKAIA MISSIIA
[*f.* LONDON MISSION]
202 1756g. Kopii Vestminsterskogo dogovora mezhdu Angliei i
Prussiei ot 16/I. Versal'skogo mezhdu Avstriei i Frantsiei ot
1/V [1756. Copies of the Westminster Agreement between
England and Prussia 16/I. Of the Versailles between Austria
and France 1/V].
f. SNOSHENIIA ROSSII S POL'SHEI
[*f.* RELATIONS OF RUSSIA WITH POLAND]
1755, *op.* 79/1
5 1755 Genv.–Dek. Otpuski Reskriptov k Sekretariu Posol'stva
v Pol'she Rzhichevskomu [Jan.–Dec. 1755. Dispatches of
Rescripts to the Secretary of the Embassy in Poland, Rzhi-
chevski].
8 1755 Genv.–Dek. Soobshchenii vzaimnyia i Konferentsii
Pol'sko-Saksonskago v Rossii Chrezvychainago Poslannika
Funka [Jan.–Dec. 1755. Reciprocal Communications and
Conferences of the Polish-Saxon Extraordinary Envoy in
Russia, Funck].
1756, *op.* 79/1
2 1756 Genv.–Dek. Gramoty k Imperatritse Elisavete I. ot
Pol'skago Korolia Avgusta III [Jan.–Dec. 1755. Letters to
Empress Elizabeth I from Polish King August III].
3 1756 Genv.–Dek. Pis'ma k Rossiiskim Ministram ot Pol'skikh

144

Vel'mozh i ot Saksonskikh Ministrov—s otpuskami na onyia otvetov [Jan.–Dec. 1756. Letters to Russian Ministers from Polish Magnates and from Saxon Ministers—with Dispatches of Replies on them].

5 1756 Genv.–Dek. Otpuski Reskriptov k Chrezvychainomu pri Pol'skom Dvore Poslaniku Grosu [Jan.–Dec. 1756. Dispatches of Rescripts to Extraordinary Envoy Gross at the Polish Court].

f. SNOSHENIIA ROSSII S FRANTSIEI
[*f.* RELATIONS OF RUSSIA WITH FRANCE]
1756, *op.* 93/1

1 1756 goda. Otpuski Gramot Imperatritsy Elisavety I. k Frantsuzskomu Koroliu Ludoviku XV.—tut zhe i Ego Korolia k Imperatritse Gramoty [1756. Dispatches of Letters of Empress Elizabeth I to French King Louis XV—and the Letters of the King to the Empress].

2 1756 Genv.–Dek. Perepiska Rossiiskikh Ministrov s Frantsuzskimi Statskimi Sekretariami [Jan.–Dec. 1756. Correspondence of Russian Ministers with French State Secretary].

3 1756 Iiul'–Dek. 31. Instruktsiia i otpuski Reskriptov i Kantselerskikh Tsidul k Poverennomu vo Frantsii v Delakh Nadvornomu Sovetniku Fedoru Bekhteevu [July–31 Dec. 1756. Instructions and Dispatches of Rescripts and Chancellery Letters to the *Chargé d'Affaires* in France, Court Councilor Feodor Bekhteev].

5 1756 Apr.–Dek. Priezd v Rossiiu Frantsuzskago Poverennago v Delakh Sheval'e Duglasa—tut zhe Soobshchenii i Vzaimnyia ob Nim Konferentsii [April–Dec. 1756. The Arrival in Russia of the French *Chargé d'Affaires* Chevalier Douglas—Reciprocal Communications of Conferences about it].

7 1756 Avg. 24. Delo ob Otpravlenii v Parizh Kollegii Iunkera Mikhaila Pleshcheeva Kurieram k Poverennomu v Delakh Bekhteevu [Aug. 24, 1756. Business about Sending the Courier College Junker Mikhail Pleshcheev to *Chargé d'Affaires* in Paris, Bekhteev].

8 1756 Sent.–Okt. 1761. Otpravlenie Ober Gofmarshala Grafa Mikhaila Petrovicha Bestuzheva-Riumina k Frantsuzskomu Dvoru Posolom [Sept. 1756–Oct. 1761. The Sending of Court Marshal Count Mikhail Petrovich Bestuzhev-Riumin to the French Court as Ambassador].

9 1756 Okt.–Dek. Otpuski Reskriptov k Polnomochnomu vo Frantsii Poslu Ober Gofmarshalu Grafu Mikhaile Bestuzhevu-Riuminu [Oct.–Dec. 1756. Dispatches of Rescripts to Pleni-

potentiary Ambassador in France, Court Marshal Count Mikhail Bestuzhev-Riumin].

10 1756 Dek. Reliatsii Naznachennago vo Frantsiiu Polnomo-chnago Posla Grafa Mikhaila Bestuzheva Riumina [Dec. 1756. Relations of the Appointed Plenipotentiary Ambassa-dor to France, Count Mikhail Bestuzhev-Riumin].

1757, op. 93/1

1 1757 goda. Otpuski Gramot Imperatritsy Elisavety I. k Frant-suzskomu Koroliu Ludoviku XV.–s Otvetami Ego na onyia [1757. Dispatches of Letters of Empress Elizabeth I. to the French King Louis XV–with His Replies to them].

2 1757 Genv.–Dek. Perepiska Rossiiskikh Ministrov s Frant-suzskimi Statskimi Sekretariami [Jan.–Dec. 1757. Correspon-dence of Russian Ministers with French State Secretaries].

3 1757 Genv.–Iiul. 31. Reskripty i Tsiduly Poverennomu vo Frantsii v Delakh Nadvornomu Sovetniku Fedoru Bekhteevu po den otzyva ego iz Parizha [Jan.–July 31, 1757. Rescripts and Letters to the *Chargé d'Affaires* in France, Court Coun-cilor Feodor Bekhteev on the day of his departure from Paris].

5 1757 Genv.–Dek. Otpuski Reskriptov k Polnomochnomu vo Frantsii Poslu Ober Gofmarshalu Grafu Mikhaile Petrovich Bestuzhevu Riuminu [Jan.–Dec. 1757. Dispatches of Res-cripts to Plenipotentiary Ambassador in France, Court Mar-shal Count Mikhail Petrovich Bestuzhev-Riumin].

7 1757 Genv.–Iiul. Soobshchenii vzaimnyia i Konferentsii Byvshikh v Rossii 1) Frantsuzskago Poverennago v Delakh Sheval'e Duglasa, i 2) Polnomochnago Posla Markiza Lop-italia, v Iiune Mtse priekhavshago v Rossiu. Pervaia Polovina. [Jan.–July 1757. Reciprocal Communications and Former Conferences in Russia (1) of the French *Chargé d'Affaires* Chevalier Douglas and (2) of the Plenipotentiary Ambassa-dor Marquis l'Hôpital, who arrived in Russia in June. First Half.].

8 1757 Iiul–Dek. 31. Soobshchenii vzaimnyia i Konferentsii byvshikh v Rossii 1) Frantsuzskago Poverennago v Delakh Shevale Duglasa, po den' (8 Avg.) ego iz Rossii otezda–i 2) Posla Markiza Lopitalia v Iiune Mtse Priekhavshago v Rossiiu. Vtoraia Polovina. [July–Dec. 31, 1757. Reciprocal Communications and Former Conferences in Russia (1) of the French *Chargé d'Affaires*, Chevalier Douglas on the day (8 Aug.) of his departure and (2) of Ambassador Marquis l'Hôpital who arrived in Russia in June. Second Half.].

TSENTRAL'NYI GOSUDARSTVENNYI ARKHIV DREVNIKH AKTOV (*Ts GADA*)
[*Central State Archives of Ancient Acts*]
f. 11, RAZRIAD XI. PEREPISKA RAZNYKH LITS
[*f.* 11, CATEGORY XI. CORRESPONDENCE OF VARIOUS PERSONS]
Delo
246 Prosheniia k Imperatritse Elizavete Grafa Aleksei Bestuzheva-Riumina [Petitions of Count Aleksei Bestuzhev-Riumin to Empress Elizabeth].
643 Pis'ma Stepena Apraksina k Imperatritse Elizavete [Letters of Stepan Apraksin to Empress Elizabeth].
f. 178, KONFERENTSIIA PRI VYSOCHAISHEM DVORE
[*f.* 178, CONFERENCE AT THE IMPERIAL COURT]
1 Protokoly Byvshei Dvore Konferentsii 1756 Mart 14–Dekabr 31 [Protocols of the Former Conference at the Court, Mar. 14–Dec. 31, 1756].
2 Protokoly Byvshei Dvore Konferentsii 1757 Jenvar 3–Iiun 30 [Protocols of the Former Conference at the Court, January 3–June 30, 1757].
3 Protokoly Byvshei Pri Dvore Konferentsii 1757 goda. Vtoraia Polovina [Protocols of the Former Conference at the Court, 1757. Second Half].
f. 276, *op.* 1, KOMMERTS-KOLLEGIIA
[*f.* 276, *op.* 1, COMMERCE COLLEGE]
1328 Po Ukazu Prav. Senata, ob Otdache Grafu Shuvalovu s 1757 goda vpred na 20 let na Otkup Tabaka, dlia Otpuska za More, 1757–1761 [According to the Decree of the Governmental Senate about Giving Count Shuvalov from 1757 on for 20 years the Control of Tobacco for Export by Sea, 1757–1761].
1329 Po Ukzau Prav. Senata, o Neotpuske za More i za Granitsu iz Malorussii Tabaka Nikomu, krome Ego Ciiatel'stvu Grafu Shuvalovu i Ego Poverennym 1757g. [According to the Decree of the Governmental Senate about Nobody, Except His Excellency Count Shuvalov and His Chargé, Exporting Tobacco by Sea or Land from Little Russia, 1757].
1393 Po Ukazu Prav. Senata, ob Otpuske Ego Velichestvu Koroliu Shvedskomu Trebuemago Im Kolichestva Khleba, do 20,000 bochek [According to the Decree of the Governmental Senate about Exporting to His Majesty the King of Sweden up to 20,000 barrels of Grain which he requested].

f. 1261, *op*. 1, VORONTSOVYKH
[*f*. 1261, *op*. 1, VORONTSOVS]

94 Akty diplomaticheskoi perepiski mezhdu russkim pravitel-'stvom i saksonskim dvorom, 15 II 1745–1755g. [Acts of Diplomatic Correspondence between the Russian Government and Saxon Court, 15 Feb. 1745–1755].

144 Reliatsiia russkogo rezidenta v Turtsii Obrezkova Imperatritse Elizavete Petrovne o reaktsii turetskogo pravitel'stva na reshenie Rossii pristupits k postroike na Dnepre kreposti "Sv. Elizavety." 26 VI 1754 [Relations of the Russian Resident in Turkey Obreskov to Empress Elizabeth Petrovna about the Reaction of the Turkish Government to the Decision of Russia to Construct a Fortress "St. Elizabeth" on the Dnieper. 26 June 1754].

154 Pis'mo Frantsuzskogo Stats-Sekretaria Rul'e Frantsuzskomu Ministru v Berline De-Liatush (De la Touch) o sodeistvii Shevale Duglasu v Ego poezdke v Rossiu. 11 II 1756 [Letter of French State Secretary Rouillé to French Minister in Berlin De la Touch about assisting Chevalier Douglas in his Journey to Russia. 11 Feb. 1756].

156 Ukaz Imperatr. Elizavety Petrovny rizhskomu Vitse-Gubernatoru gener-poruchiku Voeikovu ob okazanii podobaiushchei vstrechi i sodeistviia proezdu v Peterburg Frantsuzskogo Posla Duglasa. 19 III 1756 [Decree of Empress Elizabeth Petrovna to the Vice-Governor of Riga, Lieutenant-General Voeikov, about Rendering a Proper Reception and Assistance to the Journey to Petersburg of the French Envoy Douglas. 19 Mar. 1756].

160 Pis'mo Terc'e (?) Frantsuzskomu Poslu v Peterburge Duglasu s soobshcheniem raznykh cvedenii: o zemletriasenii, ob Anglii, o Shvetsii i Danii, o formirovanim armii i flota dlia voennykh tselei i dr. 28 IV/7 V 1756 g. [Letter of Tercier to the French Envoy in Petersburg, Douglas, with Communication of various informations: about an Earthquake, about England, about Sweden and Denmark, about the Formation of an Army and Fleet for Military Purposes etc. 28 Apr.–7 May 1756].

162 Pis'ma Frantsuzskogo Ministra Inostrannykh Del Rul'e Frantsuzskomu Poslu v Peterburg Duglasu. 18 VI 1756–14 VIII 1756 [Letters of the French Minister of Foreign Affairs Rouillé to the French Envoy in Petersburg, Douglas. 18 June–14 Aug. 1756].

163 Zapiska o Duglase i Ego Otnosheniakh s Semaei Voront-
     sovykh, o Upominaniem Faktov i Sobytii iz Pridvornei i
     Politicheskoi Zhizni. 12 VIII 1756 [Notes about Douglas and
     His Relations with the Vorontsov Family, about the Mention
     of Facts and Events from Court and Political Life. 12 Aug.
     1756].

169 Reskripty Marii Terezii gr. Estegazi, s Prilozheniem Proekta
     Konventsii Mezhdu Rossiei i Avstriei o Sovmestnoi Bor'be
     Protiv Domogatel'stv Prusskogo Korolia. 5 XI 1756–29 XI
     1756g. [Rescripts of Maria Theresa to Count Esterhazy,
     with Supplements of the Project of the Convention between
     Russia and Austria about Uniting in the Struggle Against the
     Importunity of the Prussian King. 5 Nov.–29 Nov. 1756].

170 Pis'ma Frantsuzskogo Rezidenta v Dantsige Diumona Dug-
     lasu. 30 XI 1756–10/21 I 1757g. [Letters of the French
     Resident in Gdańsk, Dumont, to Douglas. 30 Nov. 1756–10/21
     Jan. 1757].

171 Konventsiia mezhdu Rossiei i Avstriei v sviazi s obshchei
     bor'boi protiv Prussii. 1756g. [Convention between Russia
     and Austria in Connection with the Common Struggle
     Against Prussia. 1756].

175 Soobshchenie "Sheval'e" Duglasa Kantsleru [Bestuzhevu-
     Riuminu] o vstuplenii Fridrikha IIgo s voiskom v Saksonim,
     1756 [Communication of Chevalier Douglas to Chancellor
     Bestuzhev-Riumin about the entry of Frederick II with an
     army into Saxony, 1756].

177 Pis'mo Frantsuzskogo Poslannika v Shvetsii Markiza Dav-
     renkura Frantsuzskomu Poslu v Rossii Duglasu o Besedakh
     s Russkim Poslannikom v Shvetsii Paninym po Voprosam
     Vneshnei Politiki. 4 I 1757g. [Letter of French Envoy in
     Sweden Marquis d'Harincourt to French Envoy in Russia
     Douglas about Conversations with the Russian Envoy in
     Sweden, Panin, on Questions of Foreign Policy. 4 Jan. 1757].

178 Soobshcheniia Pol'skogo i Saksonskogo Sekretaria Polsol'stva
     Prasse Kantsleru [Bestuzhevu-Riuminu] o Sostoianii Pruss-
     kikh Voiny, o Kachestve Rukovodiashchikh Prusskikh Gen-
     eralov i Territorialnom Razmeshchenii Prusskikh Voisk. 19 I
     1757g. [Communications of the Polish and Saxon Secretary
     of the Embassy, Prasse, to Chancellor Bestuzhev-Riumin
     about the Condition of the Prussian Army, about the Qual-
     ity of Prussia's Leading Generals and the Territorial Distri-
     bution of the Prussian Army. 19 Jan. 1757].

308 Zapis' ob usloviiakh sovmestnoi podgotovki russkogo i vens-

kogo dvorov k bor'be protiv Prussii. XVIIIv.(?) [Record of the Conditions of the United Preparations of the Russian and Vienna Courts toward the Struggle Against Prussia. 18th century (?)].

312 Zapiska [Vorontsova, M.I.] o russko-turetskikh otnoshe-niiakh. Vt. Pol. XVIIIv. [Note of M. I. Vorontsov about Russo-Turkish Relations. 2nd half 18th century].

321 Protokol Konferentsii 9 Iiulia 1756g. [Protocol of the Conference, 9 July 1756].

353 Reliatsiia gen. Fel'dmarshala Apraksina Stepana Fedorovi-cha Imperatritse Elizavete Petrovne o Pobede pri Gros-Egersdorfe. 20 VIII 1757–14 XII 1757g. [Relations of General Field Marshal Stepan Fedorovich Apraksin to Empress Elizabeth Petrovna about the Victory at Gross Egersdorf. 20 Aug. 1757–14 Dec. 1757].

2780 Zapiski [M. I. Vorontsova] 1) "Opisanie Sostoianie Del vo Vremia Imp. Elizavety Petrovy"—Obzor Mezhdunarodnoi Obstanovki i Vneshnei Politiki Rossii i 2) "Kratkoe Izvestie" o Pogranichnykh s Rossiei Narodakh. 1762 [Notes of M. I. Vorontsov (1) "Description of the State of Affairs during Empress Elizabeth Petrovna," Review of the International Position and Foreign Policy of Russia, and (2) "Brief News" about the nations on the frontiers with Russia. 1762].

2812 Zapiska Neizvestnogo Litsa o Lichnost Imp. Elizavety Pet-rovny. XVIIIv. [Note of an Anonymous Person about the Personality of Empress Elizabeth Petrovna. 18th century].

f. 1261, op. 9.

25 1756 Iiulia 9–Okt. 15. Pis'ma Vitse-Kantslera Grafa Mikhaila Vorontsova k Gospodinu Bekhteevu o Politicheskakh De-lakh [July 9–Oct. 15, 1756. Letters of Vice-Chancellor Count Mikhail Vorontsov to Mr. Bekhteev about Political Affairs].

29 1756 Noiabria 27. Pis'mo (v kopii) Frantsuzskogo Ministra Rul'e k Poverennomu v Delakh Duglasu [Nov. 27, 1756. Letter (copy) of French Minister Rouillé to Chargé d'Affaires Douglas].

30 1757 Jenv. 4. Iz Stokgolma. Kopiia s Pis'ma Duglasa k Kant-sleru Grafu Bestuzhevu s Politicheskoi sistemy Shvedskago Pravleniia [Jan. 4, 1757. From Stockholm. Copy of a Letter of Douglas to Chancellor Bestuzhev of the Conduct of the Political System of Sweden].

f. 1263, op. 1, GOLITSYNYKH
[f. 1263, op. 1, GOLITSYNS]

27 1755g. Kniga Vkhodiashchikh Del Pokhodnogo-Voennogo

Kantseliarii Admirala Golitsyna, Mikhaila Mikhailovicha [1755. Incoming Communications on Naval Operations, Chancellery of Admiral Mikhail Mikhailovich Golitsyn].

29   1757god. Kniga Vkhodiashchikh Del Pok ..odnogo-Voennogo Kantseliarii Admirala Golitsyna, Mikhaila Mikhailovicha [1757. Incoming Communications on Naval Operations, Chancellery of Admiral Mikhail Mikhailovich Golitsyn].

56   1755g. Zhurnal Iskhodiashchim Delam Pokhodnogo Voennogo Kantseliarii Admirala Golitsyna, Mikhaila Mikhailovicha [1755. Outgoing Communications on Naval Operations, Chancellery of Admiral Mikhail Mikhailovich Golitsyn].

57   1756g. Zhurnal Iskhodiashchim Delam Pokhodnogo-Voennoge Kantseliarii Admirala Golitsyna, Mikhaila Mikhailovicha [1756. Outgoing Communications on Naval Operations, Chancellery of Admiral Mikhail Mikhailovich Golitsyn].

58   1757g. Protokoly Iskhodiashchim Delam Pokodnogo-Voennogo Kantseliarii Admirala Golitsyna, Mikhaila Mikhailovicha [1757. Outgoing Protocols on Naval Operations, Chancellery of Admiral Mikhail Mikhailovich Golitsyn].

92   1755g. Ukaz Elizavety Petrovny o Naznachenii Kniazia Golitsyna, Aleksandra Mikhailovicha Chrezvychainym Poslannikom v Angliiu i ob Otozvanii Polnomochnogo Ministra Grafa Chernyshova [1755. Decree of Elizabeth Petrovna about the Appointment of Prince Alexander Mikhailovich Golitsyn Extraordinary Envoy to England and about the Recall of Plenipotentiary Minister Count Chernyshev].

93   1755g. Gramoty Elizavety Petrovny k Angliiskomu Koroliu Georgu II ob Otozvanii Polnomochnogo Ministra Grafa Chernyshova i o Naznachenii Russkim Polnomochnym Poslannikom v Anglii Kniazy Golitsyna, Aleksandra Mikhailovicha [1755. Letters of Elizabeth Petrovna to the English King, George II, about the Recall of Plenipotentiary Minister Count Chernyshev and about the Appointment of Prince Alexander Mikhailovich Golitsyn Russian Plenipotentiary Envoy to England].

469 1757g. Pis'ma Fel'dmarshala Apraksina, Stepana Fedorovicha k Golitsynu, A. M. [1757. Letters of Field Marshal Stepan Fedorovich Apraksin to A. M. Golitsyn].

470 1756g. Pis'mo Fel'dmarshala Apraksina, Stepana Fedorovicha

k Golitsynu, A. M. [1756. Letter of Field Marshal Stepan Fedorovich Apraksin to A. M. Golitsyn].

576 1757g. Pis'mo Bernstorfa (Bernstorff) k Golitsynu, A. M. [1757. Letter of Bernstorff to A. M. Golitsyn].

581 1756, 1757gg. Pis'ma Berensa (Berens) iz Rigi k Golitsynu, A. M. [1756, 1757. Letters of Berens from Riga to A. M. Golitsyn].

585 1749, 1750, 1755–1758 gg. Pis'ma Grafa Bestuzheva-Riumina k Golitsynu, A. M. [1749, 1750, 1755–1758. Letters of Count Bestuzhev-Riumin to A. M. Golitsyn].

586 1757g. Pis'ma Bekhteeva, Fedora k Golitsynu, A. M. [1757. Letters of Feodor Bekhteev to A. M. Golitsyn].

684 1757g. Pis'ma Rezidenta Biutnera, M. (Büttner, M.) k Golitsynu, A. M. [1757. Letters of Resident M. Büttner to A. M. Golitsyn].

793 1755g. Pis'ma Kantslera Vorontsova, Mikhaila Larionovicha k Golitsynu, A. M. [1755. Letters of Chancellor Mikhail Larionovich Vorontsov to A. M. Golitsyn].

794 1756g. Pis'ma Kantslera Grafa Vorontsova, Mikhaila Larionovicha k Golitsynu, A. M. [1756. Letters of Chancellor Mikhail Larionovich to A. M. Golitsyn].

1000 1755g. Pis'ma Kn. Golovkina, Ivana k Golitsynu, A. M. [1755. Letters of Prince Ivan Golovkin to A. M. Golitsyn].

1001 1756g. Pis'ma Golovkina, Ivana k Golitsynu, A. M. [1756. Letters of Ivan Golovkin to A. M. Golitsyn].

1002 1757g. Pis'ma Posla Kniazia Golovkina, Ivana k Golitsynu, A. M. iz Gagi [1757. Letters of Ambassador from The Hague, Prince Ivan Golovkin to A. M. Golitsyn].

1028 1756g. Pis'mo Gol'dernessa (Holdernesse) k Golitsynu, A. M. [1756. Letter of Holdernesse to A. M. Golitsyn].

1089 1755g. Pis'mo Grossa iz Drezdena k Golitsynu, A. M. [1755. Letter of Gross from Dresden to A. M. Golitsyn].

1090 1756g. Pis'ma Grossa, Genrikha k Golitsynu, A. M. [1756. Letters of Heinrich Gross to A. M. Golitsyn].

1091 1757g. Pis'ma Grossa, Genrikha k Golitsynu, A. M. iz Varshavy [1757. Letters of Heinrich Gross from Warsaw to A. M. Golitsyn].

1126 1757g. Pis'ma Kn. Golitsyna, Dmitriia Mikhailovicha k Golitsynu, A. M. [1757. Letters of Prince Dmitri Mikhailovich Golitsyn to A. M. Golitsyn].

1619 1756g. Pis'ma Posla Keizerlinga (Keyserling) k Golitsynu,

A. M. [1756. Letters of Ambassador Keyserling to A. M. Golitsyn].

1620   1739, 1757, 1759 gg. Pis'ma Russkogo Posla v Vene Keizerlinga k Golitsynu, A. M. [1739, 1757, 1759. Letters of the Russian Ambassador in Vienna, Keyserling, to A. M. Golitsyn].

1659   1757g. Pis'ma i Kopiia Pis'ma ot 21 Iiunia Generala Kobenua (Cobenzl) k Golitsynu, A. M. iz Briusselia [1757. Letters and Copies of Letters from June 21 of General Cobenzl from Brussels to A. M. Golitsyn].

1685   1757g. Pis'ma Kolloredo (Colloredo) iz Veny k Golitsynu, A. M. [1757. Letters of Colloredo from Vienna to A. M. Golitsyn].

1702   1757g. Pis'ma Kanits (Kaunitz) k Golitsynu, A. M. [1757. Letters of Kaunitz to A. M. Golitsyn].

1764   1756g. Pis'ma Barona Korfa k Golitsynu, A. M. iz Kopengagena [1756. Letters of Baron Korf from Copenhagen to A. M. Golitsyn].

1765   1757g. Genvar'-Iiul'. Pis'ma Barona Korfa k Golitsynu, A. M. iz Kopengagena [Jan.–July, 1757. Letters of Baron Korf from Copenhagen to A. M. Golitsyn].

1766   1757g. Avgust-Dekabr. Pis'ma Barona Korfa k Golitsynu, A. M. iz Kopengagena [Aug.–Dec. 1757. Letters of Baron Korf from Copenhagen to A. M. Golitsyn].

2249   1757g., 1761g. Pis'ma Mishelia (Michel) k Golitsynu, A. M. [1757, 1761. Letters of Michel to A. M. Golitsyn].

2448   1756g. Pis'ma Nevkaetelia (Newcastle) k Golitsynu, A. M. [1756. Letters of Newcastle to A. M. Golitsyn].

2484   1755g. Pis'ma Russkogo Posla v Turtsii Obrezkova, Alekseia k Golitsynu, A. M. [1755. Letters of the Russian Ambassador in Turkey Aleksei Obreskov to A. M. Golitsyn].

2485   1756g. Pis'ma Obreskova, Alekseia k Golitsynu, A. M. [1756. Letters of Aleksei Obreskov to A. M. Golitsyn].

2486   1757g. Pis'ma Russkogo Posla v Turtsii Obrezkova k Golitsynu, A. M. [1757. Letters of the Russian Ambassador in Turkey, Obreskov, to A. M. Golitsyn].

2652   1756g. Pis'ma Kamergera Grafa Panina, Nikita Ivanovicha k Golitsynu, A. M. [1756. Letters of Chamberlain Count Nikita Ivanovich Panin to A. M. Golitsyn].

2653   1757g. Pis'ma Kamergera Grafa Panina, Nikita Ivanovicha Golitsynu, A. M. [1757. Letters of Chamberlain Count Nikita Ivanovich Panin to A. M. Golitsyn].

3104 1755g. Pis'mo Grafa Saltykova, Sergeia Vladimirovicha k Golitsynu, A. M. [1755. Letter of Count Sergei Vladimirovich Saltykov to A. M. Golitsyn].

3105 1756g. Pis'ma Grafa Saltykova, Sergeia Vladimirovicha k Golitsynu, A. M. [1756. Letters of Count Sergei Vladimirovich Saltykov to A. M. Golitsyn].

3106 1757g. Pis'ma Grafa Saltykova, Sergeia Vladimirovicha k Golitsynu, A. M. [1757. Letters of Count Sergei Vladimirovich Saltykov to A. M. Golitsyn].

3130 1756g. Pis'ma Grafa Saltykova iz Gamburge k Golitsynu [1756. Letters of Count Saltykov from Hamburg to Golitsyn].

8369 1756g. Kniga Vkhodiashchikh Del Pokhodnogo-voennogo Kantseliarii Admirala Golitsyna, Mikhaila Mikhailovicha [1756. Incoming Communications on Naval Operatons, Chancellery Admiral Mikhail Mikhailovich Golitsyn].

TSENTRAL'NYI GOSUDARSTVENNYI VOENNO-ISTORICHESKII ARKHIV SSSR
(TsGVIA) [Central State Archives of Military History of the USSR]
f. 48, op. 202, P. SHUVALOV
[f. 48, op. 202, P. SHUVALOV]

6 Iz Del Grafa P. Shuvalova [From the Business of Count P. Shuvalov].

10 Iz Del Grafa P. Shuvalova [From the Business of Count P. Shuvalov].

13 Iz Del Grafa P. Shuvalova [From the Business of Count P. Shuvalov].

15 Iz Del Grafa P. Shuvalova [From the Business of Count P. Shuvalov].

f. VUA: VOENNO-UCHENNOGO ARKHIVA
GL. SHTABA
[f. VUA: MILITARY-EXERCISE ARCHIVES OF
THE CHIEF OF STAFF]

1655 Iz Reliatsii Voennoi Kollegia, 1756. V Arkhiv Voenno-Topograficheskago Delo [From the Relations of the War College, 1756. In the Archives of Military Topographical Affairs].

1657a Reliatsii Grl. Apraksina 1757. V. Voennotopografi Delo [Relations of General Apraksin, 1757. In Military Topografical Affairs].

1657 II Iz Reliatsii Generala Fermora, 1757. V Arkhiv Voenno Topograficheskago Delo [From the Relations of General Fermor, 1757. In the Archives of Military Topographical Affairs].

United States

THE CORRESPONDENCE OF SIR CHARLES HANBURY WILLIAMS (*CHW*)
(Owned by Shelden Wilmarth Lewis, Farmington, Connecticut)
Vols.: 20–10884
        21–10878
        22–10885
        64–10911

PRIMARY SOURCES

Bartenev, P. J., ed. *Arkhiv Kniazia Vorontsova* [The Archives of Prince Vorontsov]. Moscow, 1870–1895. Vols. III, VI.

Boutaric, M. E., ed. *Correspondance secrète inédite de Louis XV*. 2 vols. Paris, 1866.

Broglie, Duc de, ed. *The King's Secret: Being the Secret Correspondence of Louis XV with His Diplomatic Agents from 1752 to 1774*. 2 vols. London, 1879.

Frederick II. *Politische Correspondenz Friedrichs des Grossen*. Berlin, 1879–1939. Vols. XI, XII, XIII, XIV. (Cited as PC.)

———. *Die politischen Testamente Friedrichs des Grossen*. Ed. G. B. Volz. Berlin, 1920.

Goriaïnow, S., ed. *Correspondance de Catherine Alexeievna, Grande Duchesse de Russie, et de Sir Charles H. Williams, Ambassadeur d'Angleterre, 1756 et 1757*. Moscow, 1909.

———. *Memoires du roi Stanislas-Auguste Poniatowski*. 2 vols. St. Petersburg, 1914–1924.

Hertzberg, Ewald Friedrich, Graf von. *Recueil des déductions, manifestes, déclaration traités et autres actes et écrits publiés, qui ont été rédigés et publiés pour la cour de Prusse par le ministre d'état Comte de Hertzberg depuis l'année 1756 jusqu' à l'année 1790*. 3 vols. Berlin, 1790–1795.

Ilchester, the Earl of & Mrs. Langford-Brooke, eds. and trans. *Correspondence of Catherine the Great When Grand-Duchesse, with Sir Charles Hanbury-Williams and Letters from Count Poniatowski*. London, 1928. (Cited as ICC.)

Maroger, Dominique, ed. *The Memoirs of Catherine the Great*. London, 1955.

Martens, F. de, ed. *Recueil de traités et conventions, conclus par la Russie avec les puissances étrangères*. St. Petersburg, 1874–1909, Vols. I, IX.

Ozanam, D. and M. Antoine, eds. *Correspondance secrète du Comte de Broglie avec Louis XV: 1756–1774*. 2 vols. Paris, 1956–1961.

Publicationen aus den K. Preussischen Staatsarchiven. Vol. 74. *Pre-*

ussische und österreichische Acten zur Vorgeschichte des siebenjährigen Krieges. Ed. G. Küntzel and G. B. Volz. Leipzig, 1899.
(Cited as PPS.)

Recueil des instructions données aux ambassadeurs et ministres de
France depuis les traités de Westphalie jusqu' à la révolution fran-
çaise. Paris, 1884. Vol. IX.

Sbornik imperatorskago russkago istoricheskago obschestva [The
Collection of the Imperial Russian Historical Society]. St. Petersburg, 1867–1916. Vols. CXXXVI, CXLVIII. (Cited as SIRIO.)

Semiletniaia voina (materialy o deistviiakh russkoi armii i flota v
1756–1762 gg.) [The Seven Years' War (Materials about the Operations of the Russian Army and Fleet: 1756–1762)]. Moscow,
1948.

SELECTED SECONDARY WORKS

Albion, Robert G. Forests and Sea Power: The Timber Problem of
the Royal Navy, 1652–1862. Cambridge, Mass., 1926.

Andreas, Willy. Friedrich der Grosse und der siebenjährige Krieg.
Leipzig, 1940.

Arneth, Alfred Ritter von. Geschichte Maria Theresias. Vienna,
1863–1879. Vols. I–III.

Aster, Heinrich. Beleuchtung der Kriegswirren zwischen Preussen
und Sachsen von Ende August bis Ende Oktober 1756. Dresden,
1848.

Bamford, Paul W. Forests and French Sea Power, 1660–1789. Toronto, 1956.

Beer, Adolf. Aufzeichnungen des Grafen William Bentinck über
Maria Theresia. Vienna, 1871.

———. "Denkschriften des Fürsten Wenzel Kaunitz-Rittberg," Archiv
für österreichische Geschichte, XLVIII (Vienna, 1872), 1–162.

———. "Die österreichische Politik in den Jahren 1755 und 1756,"
Historische Zeitschrift, XXVII (Munich, 1872), 282–373.

———. "Zur Geschichte des Jahres 1756," Mittheilungen des Instituts
für oesterreichische Geschichtsforschung, XVII (Innsbruck, 1896),
109–160.

Beskrovnyi, L. G. Khrestomatiia po russkoi voennoi istorii [Reader
in Russian Military History]. Moscow, 1947.

———. Ocherki voennoi istorografii Rossii [Outline of Military Historiography of Russia]. Moscow, 1962.

Bilbassoff, B. Geschichte Katharina II. 2 vols. Berlin, 1891–1893.

Braubach, Max. Versailles und Wien von Ludwig XIV bis Kaunitz.
Bonn, 1952.

Broglie, Albert, Duc de. *L'alliance autrichienne, par le duc de Broglie.* Paris, 1895.

Brüggemann, Fritz. *Der siebenjährige Krieg im Spiegel der zeitgenössischen Literatur.* Leipzig, 1935.

Butterfield, Herbert. "The Reconstruction of an Historical Episode: The History of the Enquiry into the Origins of the Seven Years War," *Man on His Past.* Cambridge, 1955.

Daniels, E. "Friedrich der Grosse und Maria Theresia am Vorabend des siebenjährigen Krieges," *Preussische Jahrbücher,* C (Berlin, 1900), 11–62.

Delbrück, Hans. "Friedrich der Grosse und der Ursprung des siebenjährigen Krieges," *Preussische Jahrbücher,* LXXXIV (Berlin, 1896), 32–53.

———. "Ueber den Ursprung des siebenjährigen Krieges," *Preussische Jahrbücher,* LXXXVI (Berlin, 1896), 416–427.

———. "Der Ursprung des siebenjährigen Krieges," *Preussische Jahrbücher,* LXXIX (Berlin, 1895), 254–282.

Dorn, Walter L. *Competition for Empire, 1740–1763.* New York, 1940.

Duncker, Max. "Preussen und England im siebenjährigen Kriege," *Preussische Jahrbücher,* LV (Berlin, 1885), 125–150.

———. "Der siebenjährige Krieg," *Historische Zeitschrift,* XIX (Munich, 1868), 103–180.

Dzhincharadze, V. Z. "Obzor fonda Vorontsovykh, khraniashchegocia v TsGADA" [Review of the fund Vorontsovs preserved in TsGADA], *Istoricheskie Zapiski,* XXXII (Moscow, 1950), 242–265.

Eldon, Carl William. *England's Subsidy Policy Towards the Continent During the Seven Years' War.* Philadelphia, 1938.

Firsov, N. N. *Usloviia, pri kotorykh nachalas semiletniaia voina* [Conditions under which the Seven Years' War began]. Moscow, 1916.

Fitzlyon, Kyril, trans. and ed. *The Memoirs of Princess Dashkov.* London, 1958.

Gerhard, Dietrich. *England und der Aufstieg Russlands.* Munich, 1933.

Herrmann, Ernst. "Sächsisch-polnische Beziehungen während des siebenjährigen Krieges zum russischen Hof und insbesondere zum Grosskanzler Bestuschew," *Preussische Jahrbücher,* XLVII (Berlin, 1881), 558–589; XLVIII (Berlin, 1881), 1–23.

Herrmann, Otto. "Eine Beurteilung Friedrichs des Grossen aus dem Jahre 1753," *Forschungen zur brandenburgischen und preussischen Geschichte,* XXXIV (Munich and Berlin, 1922), 239–264.

Horn, David Bayne. *Sir Charles Hanbury Williams & European Diplomacy (1747–58)*. London, 1930.

Horowitz, Sidney. "Franco-Russian Relations, 1740–1746," unpublished Ph.D. dissertation (New York University, 1951), 641 pp.

Ilchester, the Earl of, and Mrs. Langford-Brooke. *The Life of Sir Charles Hanbury-Williams: Poet, Wit and Diplomatist*. London, 1928.

Kirchner, Walther. "Relations économiques entre la France et la Russie au XVIIIe siècle," *Revue d'histoire économique et sociale*, XXIX:2 (Paris, 1961), 158–197.

Kistler, Charles Edward. "British Diplomacy and Russia During the Seven Years' War," unpublished Ph.D. dissertation (University of Michigan, 1946), 311 pp.

Konopczyński, Władysław. *Polska w dobie wojny siedmioletniej* [Poland during the Seven Years' War]. 2 vols. Kraków, 1909–1911.

Korobkov, N. *Semiletniaia voina (deistviia rossii v 1756–1762 gg.)* [The Seven Years' War: Operations of Russia, 1756–1762]. Moscow, 1940.

Koser, Reinhold. "Neue Veröffentlichungen zur Vorgeschichte des siebenjährigen Krieges," *Historische Zeitschrift*, LXXVII (Munich and Leipzig, 1896), 1–40.

———. "Preussen und Russland im Jahrzehnt vor dem siebenjährigen Kriege," *Preussische Jahrbücher*, XLVII (Berlin, 1881), 285–305, 466–493.

———. "Die preussische Kriegsführung im siebenjährigen Kriege," *Historische Zeitschrift*, XCII (Munich and Berlin, 1903–1904), 239–273.

———. "Die preussischen Finanzen im siebenjährigen Kriege," *Forschungen zur brandenburgischen und preussischen Geschichte*, XIII (Leipzig, 1900), 153–217, 329–375.

Küntzel, Georg. "Zur Geschichte Friedrichs des Grossen," *Forschungen zur brandenburgischen und preussischen Geschichte*, XV (Leipzig, 1902), 497–519.

Lehmann, Max. *Friedrich der Grosse und der Ursprung des siebenjährigen Krieges*. Leipzig, 1894.

———. "Urkundliche Beiträge zur Geschichte des Jahres 1756," *Mittheilungen des Instituts für oesterreichische Geschichtsforschung*. XVI (Innsbruck, 1895), 480–491.

Lodge, Sir Richard. *Great Britain & Prussia in the Eighteenth Century*. Oxford, 1923.

———. *Studies in Eighteenth Century Diplomacy (1740–1748)*. London, 1930.

Luckwaldt, Friedrich. "Die Westminsterkonvention," *Preussische Jahrbücher*, LXXX (Berlin, 1895), 230–267.

Mayer, Franz M. "Zur Geschichte des siebenjährigen Krieges," *Mittheilungen des Instituts für oesterreichische Geschichtsforschung*, VII (Innsbruck, 1886), 378–435.

Masslowski, E. I. *Der siebenjährige Krieg nach Russischer Darstellung*. 3 vols. Berlin, 1888–1893.

McGill, William James, Jr. "The Political Education of Wenzel Anton von Kaunitz-Rittberg," unpublished Ph.D. dissertation (Harvard University, 1960), 230 pp.

Mediger, Walther. *Moskaus Weg nach Europa*. Braunschweig, 1952.

Meyer, Robert. *Die Neutralitätsverhandlungen des Kurfürstentums Hannover beim Ausbruch des siebenjährigen Krieges*. Kiel, 1912.

Naudé, Albert. "Aus ungedruckten Memoiren der Brüder Friedrichs des Grossen. Die Entstehung des siebenjährigen Krieges und der General von Winterfeldt," *Forschungen zur brandenburgischen und preussischen Geschichte*, I (Leipzig, 1888), 231–269.

——. "Beiträge zur Entstehungsgeschichte des siebenjährigen Krieges. Teil I," *Forschungen zur brandenburgischen und preussischen Geschichte*, VIII (Leipzig, 1895), 523–618.

——. "Beiträge zur Entstehungsgeschichte des siebenjährigen Krieges. Teil II," *Forschungen zur brandenburgischen und preussischen Geschichte*. IX (Leipzig, 1897), 101–328.

Novotny, Alexander. *Staatskanzler Kaunitz als geistige Persönlichkeit*. Vienna, 1947.

Oliva, L. Jay. "French Policy in Russia: 1755–1762," unpublished Ph.D. dissertation (Syracuse University, 1960), 411 pp.

——. *Misalliance: A Study of French Policy in Russia During the Seven Years' War*. New York, 1964.

Oncken, Wilhelm. *Das Zeitalter Friedrichs des Grossen*. 2 vols. Berlin, 1881–1882.

Porsch, R.O.K. *Die Beziehungen Friedrichs des Grossen zur Turkei bis zum Beginn und während des siebenjährigen Krieg*. Marburg, 1897.

Ranke, Leopold von. *Der Ursprung des siebenjährigen Krieges*. Leipzig, 1871.

Reading, Douglas K. *The Anglo-Russian Commercial Treaty of 1734*. New Haven, Conn. 1938.

Rojdestvensky, S. and I. Lubimenko. "Contribution à l'histoire des relations commerciales franco-russes au XVIIIe siècle," *Revue d'histoire économique et sociale*, XVII (Paris, 1929), 363–402.

Ropes, Arthur R. "The Causes of the Seven Years' War," *Transactions of the Royal Historical Society*, New Series, IV (London, 1889), 143–170.

――. "Frederick The Great's Invasion of Saxony and the Prussian 'Mémoire Raisonné,' 1756," *Transactions of the Royal Historical Society*, New Series, V (London, 1891), 157–175.

Rothfels, Hans. "Friedrich der Grosse in den Krisen des siebenjährigen Krieges," *Historische Zeitschrift*, CXXXIV (Berlin and Munich, 1926), 14–30.

Rulhière, Claude de. *Histoire de l'anarchie de Pologne*. Paris, 1819. Vols. I, II.

Schaefer, Arnold. *Geschichte des siebenjährigen Krieges*. 2 vols. Berlin, 1867–1874.

――. "Der Ursprung des siebenjährigen Krieges nach den Acten des österreichischen Archivs," *Historische Zeitschrift*, XXIV (Munich, 1870), 365–405.

Schmidt, K. Rahbek. "Wie ist Panins Plan zu einem Nordischen System enstanden?" *Zeitschrift für Slawistik*, II:3 (Berlin, 1957), 406–422.

Schmidt, Otto Eduard. *Minister Graf Brühl und Karl Heinrich von Heinecken: Briefe und Akten, Charakteristiken und Darstellungen zur sachsischen Geschichte (1733–1763)*. Leipzig and Berlin, 1921.

Schwarze, Karl. *Der siebenjährige Krieg in der zeitgenössischen deutschen Literatur*. Berlin, 1936.

Seraphim, Ernst. *Geschichte Liv-,Est-und Kurlands*. Reval, 1895–1896. Vol. II.

Shchepkin, Evgenii. *Russko-Avstriiskii soiuz vo vremia Semiletnei Voiny, 1746–1758 gg.* [The Russo-Austrian union during the Seven Years' War, 1746–1758]. St. Petersburg, 1902.

Sistematicheskii katalog delam gosudarstvennoi Kommerts-Kollegii [Systematic catalog of the affairs of the State Commerce College]. St. Petersburg, 1884.

Solov'ëv, S. M. *Istoriia rossii s drevneishikh vremën* [History of Russia from the oldest times]. Moscow, 1959–1966. Vol. XXIV.

Stenzel, G. A. H. *Geschichte des preussischen Staats*. Hamburg and Gotha, 1830–1854. Vol. IV.

Strieder, Jakob. *Kritische Forschungen zur österreichischen Politik vom Aachener Frieden bis zum Beginne des siebenjährigen Krieges*. Leipzig, 1906.

――. "Maria Theresia, Kaunitz und die österreichische Politik von 1748–1755," *Historische Vierteljahrschrift*, XIII (Leipzig, 1910), 494–509.

Stuhr, P. F. *Forschungen und Erläuterungen über Hauptpunkte der Geschichte des siebenjährigen Krieges.* Hamburg, 1842.

Vandal, Albert. *Louis XV et Elizabeth de Russie.* Paris, 1882.

Vitzthum von Eckstädt, Karl Friedrich. *Die Geheimnisse des sächsischen Cabinets, Ende 1745 bis Ende 1756.* 2 vols. Stuttgart, 1866.

Volz, Gustav Bertold. *Kriegfuhrung und Politik König Friedrichs der Grossen in dem ersten Jahren des siebenjährigen Krieges.* Berlin, 1895.

——. "Zur Entstehung der Politischen Testamente Friedrichs des Grossen von 1752 und 1768," *Forschungen zur brandenburgischen und preussischen Geschichte,* XXXII (Munich and Leipzig, 1920), 369–384.

——. "Ungedruckte Briefe und Dichtungen Friedrichs des Grossen," *Forschungen zur brandenburgischen und preussischen Geschichte,* XLV (Berlin, 1933), 366–374.

Waddington, Richard. *Louis XV et le renversement des alliances: Préliminaires de la guerre de sept ans (1754–1756).* Paris, 1896.

——. *La guerre de sept ans; histoire diplomatique et militaire.* 5 vols. Paris, 1899–1914.

Wagner, Ferdinand. "Die europäischen Mächte in der Beurtheilung Friedrichs des Grossen 1746–1757," *Mittheilungen des Instituts für oesterreichische Geschichtsforschung,* XX (Innsbruck, 1899), 397–443.

Weiss, Joseph. "Der Streit über den Ursprung des siebenjährigen Krieges," *Historisches Jahrbuch,* XVIII (Munich, 1897), 311–321, 831–848.

Winter, Gustav. "Die Gründung des kaiserlichen und königlichen Haus-,Hof-und Staatsarchivs, 1749–1762," *Archiv für österreichische Geschichte,* XCII (Vienna, 1902), 1–82.

Wolf, Gustav. "Friedrichs des Grossen Angriffspläne gegen Österreich im siebenjährigen Kriege," *Forschungen zur brandenburgischen und preussischen Geschichte,* XIII (Leipzig, 1900), 552–555.

Index

Anglo-Russian Subsidy Treaty: negotiations for, 7–10, 15–16, 22–24; provisions of, 22; Empress Elizabeth's additions to, 22–24, 41–45; British reaction to appended declaration, 22–24, 67–69; final signing of, 24; Elizabeth's refusal to ratify, 36–41; ratification of, 41; reaction of pro-French group to declaration, 45; Russian proposal to reject treaty, 53–54; as barrier to Franco-Russian rapprochement, 63

Apraksin, General Stepan: allies himself with Peter and Catherine, 102–103, 111–112; headquarters at Riga, 114, 124

Augustus III of Poland: dilemma over invasion of Saxony, 96–98; asks assistance from Empress Elizabeth, 115

Austria: as traditional ally of England, 5; negotiations for Austro-Russian military alliance against Prussia, 54, 55, 58–60, 121–123; decline in diplomatic relations with Great Britain, 71–73; Treaty of Versailles, 73–74; fears of Russian expansion, 74–75; asks Russia for delay in attack on Prussia, 84–85; mobilization, 86; decline in Austro-Russian relations, 99–100; effect of Russian military inaction on, 112; sought military aid from Russia, 116. See also

Maria Theresa

Austro-Russian treaty against Prussia: negotiations for, 4, 54, 55, 58–60, 121–123; terms of treaty, 122–123; Maria Theresa's secret declaration to, 123

Bekhteev, Feodor, 75, 76

Bestuzhev-Riumin, Alexis Petrovich (Russian grand chancellor): director of Russian foreign policy, 12; Anglo-Russian Subsidy Treaty negotiations, 16, 38, 39–41; Michael Vorontsov's intrigues against, 25–28, 44–45, 49, 51–54, 77–78, 126–127; instigated Conference at the Imperial Court against Prussia, 40, 47, 48; comments on Convention of Westminster, 42–43; presents Russian position in European politics, 49, 52–53; collapse of his French policies, 77–78, 126–127; relations with Grand Duchess Catherine, 106–107; changes his attitude toward Prussia, 107–108; delay of Russian military offensive against Prussia, 111–112, 123–124; concern with protection of Hanover, 118, 119–120

Bestuzhev-Riumin, Michael: as Russian ambassador to Poland, 61, 115–116; named ambassador to France, 78–79, 94

Betskoi, Ivan, argues for French

164

INDEX

British foreign policy, 71–73; presents foreign policy statement to Russian court, 100; secret declaration to Austro-Russian treaty, 123. *See also* Austria

Memel, surrender of, 124

Michell, Prussian envoy to Great Britain, 30–31

Mitchell, Andrew, British ambassador to Prussia, 81, 81n, 82, 88–89

Newcastle, Duke of, chief minister of England, 8, 9, 15, 17–20 *passim*, 30, 69, 69n

Ottoman Empire: reaction to Convention of Westminster, 60; reaction to Russia's accession to Treaty of Versailles, 98; Russian fear of, 102, 117–119; secret declaration to Treaty of Versailles concerning, 119

Peter, Grand Duke: political attitudes of, 50, 101–103; as Peter III, effects treaty with Prussia taking Russia out of Seven Years' War, 101; comparison with Grand Duchess Catherine, 103

Peter the Great, 3–4

Peter III. *See* Peter, Grand Duke

Podewils, Prussian minister of state, disregarded by Frederick II, 90

Poland: Empress Elizabeth's plans for, 4, 55–56; negotiations for passage of Russian troops through Poland, 94–98, 115–117. *See also* Polish-Lithuanian Commonwealth

Polish-Lithuanian Commonwealth: Russia strengthens interests in, 60–62; fear of Russian influence in, 74; France and Russia's interest in, 94–95; Empress Elizabeth's negotiations for crossing, 94–98, 115–117

Pomerania, Frederick II marches into, 88–89

Poniatowski, Stanislas: lover of Grand Duchess Catherine, 105, 106; states terms of Russian

march through Poland, 117

Prussia: Frederick II as ruler of, 3–4; as threat to Hanover, 5, 17, 19–20; general mobilization, 80–90; begins hostilities, 91–100; defeated at Memel and Gross-Jägersdorf, 124. *See also* Frederick II

Rouen, Michel de, 26, 65–66, 75

Rouillé, Antoine Louis, 13, 97

Russia: Westernization under Peter the Great, 3–4; foreign policy aims under Empress Elizabeth, 4; Anglo-Russian Subsidy Treaty, 7–10, 22–24, 36–45; pro-French interest at Russian court, 26–28, 102–103, 109–110; preparations for war with Prussia, 31–32, 47–56; establishment of Conference of the Imperial Court, 40, 47–56, 126; foreign policy clashes between Bestuzhev-Riumin and Vorontsov, 25–28, 44–45, 49, 51–54, 77–78, 126–127; plans for Austro-Russian alliance against Prussia, 54, 55, 58–60, 121–123; relations with Polish-Lithuanian Commonwealth, 55–56, 60–62, 94–98, 116; army strength, 57–58, 114; mobilization for war against Prussia, 57–66; naval strength, 58n; rapprochement with France, 61–66, 74, 75–79; decline in diplomatic relations with Great Britain, 68–71; Treaty of Versailles, 73–74, 98–99, 119; effect of Treaty of Versailles on foreign policy, 74–75; delay in invasion of Prussia, 87–88, 111–112, 123–124; decline in Austro-Russian relations, 99–100; illness of Empress Elizabeth, 101, 112–113, 127; crisis at Russian court, 101–113; intrigues of Grand Duchess Catherine, 101–113; fear of Turkey, 102, 117–119; unsuccessful in negotiations for accession to Treaty of Versailles, 117–120; secret declaration to Treaty of Versailles, 119–120; as